GLYNDEBOURNE

GLYNDEBOURNE

AN OPERATIC MIRACLE

John Jolliffe

JOHN MURRAY
Albemarle Street, London

ISBN 0-7195-5578-7

Typeset in 12 on 16pt Bembo by Wearset, Boldon, Tyne and Wear

Printed and bound in Great Britain by The University Press, Cambridge

To Augustus and Imogen Christie
and
the future of Glyndebourne

CONTENTS

ILLUSTRATIONS

BLACK AND WHITE

ILLUSTRATIONS

The author and publishers wish to thank the following for permission to reproduce illustrations: Colour plates 1, 17, 18 and 34, Mike Hoban; 2, 3, 4, 5, 6, 7, 8, 9, 10, 11, 12, 13, 14, 15, 16, 20, 21, 22, 23, 24, 25, 26, 27, 28, 29, 30, 31, 32 and 33, Guy Gravett; 19, Peter Brookes, Black-and-white plates pp. xv and 258, Lady Lancaster/Private Collection; 2, 9, 21, 23, 27, 40, 43, 52 and 185 (above), Glyndebourne Archive; 12, 62, 65, 69, 72, 77, 78, 80, 87, 89, 90, 100–1, 102, 103, 105, 109, 111, 112, 120–1, 124, 125, 129, 133, 134, 135, 137, 141, 145, 148, 152, 157, 163, 167, 172–3, 175, 177, 179, 193, 198, 204, 205, 211, 216, 217, 223 (below), 228, 233, 236, 242, 245 and 247, Guy Gravett; 31, Bill Brandt © Bill Brandt Archive Ltd.; 36, *Daily Herald*; 47, 50 and 55, Angus McBean; 59, Cornell Capa/Life; 75, Lady Lancaster/Guy Gravett; 149, © David Hockney/Guy Gravett; 158, Mel Calman © S. and C. Calman/Private Collection; 185 (below), Edward Reeves of Lewes; 190, 191, 249, 252 and 257, Mike Hoban; 223 (above), Gus Christie; 237, Royal Commission of Historical Monuments of England.

Every effort has been made to trace copyright holders. In a few cases this has proved impossible. The author and publishers of this book would be pleased to hear from any copyright holders not acknowledged.

FOREWORD

This book is an attempt to satisfy a wide range of readers. At one end of the spectrum are the musical experts who, consciously or otherwise, are already aware of most of what it contains, more especially those who have contributed in one way or another to the extraordinary success of Glyndebourne. At the other, there are those lovers of the place who know little or nothing of its history and inner workings, but are curious to learn. Once numbering only a small minority, they have increased to hundreds of thousands as a result of the development of Glyndebourne Touring Opera, of the annual broadcasts on television and radio, and the subsequent production of video cassettes, compact discs and 'opera bites', and more recently of the Glyndebourne Education Department. Between those two extremes lie infinite gradations, containing some readers who do not need to be told all that they will find in these pages, and others who may long for more. I regret the fact that it is impossible to produce a book perfectly suited to all.

I would like to thank George Christie for many kinds of help, but first of all for his cheerful optimism in authorizing me to undertake this task, in giving me exclusive access to the Glyndebourne archives, and in asking many leading Glyndebourne lights, past and present, to co-operate with me. I am also grateful to John Botts, the present Chairman of the Trustees of Glyndebourne Arts Trust, and especially to his predecessor but one, Lord Lloyd of Berwick, and to Brian Nicholson. I am infinitely indebted to Gillian Fane, together with her husband Julian Fane, for much hospitality as well as for information based on the many years of her service on the Board of Glyndebourne Productions Ltd. Others who have helped me greatly are Anthony Whitworth-Jones, until recently General Director at Glyndebourne, and his predecessor Brian Dickie. Michael Kennedy has been kind enough to read much of my typescript twice, with great care, and has made many helpful suggestions for which I am particularly grateful. Among star Glyndebourne performers I have had the privilege of consulting Dame Janet Baker, Dame Felicity Lott and Paolo Montarsolo. Sir Peter Hall and Raymond Leppard gave me special insights into working at Glyndebourne, as have, in their various departments, June Dandridge, Annabelle Hawtrey, John and Elizabeth Bury, Andrew Davis, Graham Vick, Graeme Jenkins, Nikolaus Lehnhoff and Ivor Green. Jenny KilBride gave me much invaluable information about the massive task of raising the funds required for the building of the new opera house, as did Eric Gabriel, the remarkable co-ordinator of the construction process. Sarah Playfair gave me a stirring account of the workings of Glyndebourne Touring Opera, especially in its darkest hour. Katie Tearle, under whom the Glyndebourne Education Project has advanced by leaps and bounds while this book was being written, has been very kind in bringing me as far as possible up to date.

I am also hugely indebted to Rosy Runciman, whose work in transforming the Glyndebourne archives just before I started working on them made an immense difference to my task. She also read much of my text, and made many helpful comments. Her successor Jayne Fenwick-White's work in that department coincided almost exactly with the period when I was working there, and I am more than grateful for her patience and speedy help in tracing recondite details. And as regards the vast pictorial archive, I would have drowned in it without the unique help of Helen Gravett, whose late husband Guy had taken many of the photographs. The appearance of this book and its impact on the reader owe more than I can say to her selection of material which genuinely illuminates the story rather than merely adorning it.

Many others have helped me and I hope they will forgive me for not naming them. In all the time that I spent at Glyndebourne I met with nothing but patience and helpfulness, arising from love of the place and pride in it, from busy people usually working to the most demanding of deadlines. But the guidance and hospitality that I received from George and Mary Christie, both of whom bear an astonishing burden, year in, year out, are in a category of their own. Mary's wonderfully natural and generous welcome to all those who contribute to Glyndebourne's success is matchless; while George combines the patience of Job, the eye of an eagle and the memory of an elephant with the stamina of a Marathon gold medalist. Glyndebourne is a living, singing monument to their unique qualities.

'Do the best you can
because I want to give my country a model
of perfection.'

JOHN CHRISTIE TO CARL EBERT, 1934

'Certain places, just like certain people, are powerhouses,
centres from which radiations come, affecting levels of achievement
far beyond their own boundaries. They have to be "special"
or "exclusive" because of the nature of their task. As such a centre,
Glyndebourne needs no justification. It succeeds totally.'

DAME JANET BAKER, 16 JUNE 1982

I

JOHN CHRISTIE
AND HIS
BACKGROUND

On 28 May 1994 a triumphant event was celebrated which has no real parallel in the history of opera, or even of the theatre in general. It was the first night of the first season of the new opera house at Glyndebourne, and it came sixty years to the day after the first opening night in the old theatre. Many other opera houses have been rebuilt, usually after fires, but Glyndebourne was unique in Europe even before the heroic plan had been formulated, seven years earlier, to pull down the original opera house, much loved but now on its last legs, and to replace it with something half as big again, to hold an audience of 1,250 instead of 830.

It had not only been a question of size. The old theatre had been built in a hurry, and although it had put on many unforgettable productions, the acoustics had become far from ideal as a result of two enlargements of the original building; the size of the auditorium had limited the repertory that could be shown; and the technical facilities had become inadequate if Glyndebourne was to hold its own against relentless competition. Not only was the rebuilding a huge gamble, it was also unique in that the vast sum of money required for it – £34 million – had all been raised, in one way or another, from individual and corporate supporters. Sir George Christie, its only begetter, rightly pointed out that not a penny of public money had been spent on his new creation, any more than it had on the original one; and there could be no more overwhelming evidence of the place that Glyndebourne had earned in the hearts of its audiences than their willingness to answer his call and produce the sum required for Glyndebourne to be able to maintain, and even improve on, the record which it had built up since its foundation.

It had already become one of the wonders of the world: an opera house, international yet distinctly English, financed at first privately and then by its devotees, without state subsidy, which by constantly aiming at perfection had established, within its natural limits, a reputation second to none. There is also its delightful situation, sheltered but not shut in by the Sussex Downs, with a high wood on one side and, on the other, a beautifully designed and maintained garden leading to a chain of long ponds fringed with willows, and from there out into a wide plain, framed to the south by the solid, spacious range of the downs, which descends sharply from Firle Beacon, five miles away. For the last sixty-five years, many

Three generations: John Christie in front of the house at Glyndebourne with his father and grandfather (1895)

who have worked there have borne witness to the unique effect which the surroundings have on the general atmosphere, and how they permeate the music created there, which seems to arise from what Pope, in his *Epistle to Lord Burlington*, called 'The Genius of the Place'.

To understand how the opera house came into being, it is necessary to examine briefly the story of its founder, George's father John Christie. He was the owner of the large Glyndebourne estate, as well as of other properties, and he had romantically married the opera singer Audrey Mildmay in 1931. They both possessed remarkable qualities, quite different but wonderfully complementary. Certainly neither could have achieved their joint triumph without the other; and not even John, with his sweeping and all-embracing self-confidence, could altogether have foreseen the position which Glyndebourne occupies in the world of international opera today.

Glyndebourne came to the Christie family in 1833 through the marriage of Daniel Christie to Elizabeth Langham, an heiress whose family were the previous owners. Born in 1882, John Christie, the founder of Glyndebourne Opera, was the great-great-grandson of that heiress. His grandfather, William Christie, had married another heiress, Agnes Cleveland, who brought considerable estates in north Devon into the family and enabled her husband to increase the size of the Glyndebourne estate to 10,000 acres. John Christie's father, Augustus, married Lady Rosamond Wallop, but suffered some form of nervous breakdown not long before his son's birth, and turned, sometimes violently, against his wife. The marriage never recovered and the couple separated in 1885. Nevertheless, despite his increasing mental instability and his cruel and insulting behaviour, interspersed with occasional apologies, his wife returned to Tapley, the family home in Devon, though she was often elsewhere. All her affection was devoted to her son John, whose own son George later summed up their difficult relationship as follows:

My father was obviously driven mad by his mother's affection for him, her sentimentality and her efforts to coddle him; he was also maddened by her lack of humour and wit and there always seems to have been a considerable lack of understanding of one another's character. But ... his relations with her changed radically for the better in the last years of her life.

Perhaps not surprisingly, by the tender age of six John had become such an unruly, solitary child that he was sent away to a barbarous boarding school. There he was pugnacious, and he was often to be punished throughout his school career. But he eventually captained the football team and showed 'fearless honesty' in never telling lies when in trouble. In 1896 he went on to Eton, where he was shown neither sympathy nor affection by his housemaster and was left to rely on his own resources: no doubt to his eventual benefit. He was still childish and unpunctual, but according to his biographer Wilfrid Blunt, who had himself been art master at Eton until 1960: 'He would work for masters whose teaching stimulated him; for others he would not make the least effort.' At the age of sixteen John was placed in the Army Class, to prepare for entry into Woolwich Military Academy for a full military career. He now had his first piece of luck, coming under a gifted teacher of science, a subject which already appealed to him strongly. The Revd Dr T. C. Porter was an inspiring eccentric who, as well as being a stimulating influence in the classroom, gave special 'good-boy lectures' to deserving pupils, preceded by a huge tea and including such excitements as a home-made volcano. Blunt records that 'there was always the thrilling element of danger and casualties were not unknown'. In 1930, no fewer than six of Porter's former pupils were Fellows of the Royal Society. But all was not going smoothly and John's housemaster comments in one of John's reports that 'he is so perfectly satisfied with himself in all circumstances apparently that he does not realise the bad impression he produces' (prophetic words, in the light of his later relations with such formidable figures as J. M. Keynes and with the management of Covent Garden). The housemaster adds that 'on two occasions I have been able to avert a catastrophe by persuasion. There is so much that is good in him, and he is such a likeable boy in himself and so much liked by others that it is a great pity he will not do himself justice.' How often, in later years, John's incomparable wife might have said the same! Finally, however, he put some of his childishness behind him and realized that a degree of discipline must be accepted, though never to the point of condoning or even showing patience with what he regarded as stupidity or incompetence in others. He passed into the military academy at Woolwich which he afterwards described as a 'pretty boring and utterly useless and rotten education'.

After eighteen months his ankle was severely crushed in a riding accident. Some time later, as a result of the invention of X-ray technology, it was revealed that his whole foot had been damaged, and the bones had to be reset under the care of Sir Thomas Barlow, the royal doctor, who considered the accident a valid reason for leaving Woolwich. John wrote a careful letter to his father saying that his own tastes 'lie and always have done in experimental science and original research. My only liking for the Artillery was the outdoor life, i.e. riding, etc. . . . but once started in Science, games and sport would come second . . . I should not merely dabble in it but work at it.' His parents agreed to his sitting the entrance examination for Cambridge which he passed in the autumn of 1901 after a spell of cramming at Antony Vicarage, near Devonport. He never hesitated to make his mother fetch and carry for him, or to complain about delays in sending him scientific books, a trouser press, X-ray photographs, boots for cricket and shooting and other clothes.

John threw himself with characteristic vigour and application into the study of science, and worked hard at Cambridge, seven hours a day, even long before his first examination approached. He also persuaded his parents that he should have a car, skilfully justifying it partly on the grounds of the considerable practical scientific knowledge required in those days to keep it on the road. He also acquired a taste for Wagner, though not for music in general; and in 1904 he combined these two principal interests by driving to Bayreuth with three friends including Dr Lloyd, who was in charge of music at Eton, and then aged over sixty. John designed a trailer for luggage and passengers, and since cross-channel steamers did not in those days cater for cars, a barge was hired and the car, with its passengers, was towed over to Calais. This was a wonderful early example of his passion for practical improvisation. His accident at Woolwich prevented him from playing the games that were so important to him, and in his first year at Cambridge he was often seen hobbling about on sticks. Worse still, when he could once more take up rackets, which he had greatly enjoyed at Eton, he was hit in the face by a ball and eventually lost the sight of one eye.

On leaving Cambridge, John took a job as a science master at Eton where, except for two years' active service in the war, he remained for sixteen years. This period, well described in Blunt's biography, is not part of the history of Glyndebourne but it is worth recording his typical method of passing the eye test required by the Army. His good eye was tested first. He then transferred the eye pad not to the other eye but to his other hand, replacing it over the same blind eye as before. He also somehow contrived to conceal his damaged ankle and knee from the medical officers, joined the 60th Rifles and was later recommended for the DSO after a fierce battle. In a battered trench, under heavy shell-fire, John took a copy of Spenser's *The Faerie Queene* out of his pocket and read it aloud to cheer up his company. He had never taught English literature, but perhaps the spirit of the classroom rose again to the surface in these hair-raising circumstances. Seeing his name on the decorations list, he struck it off, not considering that he had done more than many others; but he was later unable to avoid being awarded the MC.

In 1922 he was shortly due to start entering boys on a list with a view to becoming a housemaster. This would effectively have tied him down at Eton for at least ten years, by which time he would have been over fifty. Fortunately, he decided to turn his attention to the Glyndebourne estate which was now legally his. But it seems likely that his years as a schoolmaster, however eccentric and privileged, developed his confidence to drive his projects forward with a sense of natural authority, however capricious. In his later years he was even referred to, by those who knew him well at Glyndebourne, as the Old Master.

Until his father's death in 1930, and for one terrible year afterwards, the future of the two neighbouring estates in north Devon, Tapley and Saunton, was a nightmare to John's mother because of the increasing mental instability of her husband. There were intervals of perfect lucidity especially where his neighbours, with whom he was very popular, were concerned, and this made it harder to obtain a medical decision to the effect that he was incapable of running the estates and that Lady Rosamond should do so in his place, John himself being almost entirely taken up with Glyndebourne. A sort of persecution mania was added to his father's other derangements and in 1925 Augustus Christie made a new will leaving Tapley and a large sum of money to a second cousin called Nicholson. When Augustus died in 1930 (to cut short a long and painful story which is told in full in Blunt's biography), this second will was contested, Lady Rosamond being represented by Sir John Simon, KC, later Lord Chancellor. The judge, Lord Merrivale, pronounced against the will and Lady Rosamond, who had suffered so long and so cruelly, was finally victorious.

John's relations with his mother had greatly improved by the time of her death in 1935. Later, he wrote to the housekeeper at Tapley:

> She found so many were foes, that she asked for no friends. She was prepared to fight the battle alone and in the end she was magnificently successful. I believe she kept me out of it so that I should not incur the odium. I cannot find words to describe the pride I feel that she was my mother and the luck I have had that she did not marry Joe Chamberlain as I have heard was at one time thought possible.

And on her grave he put the following inscription:

AN HEROIC WOMAN
POSSESSED OF INTEGRITY, COURAGE,
DIGNITY AND KINDNESS, TESTED AND
PROVED BY INCESSANT DIFFICULTIES

A few months before his own death in 1962 he wrote to thank an unknown old lady for offering to contribute one week of her pension towards Glyndebourne's expenses. He added:

> I agree with you – there is something different in people here,
> and in the surroundings, to what we find elsewhere. Why it
> should be so, I do not know, but I had the most wonderful
> mother, and she had an appalling life. I think this probably
> explains the position and will enable the family to retain what
> is unusual and yet essential in our lives.

After thirty years of criticism and coolness, this is a good example of
how John could change his mind. More often, though, it was in the
opposite sense, and people whom he had taken up, encouraged and
treated like brothers could then be neglected and forgotten when a new
enthusiasm entered his fertile brain.

The organ firm of Hill, Norman & Beard which John acquired in
1923, plunging into its activities with great initial success during the
boom in the demand for organs in cinemas, provides an example.
Donald Beard, whose father had run the business, returned from a sales
trip to Australia in 1931 to find that John, having in 1920 built a magnificent organ room at the back of the house at Glyndebourne, had completely lost interest in organs and was instead absorbed in plans for opera.
The unfortunate Donald Beard, to whom Glyndebourne had previously
been a second home, now found himself completely ignored, and wrote
a letter of resignation as a director of the firm. John never replied, and
Beard never saw nor heard from him again. John had tinkered with the
organ so often and extended its range so much that its power was finally
far too great for the room. The works were carefully removed some
years after the war, leaving only the magnificent carved oak façade
behind.

It should be remembered that the Organ Room, his first major addition to the house, which survives almost in its splendid original form
today, is itself a monument to John's natural generosity and his already
powerful sense of hospitality, which was given full rein when he inherited Glyndebourne as a forty-year-old bachelor schoolmaster. He loved

Glyndebourne.

Concerts, September 6, 7, 8, 1921.

Music, selected from the following pieces, will be given by
Miss NORAH DESMOND & Mr. EDWARD POTTER, F.R.C.O.

MISS NORAH DESMOND.

1.	LARGO	G. F. Handel (1685-1759).
2.	"O REST IN THE LORD"	J. L. F. Mendelssohn-Bartholdy.
3.	"THERE IS A GREEN HILL"	C. F. Gounod (1818-1893).
4.	"REQUEST"	Amy Woodford-Finden.
5.	"BEYOND THE DAWN"	Wilfrid Sanderson.
6.	"THE STRING OF PEARLS"	N. L. Phillips.
7.	"ABIDE WITH ME"	Liddle.
8.	"DOWN HERE"	May H. Brahe.
9.	"HOMING"	Teresa del Riego.

MR. EDWARD POTTER.

10.	PAVANE	William Byrd (1542 ?-1623).
11.	PASSACAGLIA	J. S. Bach (1685-1750).
12.	TOCCATA IN F	,, ,,
13.	2ND CONCERTO—1ST MOVEMENT	G. F. Handel (1685-1759).
14.	MINUET IN F	,, ,,
15.	"SEE THE CONQUERING HERO COMES" (Judas Maccabaeus) ...	,, ,,
16.	MARCH FROM SCIPIO	,, ,,
17.	2ND PIANO SONATA—2ND MOVEMENT	L. van Beethoven (1770-1827).
18.	MINUET IN E FLAT (Piano Sonata, Op. 122)	Schubert (1797-1828).
19.	UNFINISHED SYMPHONY	,, ,,
20.	IMPROMPTU IN A FLAT (Piano)	,, ,,
21.	FUNERAL MARCH (Liede ohne Worte)	J. L. F. Mendelssohn-Bartholdy (1809-1847).
22.	"SLEEPERS, WAKE" (St. Paul) ... ,, ...	,, ,,
23.	MARCH IN C (from the Pianoforte Duet)	C. M. von Weber (1841-1904).
24.	MELODY IN F	A. Rubinstein (1830-1881).
25.	8TH ORGAN SONATA—2ND MOVEMENT	S. G. Rheinberger (1839-1901).
26.	,, 3RD AND 4TH MOVEMENTS ...	,, ,,
27.	20TH ORGAN SONATA—3RD MOVEMENT	,, ,,
28.	,, 4TH MOVEMENT	,, ,,
29.	THE DEATH OF ASE (Peer Gynt)	E. H. Grieg (1843-1902 ?).
30.	1ST HUMORESKE IN E FLAT MINOR	A. Dvorák.
31.	3RD HUMORESKE IN A FLAT	,,
32.	LARGO (from the "From the New World" symphony)	,,
33.	5/4 MOVEMENT FROM THE PATHETIC SYMPHONY	Tchaikovsky (1840-1893).
34.	ETON MEMORIAL MARCH (written in memory of those Etonians who fell in the South African War)	C. H. Lloyd (1849-1918).
35.	SOLEMN MELODY	H. Walford Davies (1869-).

Visitors, including those outside the windows and those in the organ room passage, are earnestly requested not to talk or shuffle during the performance of the pieces. They are invited to talk and shuffle as much as they wish between the pieces.

The arrangement of the Programme depends on the number of visitors. It is proposed to give either two or three concerts with 15 minutes interval between them. In order that everyone who wishes may obtain a seat, visitors are asked to "forego a second help," and at the end of each of the first two concerts vacate the room in favour of others who wish to attend the next concert. Visitors are asked, as far as they can, to assist others to get places at the tea tables, and (if they can be trusted) to look after the children of those parents who are at the time attending a concert.

It is only fair to the organ builders to remind visitors that the organ is not finished. The final "voicing" has not been begun and some of the stops are not yet "speaking." The treble notes are too loud and the reeds on the "Great" Organ are at present noisy and unpleasant. They will be much altered before the organ is finished.

Programme of early concerts given in the Organ Room

to fill the house with his friends, the chief forms of entertainment being various outdoor games in the summer, shooting in the winter, and a wide range of music all the year round. He would write to his mother, describing his parties, no doubt to her great satisfaction, though she was often anxious about his capacity for spending money. Years later, he would not only continue to treat all those who were professionally working in the opera as an extension of the circle of his own family and friends, but would also greet strangers in the opera interval and enquire whether they were enjoying themselves as much as he thought they should. His personal warmth, his general enthusiasm and his sometimes teasing sense of humour all came to play a part in the development of the unique Glyndebourne atmosphere, and the Organ Room became a natural link between the house itself and the opera house.

The furious concentration and single-mindedness, without which the Glyndebourne Opera could never have been successfully created, could sometimes have its less attractive side, as in the case of John's treatment of Beard. But to a later, crucial employee, Frank Harvey, who became head gardener at Glyndebourne in 1924 and whose name for many years appeared in the opera programmes, John always gave a free hand. An American visitor once asked him the secret of so perfect a lawn. 'It's easy,' was the reply, 'Just mow it for two hundred years.' Anyone who has been to Glyndebourne in the summer is aware of the degree to which the gardens increase the pleasure of attending the opera, but as justice has been done to them in Anne Scott-James's book, it is only necessary to add here that under the present management by Chris Hughes they have been extended, and are still looked after with the greatest imagination and care. They continue to give delight to picnick-ers and strollers alike, as well as to those members of the company and the orchestra who find relaxation, or at least distraction, in croquet.

Throughout the 1920s John had also been developing the Ringmer Building Works, which had started as an estate facility with a weekly wages bill of £20. He claimed that it later grew into one of the biggest building concerns in the south-east, and if this was an exaggeration, it certainly made a profit of over £20,000 in 1939, or over half a million in today's money. By the great – unmusical – majority of local people John was remembered as a man who, during those years, brought much-needed employment to a whole district. One of his deepest beliefs was that, in order to justify their advantages, large landowners like himself were under a moral obligation to learn at first hand about all the trades that went with a country estate. Building and the conversion of timber and other materials, garages, water-works, hotels, golf courses: all these occupied his attention at one time or another. He utterly despised landowners who failed to give a lead in such matters, and often rather sweepingly denounced them as unproductive, inefficient, self-important and generally useless. His philosophy embodied a kind of feudalism, updated to the nineteen-twenties and thirties. The Swedish soprano Elis-abeth Söderström, a great Glyndebourne star towards the end of John's life, considered that he made his vision come true by giving his employees real inspiration to take pride in their work, to an extent that was almost unparalleled at the time; however different the circumstances are today, something of this original spirit still survives.

In 1925 he became involved in another local business, the Tunbridge Wells Opera House, which he leased after the previous management had foundered. His first idea was for a week of Gilbert & Sullivan, but this was replaced by Shaw's *St Joan*, and other plays. Details survive in John's ever-optimistic letters to his mother, but after 1927 he was concentrating more heavily on music at Glyndebourne itself and seldom referred to 'the theatre' again. But it was there that he found 'Jock' Gough, the stage carpenter and later chief stage technician whose experience and infinite ingenuity later made him for many years one of John's most valued right-hand men at Glyndebourne. John certainly also learnt something about the general problems of theatre management and promotion, as did his indispensable accountant W. E. Edwards whom he had engaged, along with other new brooms, in 1920.

As far as music was concerned, the greatest influence on John in the 1920s was the Mounsey family, who had first come to Glyndebourne in the summer holidays of 1923. Johnnie Mounsey was a Quaker, a director of Barclays Bank, and was in charge of its choir. His wife Fanny, a gifted

John Christie and Jock Gough inspect building work in the theatre, winter 1952

pianist with a general passion for music, soon became John's musical mentor, discussing the subject with him at length during a business visit to Egypt with her husband and other friends, in February 1924. Much music-making went on in the Mounseys' house in London, where a spare bedroom was at John's disposal; and the entire Mounsey family, which included four children, three maids and a pony, spent the following Christmas at Glyndebourne.

In effect, it was Fanny Mounsey who turned John's mild interest in music into a serious enthusiasm, which led to the pre-operatic music-making at Glyndebourne, which in turn led to the providential appearance there of Audrey Mildmay. The Lewes Music Festival, which had been started a few years earlier, soon took up John's attention. Preparations would begin in the autumn, with rehearsals in the Organ Room at Glyndebourne under professional conductors who included Malcolm Sargent. Local choirs would compete against each other and then combine to perform a major choral work on the last day of the Festival.

In August 1925 John went with the Mounseys and other friends to hear Wagner and Mozart operas at Bayreuth and Munich. Not surprisingly, Bayreuth had not recovered from the war and from Germany's bad economic state. John wrote to his mother that the scenery was over forty years old and was seldom adequately lit because it would have looked so shabby. 'However the copious use of steam for transformation and the fire effects are admirable'; no doubt they kindled John's later absorbing interest in stage mechanics and lighting. While he had a love of music, and could often spot a promising voice and notice when a good singer was off form, John was first a scientist, fascinated by lighting and sound effects and other production devices, and a music-lover only second.

Besides the rehearsals for the Lewes Music Festival, the Organ Room was increasingly used for concerts, recitals and scenes from operas, with widening audiences of neighbours, tenants and employees, as well as guests invited to stay in the house. But the visits to Germany with the Mounseys were the strongest formative influence on John's musical interests. Their base was near Garmisch in Bavaria, where Walter and Johanna Hirth took in selected paying guests. Frau Hirth was the sister of a stage designer, Emil Praetorius, and music-lovers from far and wide assembled there. This pre-Hitler Germany suited John perfectly and the communal spirit of Munich had a special appeal.

For the next few years concert sessions and, later, costume productions of scenes from *Le nozze di Figaro* and *Die Entführung aus dem Serail* were given at Glyndebourne, and a photograph survives of John himself as Beckmesser in Act I of *Die Meistersinger von Nürnberg*. Thornley and Dorothy Gibson were among the professional contributors to these performances and thirty years later their son Patrick, later Lord Gibson and Chairman of Pearsons, became a valued trustee of Glyndebourne Opera. Besides these operatic extracts, there were also concerts of Bach (Fanny Mounsey's great hero) and Brahms *Lieder*.

In 1929, after a Whitsun weekend at Glyndebourne, Johnnie Mounsey killed himself in a wood near Redhill. It has never been established whether the cause was overwork at the bank and strain at the time of the slump, or whether he felt that after his initial delight in John's friendship, his family life had been swamped and devoured by Glyndebourne. In any event, a great gloom naturally fell on Glyndebourne. John could not face the house alone, and moved briefly into the cottage occupied by Childs, his butler, who was later not only to be best man at his wedding and godfather to his son, but also acted the part of the Mute in *Die Ent-führung* in 1935.

In 1930 John decided to put on Act I of *Die Entführung*, again in a largely amateur way. Dolly Gibson was not available, and the part of Blonde was taken by a thirty-year-old singer by the name of Audrey Mildmay, who had been a member of the great Carl Rosa Company, which had been touring opera in England since 1870. She and John became engaged, after a characteristically single-minded courtship and a shower of lavish presents, in the following April and were married in June. The story goes that on one of the three occasions when they heard *Der Rosenkavalier* together that spring, at Covent Garden, at the moment when Oktavian hands Sophie the silver rose, John took Audrey's hand and pressed into it a diamond brooch – itself in the shape of a rose, and now owned by their granddaughter Louise.

2

THE
PRE-WAR SEASONS

For the world of opera in England, nothing has ever been more fortunate than John and Audrey's marriage. Without John's determination, energy and single-mindedness (not to mention money – by 1939 he had spent, or invested, £100,000 in the project), the opera house would never have been built. Without Audrey's years of practical experience as a professional opera singer, and her charm, tact and thoughtfulness for others, John's characteristics would have derailed him into any number of prohibitive obstacles.

Sadly, the illnesses which were to plague Audrey on and off for the rest of her life began ominously to appear on their honeymoon, which was largely spent attending operas in Munich. Tonsillitis, rheumatism and anaemia were followed by appendicitis. At the same time, John also had his appendix out ('a useless organ'), as he afterwards said, 'to keep Audrey company'. On their return, plans began to take shape for the construction of an opera house as an extension of the Organ Room, but on a modest scale, only seating about 150. However, Audrey providentially decided, at the last minute, that it would fall between two stools: too big for the mainly amateur productions that had gone before, and too small for fully professional productions with paying audiences. She is said to have told her husband that if so much money was going to be spent, 'for God's sake do the thing properly'. A fresh start was made and a new building, to hold 311, was planned with a haste which resulted from John's vague idea that, as a result of the country's coming off the Gold Standard, 'we must build at once, or we shan't have any pounds left'.

He was largely his own architect, with some help from a professional known as 'Bear' Warre, the son of a former headmaster and provost of Eton. The building materials used were known locally as 'plum pudding', a brownish mixture of brick and stone (salvaged from a house which was being demolished by the Ringmer Building Works) which eventually blended harmoniously into its surroundings and can still be seen in the rooms which survive from the original buildings overlooking the garden. Audrey was a friend of the great critic Ernest Newman, who wisely advised John to study all the German books and periodicals dealing with theatre design that he could find. Building began in late 1931, and John plunged happily into all the details of the interior, including the purchase of a second-hand 'cloud apparatus', reduced, perhaps through a shortage of demand, from £700 to £95.

Audrey spent the autumn of 1932 taking singing lessons in Vienna from Jani Strasser, a young Hungarian who was to play a key role as a coach at Glyndebourne, both before and after the war. John joined her there in December, when possible operas for Glyndebourne were discussed; *Le nozze di Figaro* and *Don Giovanni* were tentatively decided on, and Audrey began to study the parts of Susanna and Zerlina. The night before leaving for home John characteristically invited Strasser to accompany them, and was surprised that this was considered short notice. However, in February 1933 the Strassers duly arrived at Glyndebourne and remained there for five months. David Franklin, who played many main roles at Glyndebourne over the years, later summed Strasser up in carefully chosen words:

> He dominated my life while I was learning my trade, and I learnt more from him than I can ever acknowledge. He has great charm, stamina and an insatiable appetite for work, and

for the best he can get out of you; and over and over again he can be quite insufferable.

Fortunately, to Audrey at least, he was never insufferable.

Structural work on the theatre continued, while Hamish Wilson, whom Audrey had known at the Carl Rosa, was designing and building sets for projected productions. As well as being a designer, he had at least some practical experience of the general requirements of an opera house, whereas John had none. John was, however, determined to master the subject, above all the question of lighting; and after meticulous study of systems both in England and Europe, he eventually acquired some of what he wanted in Vienna, having the rest made in his own workshops at a fraction (as he proudly claimed) of the cost quoted elsewhere. The mechanics and gadgetry of the theatre were his chief fascination, to the considerable neglect of orchestral considerations. He himself had enorm-ous physical strength, and often led operations from the front. One employee at Glyndebourne has recalled that 'whenever there was any-thing large to be moved (which was often) Mr Christie always took the heavy end'. John now cheerfully announced that the pit would accom-modate an orchestra of a hundred. It could, no doubt, have done so had they been packed into it like sardines, but with instruments, music stands and elbow room, the idea was preposterous.

Nor was the matter of the operas themselves at all clear. Although John was coming round to the idea of Mozart, as suitable both for the dimensions of the opera house and for the nature of his wife's voice, his chief preoccupation was still with Bayreuth and Munich, rather than Salzburg. In fact, Mozart's operas were very little performed, or even known, in England at this time, and it was the pioneering spirit of Glyndebourne which was to put this right. A vague statement was made in the *Evening News* on 29 June 1933 that either *Don Giovanni* or *Die Walküre* would be put on in the following year and there was also the intention of producing the *Ring* cycle and *Parsifal*, 'probably' at Easter. Sir Thomas Beecham had been invited to bring down his orchestra, but 'that is not settled yet' – chiefly because Beecham had not bothered to answer what even he considered was such an improbable suggestion.

This made no great impact on the public. Beecham had been connected, in theory and practice, with dozens of operatic ventures in the past quarter of a century, and John's brief statement that 'my wife will take part' sounded like yet another rich man trying to make his wife a star. Rather touchingly, he wrote to her in January 1934: 'I love you as much and more than Mozart loved Constanze. And you are a better singer.' In October 1933, a daughter, named Rosamond after John's mother, was born. That same month, he published an article in the *Monthly Musical Record*, hinting (though not confirming) that his policy would be 'to offer superb performances' ('superb' was always a favourite) 'to dedicated audiences who would show their appreciation by taking the time and trouble to savour them', rather than an alternative, more schoolmasterish plan 'to give educational performances for the ordinary public'. It should not be forgotten that genuine music-lovers were a small band in those days, and that in general the philistine majority was much larger than it is today. One of John's closest friends, C. M. Wells, a fellow schoolmaster at Eton and a considerable scholar, athlete and connoisseur of wine, insisted that his visits to Glyndebourne should be in the winter, when there would be, as he put it, 'no caterwauling'.

At this uncertain point, Glyndebourne suddenly had the vital stroke of luck that the Christies so richly deserved. Adolf Busch, leader of the Busch Quartet, gave a recital at Eastbourne in November 1933, and on the next day was taken to Glyndebourne by his great supporter and promoter in England, Frances Dakyns, who persuaded John that Adolf's brother Fritz could provide the solution to the unresolved problem of who should conduct at Glyndebourne. She wrote to him in Copenhagen, where he had moved in disgust at the Nazis, though not himself Jewish. At first, he was prevented from considering the idea by an existing commitment to the Teatro Colón in Buenos Aires. Suddenly, however, this was curtailed and Busch was free. Entirely on the recommendation of Frances Dakyns, whose judgement John respected, Busch was put in charge of a fortnight's Mozart Festival at Glyndebourne, scheduled for the end of May 1934. John met him for the first time in Amsterdam in that January, though he had already greatly admired Busch's work at Dresden on his visit there in 1930, and thought it superior to what he had often heard in Munich. Busch's advice was to engage as producer Carl Ebert, who, after a successful career as an actor and assistant to Max Reinhardt, had become general manager at Darmstadt (where concerts and operas were put on as well as plays), and then general director of the Berlin State Opera, a post he had secured in competition with many highly qualified musicians. Like Busch, he could no longer endure Nazi pressure to surrender his artistic integrity, and had already found work elsewhere, in Switzerland, Austria and Italy. Like Beecham, he at first ignored John's letters. But when telegrams followed and he discovered that Busch had committed himself, he too came to have a look at Glyndebourne. He recognized the potential of what he later called John's 'marvellous stubbornness' and his dream of producing truly 'superb' work. Twenty-five years later, when he relinquished the post of Artistic Director of Glyndebourne, he referred to 'the staggering combination of a comfortable English country house on the one hand and the intense artistic idealism on the other'.

David Franklin, whose singing career at Glyndebourne stretched from 1936 to 1959, has observed that he often thought Glyndebourne was more interested in rehearsals than performances 'which are treated almost as extra rehearsals'. Ebert was forever pulling a scene to pieces and rebuilding it, just as John was always extending and improvising the physical structure of Glyndebourne. (In 1938 Ebert, no doubt egged on by John, was to spend ten whole days on the lighting for *Macbeth* alone). He summed it up majestically when he said that 'when an artist has no more to learn he is ready to die'. One of his greatest virtues was his commitment to fulfilling the composer's intentions (like Peter Hall forty years later) instead of imposing anything of his own on the music. Franklin also paid tribute to Ebert's powers as an actor:

> The maddening thing was that although he could not sing, he could act any of our parts better than we could . . . resourceful,

ingenious and imaginable – he could even act a woman better than the women could . . . no technical detail was too small to escape planning.

A notable feature of Glyndebourne, often mentioned by performers, is the uninterrupted preparation devoted to each production. This level of concentration is conducive to true happiness among singers, in spite of the acute pressure laid upon them, especially by the exacting genius of Ebert, to produce their very best. For him, even experienced artists were prepared to forget the way in which they had played a part in the past, and to have it built up for them from the beginning, step by step, by 'the Professor', as Ebert was universally known. Ian Wallace, who sang in many productions after the war, has well described his 'restless eyes, his expression of agony at some shortcoming, followed by a roar of satisfaction if it was corrected, and of rage if it wasn't'. Again like Hall, Ebert had moved on from the theatre because he had come to regard opera as 'a heightened method of expressing drama'. He knew that Mozart's operas were very little known in England at the time, and he soon observed that the scale of Glyndebourne was well suited to them. Not surprisingly however, since many singers are strong individualists, there have been exceptions, and not all singers, or even producers, have been equally happy in the Glyndebourne atmosphere. Occasionally, for example, an experienced singer who already knows a part through and through, will fret at the long period of rehearsal.

Not since Count Esterházy built his opera house for Haydn at Eszter-háza had there been such a magnificent example of private musical enterprise. Busch steered John away from his idea that a combination of the Busch Quartet and the organ could provide a satisfactory accompaniment, rather than a full orchestra. Under George Stratton, players from the London Symphony Orchestra eventually formed the orchestra for the early seasons at Glyndebourne. Half of the main cast of the earliest productions of *Figaro* and *Così fan tutte* were English: Audrey Mildmay herself, Roy Henderson, Constance Willis, Heddle Nash and Ina Souez (American by birth but British by marriage); from Germany came Willi

Figaro, 1935: Aulikki Rautawaara, Audrey Mildmay, Willi Domgraf-Fassbänder, Roy Henderson, Heddle Nash, Ronald Sears, Constance Willis

Domgraf-Fassbänder and Lucie Manén; from Austria Luise Helletsgruber, who had sung the part of Zdenka in the first Vienna performance of Strauss's *Arabella* the year before; from Czechoslovakia Irene Eisinger; from Italy Vincenzo Bettoni; and finally, from Finland the great soprano Aulikki Rautawaara.

In an interview in 1936, John summed up his policy on casting, and the intention behind it, as follows:

> We give the best possible welcome to every foreigner who is better than our own countrymen; and we do everything we can to make our own countrymen better than the foreigners. . . . It is a very serious venture and its purpose is the export of British music and musicians. We cannot do that until the

world respects music done in England by British executants, and British music.

He would certainly have liked to put on an English opera at Glynde-bourne, but Vaughan Williams was for some reason unwilling for his work to be performed there, and nothing suitable was found until after 1945.

After much consultation, Busch and Ebert formally accepted the invitation on one absolute condition, which they could not believe would be acceptable. It was that the final decision on all musical and artistic matters should be theirs. More than money, they longed for the artistic freedom, in their self-imposed exile, to express their own gifts and powers. They would discuss everything with John first – choice of operas and casts, and amount of rehearsal time – but the last word must be theirs. Here John showed his true greatness. He knew he was only an amateur, with a dream but without the full qualifications necessary for turning it into reality, and characteristically he was prepared to put his full trust in those whom he accepted as experts. There was occasional friction; but he kept the bargain. In return, they did their best to respect his ideas. Peter Gellhorn, chorus master at Glyndebourne in the fifties, recalled both Ebert and Busch occasionally commenting: 'I don't think John would like it.' Gellhorn, whose valuable help has been saluted by many singers, summed up his own feelings thus: 'Glyndebourne is a place where I look for a realization of what one is dreaming of . . . there are places where it's no use dreaming; at Glyndebourne I always feel that it is.'

In many ways, Glyndebourne modelled itself on German lines, as a result of John's considerable experience of opera in Germany, his lack of experience of Italy, his aversion to France, and the absence of a worth-while tradition in England. Until the rise of Hitler, there was quite a vogue for things Bavarian in England. John often wore lederhosen, a kind of informal and comfortable buckskin shorts, and the Glynde-

John Christie in the 1930s

bourne lavatories were quaintly labelled '*Damen*' and '*Herren*' rather than 'Ladies' and 'Gentlemen'. The extended period of preparation and rehearsal, unknown in England, was actually quite common in a number of German opera houses, though it covered a larger repertory there. It has survived at Glyndebourne to this day, whereas in Germany and elsewhere there has been a growing tendency to import international stars who only arrive a day or two before the performances, as at Covent Garden. By early 1934 the Big Four – John, Audrey, Busch and Ebert – were in place but there were only three months to go before the opening. Plans for a second season of three or four more operas in September were wisely shelved, but as if Audrey's tasks as wife, hostess and singer were not sufficiently taxing, she discovered in May that she was again pregnant. George William Langham Christie, heir to Glyndebourne, was born on the following New Year's Eve, and he could therefore justly claim in later life that he had been on stage at Glyndebourne even before he was born.

Audrey Christie's diary records the turmoil that continued right up to the opening nights and also the fact that important decisions were only taken at a very late stage. On 16 February 1934 she writes: 'Everything getting very difficult. Singers' fees seem very high. They want to engage Bing as agent and discussion raged until 2 am.' On the 17th: 'Hateful atmosphere of "sides" in the house – awful.' But the following morning, she comments: 'Atmosphere at breakfast most peaceful and friendly.' On the 21st: 'I sang and Busch was enthusiastic to John. Said I was "künstlich" (artistic) etc. Is satisfied, in fact keen, for me to sing in the season.'

Rehearsals began in the Wigmore Studios in London, with the arrival of the stately soprano Aulikki Rautawaara, speaking not a word of English, and 'not knowing her part at all'. The importance of Jani Strasser as a coach to an international cast of singers can hardly be exaggerated. His command of languages was exceptional, and he was particularly helpful, for example, to singers not accustomed to singing in Italian. In more recent years, there has been nobody in quite the same league to take his place in this respect, as has been confirmed by one singer who had witnessed Strasser's work in the 1960s and returned

thirty years later, to find a considerable falling off in the casts' enuncia-
tion – to some extent inevitably, in view of the wider repertory in a
variety of languages. It has, however, to be admitted that – as is often the
case with original and influential characters who become legends in their
lifetime – a minority of singers could not stand Strasser and found him
devious. But the great majority, from Audrey Mildmay herself onwards,
felt greatly indebted to him.

By 25 May, Audrey noted: 'Public rehearsal of *Così* at 5. Good audience, good performance, great enthusiasm'; and at another rehearsal next
day: 'Everyone did well.' On the 28th, the first night of *Figaro* proper,
there was a 'packed, fashionable audience', though John later claimed
that only seven of them had taken the special train from Victoria.
Audrey, who was generally critical of herself as well as of others,
recorded: 'I did, I think, a good performance and enjoyed it.'

A whole book could be compiled from the press notices, good and
bad, ignorant and well informed, then and later, but the *Daily Telegraph*
represented the general view when its critic announced solemnly that:
'We would like our readers to take note of our opinion that such a performance has not before been seen in this or in any other country.' This
was despite (or perhaps in the end because of) John's statement that:
'The aim of the performance would be not so much to please the audience or the critics as to serve the designs of the composer and to serve
the dramatic side with equal faithfulness.' In fact, his general intention
was to discourage people who were not ready to put up with inconve-
niences of various kinds, in order to attend performances of the highest
possible quality, from coming to Glyndebourne at all. This was the logic
behind his insistence on evening dress. Late in life he even told the well-
known tenor Nigel Douglas that he would, if he could, have surrounded
Glyndebourne with barbed wire in order to keep out the unworthy.

It is interesting to note the verdict of the great music critic Neville
Cardus on his first visit to Glyndebourne:

> A feeling overcame me that I had wandered out of the modern
> world into a world of the past, when culture and wealth meant

much the same thing. When an Englishman does get art and beauty on the brain, there is nobody who can compare with him for idealism, enthusiasm, love or risk and mingled quixotry and instinct for a sporting chance.

And on 13 June, John's old friend Sir Alan Lascelles, private secretary to the then Prince of Wales, wrote to him saying: 'You have done what no Englishman has ever had the guts to do before – much more valuable than climbing Everest and so forth.' Subsequently, John remained keen to make use of his grand connections whenever there was a chance to promote Glyndebourne. He planned with Lascelles to get himself invited to Sandringham, and for the new King and Queen to visit Tapley when they were next touring the properties of the Duchy of Cornwall, and though neither of these projects came off he never hesitated to invite famous or influential people to Glyndebourne.

But all was not plain sailing, least of all for Audrey herself. Her diary for 31 May records: 'Busch better [from pains in the chest the day before]. Fassbänder still feeling rotten. Not feeling very well myself. Very nervous in first act of *Figaro*, but John says not noticeable.' And the next day: 'Stayed in bed all day. *Così* at 7.15. Much bigger audience, though not full. John says they were very enthusiastic.' And the following day: 'John read second lot of marvellous notices. I only made two small mistakes in the whole opera (*Figaro*). My best performance. John enthusiastic.'

The audiences are thought to have averaged about a hundred, after fifty-four and fifty-five on the first two nights. The deficit on the season was £7,000, a large sum, but John regarded it as an investment and was unperturbed. In the winter the very inadequate conditions backstage were improved and twenty-four proper dressing-rooms were built, together with a 'Green Room', a second dining hall, a kitchen and a room for chauffeurs.

No attempt had been made to record Mozart's operas until this first season, when on 6 June Fred Gaisberg of The Gramophone Company made the first recordings at Glyndebourne, of *Le nozze de Figaro*. These recordings were not issued commercially until the following year, when

Audrey Mildmay in front of The Gramophone Company's recording van, at the time of the first HMV recording at Glyndebourne (1935)

the first six discs formed an album under the auspices of the Mozart Opera Society. A series of similar societies, covering works by Hugo Wolf, Haydn, Beethoven and Sibelius, had been formed by Walter Legge, at that time editor of HMV's house magazine, *The Voice*. Neville Cardus wrote of the *Figaro* records that: 'The performances are almost flawless; the freshness of the voices is equalled by the precision of rhythm, balance of parts, and – best of all – the suggestion of a living participation in the music's unending flow of melody.' This was the beginning of a series of recordings which has continued till this day, admirably catalogued in *Glyndebourne Recorded* (1994) by Paul Campion and Rosy Runciman, which not only covers every aspect of the records made at the time and later, but also contains much interesting back-ground information about the productions.[1]

Plans were well advanced for the next season, though various problems arose. After the initial success, several singers demanded large

---

1 In 1995 it won the Association for Recorded Sound Collections award for Best Research in the Field of Recorded Classical Music.

increases in their fees: one asked for them to be quadrupled, even though he would only be doing half as much work again as in the previous year. And there was a lot of trouble over contracts: first, because of the dilatoriness of the manager in charge of contracts for British singers, Alfred Nightingale, who had spent four years at Covent Garden and should have known better. To be fair, it should be remembered that he, like many others, had considerable difficulty in understanding Busch's English, though it was less erratic than that of Jani Strasser's wife Irene, who would replace the prosaic phrase 'hook, line and sinker' with the more arresting version 'hook, sink and knickers'. (John himself was far from fluent in German, in spite of his enthusiasm for the country, and in the early days Frances Dakyns played an invaluable role as interpreter.) Secondly, there was John's fanciful view that, given a chance to sing at Glyndebourne, an opera singer would drop any alternative, irrespective of pay or prestige. Ina Souez, who had been, perhaps, the brightest star of the first season (and whose mother-in-law, by chance, lived a mile away from Glyndebourne, at Ringmer), had verbally agreed to take the role of Fiordiligi again in 1935. But such was the delay over her contract that she had also signed up to sing the part of Micaëla in *Carmen* at Covent Garden. Busch considered her indispensable, and she in an interview said many years later that 'he was a perfect musician and a great artist in every way. He loved singers and he loved to be with them. . . . As I've often said, I'll never get to Heaven, God knows, because I was in heaven for six years at Glyndebourne before the war.' Busch threatened to resign if she was not available, and accused Glyndebourne of hopeless irresponsibility, adding that it was ridiculous to complain that she had 'behaved badly'. *All* opera singers behave badly unless prevented from doing so – everyone knew that it was the manager's job to prevent them. Amazingly – given that John would rarely pass up an opportunity, then or later, to denigrate Covent Garden both in private and in public – Covent Garden eventually agreed to release Souez on the dates when *Carmen* clashed with *Così*.

Rudolf Bing, who had worked as Ebert's assistant at Darmstadt, relates in his memoirs that he was given the very tricky task of getting this settled, and that this was only accomplished through the magnanimity of Beecham at Covent Garden. Partly as a result of this success, Bing replaced Nightingale as General Manager, having been up until then responsible only for contracts with foreign artists. Later, he also played a part in finding them. In 1938 he was invited to a cultural conference in Prague, which gave him a wonderful opportunity to visit his family and friends in Vienna. However, on the day he arrived there, the Anschluss was declared and the Czech border was sealed; anyone trying to cross it from Austria was turned back, and many of them suffered the consequences in concentration camps. By a miracle, Bing had been entrusted with a special VIP border pass issued to Sir Hugh Seely, MP, originally a member of the British delegation, who had decided to cancel his trip at the last minute. When Bing reached the Czech frontier he concealed his Austrian passport and brandished Seely's pass, loudly (though one would have thought implausibly) declaring that he did not speak German. Unwilling to have a battle with someone who was ostensibly a British Member of Parliament, the Czechs let him through. But it was a very near thing – and a massive stroke of luck for Glyndebourne, as well as for Bing.

The two operas from the year before were revived in 1935, and there were new and excellent productions of *Die Entführung* and *Die Zauberflöte*, though Mila Kocova was not a success as the Queen of Night and was replaced by Noel Eadie. The fact that the joint founder of Glyndebourne Opera was also one of the performers meant that attention was paid, in a cheerfully informal way, to details which might otherwise have been neglected. For example, on the cover of one of the early programmes, the following notice appears in John's idiosyncratic style: 'Patrons are earnestly requested not to flash TORCHES during the Performance. It is aggravating to the rest of the audience but intolerable to the Artists. It is much worse than walking behind the bowler's arm at cricket.' A far more embarrassing incident was to occur sixty years later, when an electronic alarm went off in the handbag of an unfortunate member of the audience, in the middle of a performance. One shudders to think what John's reaction would have been.

Audrey's diary again records the ups and downs of everyday life. On 16 March she writes: 'Rehearsal in Organ Room at 2.15. 304 people came. Gave them tea in the library.' By 24 May: 'Everyone in bad temper'; but at the public performance three days later she records: 'first act good, second act superb', and on the 30th, 'first performance of *Così* which was superlatively good.' On the 26 and 27 May and 2 June she was either 'tired', 'very tired' or 'dreadfully tired', and on 7 June: 'very worried about my voice'. However on the 21st: 'We did the best performance of *Figaro* we have ever made. First act heavenly, second act nervous. . . . Enormous success with the audience.'

On 25 June, Audrey comments: 'Stage dreadfully bad from where I sat. Hamish seems hopeless.' This was probably harsh. Stage design, as opposed to stage effects, was not given high priority at that time. By the standards of the day, Hamish Wilson was not 'hopeless', and, after the 1939–45 war, he had a successful career teaching and speaking on his subject in South Africa. It is said that Kenneth Clark, who was a keen Glyndebourne supporter, offered to pay for some sets by Duncan Grant about this time, which John turned down. The deficit on the 1935 season was about £8,000, of which £7,000 had been spent on the dressing-rooms and dining hall.

The following April there was a belated presentation to John and Audrey of a silver mug in honour of George's birth, and an album signed by 600 tenants and employees, many of them from Devonshire and from other Christie enterprises further afield. The *Sussex County Herald* recorded that: 'Mr Christie welcomed them with a feeling of simple friendship which has always been his lucky possession with the people with whom he had to work. He said that we are going to do our best not to rest where we are, but to extend our activities in much further and greater fields than hitherto.'

In 1936, there was indeed a further expansion. Besides the four operas given the year before, a new production of *Don Giovanni* was put on, and there were no fewer than thirty-two performances, as against twelve in the first year. Audrey had a triumphant success as Zerlina, but what Bing described as the 'plummy voice of incomparable richness' of Salvatore Baccaloni and his comic timing as Leporello went near to stealing the show. The Australian John Brownlee (whose Don Giovanni bore a faint but not inappropriate resemblance to Sir Oswald Mosley) can still be heard on the old recordings. He, too, was in quite exceptional voice, in spite of having such a busy season: he had also sung the Count in *Figaro* and Don Alfonso in *Così*, having already played Rigoletto, Scarpia (in *Tosca*) and Amonasro (in *Aida*) at Covent Garden earlier in the year.

There was, however, for the first time, some criticism in the press of Ebert's production of *Don Giovanni*. First, the trio of masks sang '*Protegga il giusto cielo*' in front of the curtain during a scene change, as if they were asking for the audience's protection rather than that of Heaven in the dark garden. And secondly, in those innocent days the presence of some near-naked courtesans at the Don's supper party in the last act was considered vulgar. For the first time, the BBC broadcast Act I of *Die Zauberflöte* on the opening night. Noel Eadie as the Queen of Night had to omit the top F's; and the next winter Ebert declared that he

Boating on the lake: Aulikki Rautawaara, Hans Oppenheim, Carl Ebert (1936)

would commit suicide if she were allowed to return to sing Constanze again.

At this stage John occasionally came near to infringing his commitment to Ebert and Busch about artistic decisions. As General Manager, Rudolf Bing wrote to John on 14 December, passing on some strongly-held opinions of Ebert's, on casting for the next season. It ends with the following significant paragraph:

> I am writing to Busch about all this and I must say the situation becomes rather difficult for us. Busch wants something different from you and Ebert, Ebert wants something different from Busch and you, and you want something different from both of them. Neither of you gives any final decision and neither of you tells the other definitively what he wants. How should I know what to make of all this? I suppose I have to assume some kind of dictatorship.

Already, at the age of thirty-three, Bing was beginning to show the formidable qualities without which he could not have controlled the Metropolitan Opera in New York with such success in his later years. Two months later, when required at Glyndebourne, Baccaloni tried to sneak off to Buenos Aires, and Bing commented to John: 'I believe his decision will depend on which he is most afraid of – us or the Teatro Colón. I therefore tried to threaten him as hard as possible!'

Busch, above all, was keenly aware of the need for growth and variety. At the end of the 1936 Glyndebourne season, he made his way to Buenos Aires, where he was paid no less than three times what he received at Glyndebourne. Nevertheless, so much did he love the circumstances of working at Glyndebourne that he curtailed his work at the Teatro Colón in 1936, and in 1937 gave it up altogether in return for a slight increase in fees. Significantly, he wrote to John from the ship:

> Another composer's work should be given next year besides the five Mozarts, for *their* standard can no longer become a better

one. . . . Played more or less by the same ensemble for three seasons, the danger of putting 'routine' in place of emotion turned rather great [sic] . . . the artistic thrill would then get lost. Singers as well as orchestra now need a change of atmosphere.

An interesting letter survives from John to Steuart Wilson, a distinguished tenor who had become President of the Solo Section of the Incorporated Society of Musicians (and who, after the war, was to become deputy general manager at Covent Garden). Wilson was a man whom John took seriously, though he was never afraid of offending him by plain speaking. The correspondence concerned Mariano Stabile, the first singer of established high reputation to appear at Glyndebourne, who had, between 1926 and 1931, sung many times at Covent Garden. He had appeared as Falstaff under Toscanini at the Salzburg Festival in 1936, and had also inspired several English critics to say that his Figaro at Glyndebourne in the same year was the best they had ever seen anywhere. John pointed out to Wilson, who was pressing for an English conductor, that great stars like Stabile would simply not bother to rehearse endlessly for any producer or conductor who was unknown to them. '*Authority* is necessary and can only be established by *experience* at first hand.' Wilson replied sharply: 'Your German crowd . . . *know* far more than you, and you will never get out of their hands . . . for all that you say, they have really got control of the show because they *know*.' John replied, with some dignity: 'It isn't a question of whether I myself know or not. My business is to see that the standard obtained is as good as we can get it.' The fact that their success was so warmly recognized by audiences and critics alike, and that the recordings of *Figaro*, *Così* and *Don Giovanni* were equally acclaimed on their release, proved once and for all that the Christies had triumphed over the odds, and that in England at least, what Glyndebourne was doing was in a class of its own.

Busch would have liked to vary the diet of Mozart with Verdi's *Falstaff* but admitted it would be very expensive and difficult to produce. The 1937 season coincided with Coronation Year, and there was a desire in musical circles for an English opera as well as English singers.

When thinking about including an English work, Busch rather surprisingly considered *The Bride of Dionysus* by Donald Tovey: 'magnificent, with a marvellous part for Audrey'. But Tovey was 'not very much estimated yet by his countrymen', and has not been since. Indeed, his Cello Concerto was described by Constant Lambert as having 'lasted longer than my first term at school'. The alternative was *Sir John in Love* by Vaughan Williams, who was indeed much appreciated in England. But the work, though delightful in its way, was not in the same league as Verdi, and even if the composer had allowed it to be put on, it would have shown up poorly beside Mozart.

In the end, the 1937 programme was identical to that of 1936, though with various changes of cast. Audrey herself completely lost her voice and retired to a nursing home in April, and the critics later sympathized with audiences who had to make do without 'their own' Zerlina. Seating-capacity had now been increased to 451, including fifty-two unmarked seats along the side walls, sold at lower prices to deserving applicants, though John untruthfully claimed that the auditorium accommodated 600, a figure not reached till 1953. Irene Eisinger gave much pleasure as Susanna, Despina and Blonde as well as in several performances as Papagena, a part she shared with Margaret Field-Hyde. Busch was never much of a hand with names other than German ones and referred to her simply as Miss Hay-Field, while he converted the Russian soprano Lissitschkina into Lisipikituziwenska when writing in his own hand, and in a typed letter she came out as Likitikimiri-kanusskawaska. (It is comforting to discover that the English are not alone in finding difficulty with foreign names.) Spike Hughes has also pointed out that the substitute Constanze, a Greek soprano called Margherita Perras, sang 'with ease and skill', but was mildly criticized for her gestures and general acting: 'This in itself is a tribute to Glyndebourne. Before 1934 people might have commented on good acting in opera; poor acting would never have been regarded as anything out of the way.'

Partly because less time was needed for rehearsals since there were no new operas, and partly because of the healthy consumption of wine (chiefly John's favourite hock and moselle, about which much trouble was taken) in the dining halls, the season actually showed a profit of £2,723, an achievement all the more creditable since Busch's fee had been raised by 50 per cent, and Ebert, too, had probably been paid more.

By 1938, the search for something to dilute Mozart was over. Donizetti's *Don Pasquale* had been selected for that reason, and posed no great problems, but Verdi's *Macbeth* was a bolder and more ambitious choice in a variety of ways. Although Ebert's production had already been put on with great success in Germany, the work was completely unfamiliar in England and had never, in fact, been professionally staged there. Secondly, a bigger orchestra was needed, and a voice of exceptional range was required for Lady Macbeth, yet not too powerful for the Glyndebourne auditorium. Busch confessed that no opera ever gave him such casting troubles. Franca Somigli was eventually engaged, and signed a contract on 24 February; however, after a whole month she decided that the part was beyond her, and disingenuously offered herself for another opera, knowing that this was out of the question. The situation was further exacerbated by her signing a better-paid contract with Beunos Aires shortly afterwards. Ebert was out of England and Audrey only returned at the end of April from Rome where she had been improving her Italian in order to do justice to the part of Norina in *Don Pasquale*. In one of her letters to John at this time she optimistically advised him against adopting an excessively aggressive attitude: 'I love and admire your tremendous driving force but what I don't want is for it to swamp your charm or your sound sense – it is *liable* to I'm afraid. Imagine that you are Beecham talking to John about Glyndebourne and be as tactful as you would like him to be!' She signed herself: 'Your admiring and adoring (if often bullying) wife'. It was only ten days before the first night that the testing part of Lady Macbeth was bravely taken on, mercifully to great acclaim, by the Croatian Vera Schwarz.

Judging by photographs, the finale looked more like a Nuremberg Rally than Birnam Wood, but the sets by the famous German expressionist designer Caspar Neher were regarded as successful, and many years later were recalled by one of the most reliable of critics, Desmond Shawe-Taylor, as having been 'magnificent', in contrast with what he referred to as the 'styleless fantasies' of Hamish Wilson.

It is worth mentioning Busch's remarkable rapport with his orchestras. They loved rather than feared him, not least for his unexpected comments. When he wanted one particular overture played as softly as possible he lifted his baton and, before a note was played, told them: 'Is already too loud.' On another occasion, after a slightly ragged start, he stopped them and said calmly: '*All* the members of this wonderful orchestra are invited to take part.' The desired effect was soon forth-coming. Toscanini attended a performance of *Macbeth*, greatly admired Busch's treatment of Verdi, and said he could not have done better himself. Both then and in 1949 there was a possibility that he might conduct at Glyndebourne, to which his attitude was more than friendly, but it came to nothing, chiefly because he was unwilling to spare the time for the sacred Glyndebourne rehearsal system. It is very sad that the

Fritz Busch rehearsing the orchestra for Macbeth *(1939)*

production was not recorded, especially in view of the great success of Margherita Grandi, who took over as Lady Macbeth in 1939, and was described in the *New Statesman* as 'the greatest dramatic soprano of the Italian school heard in this country since the war'. The various non-singing roles were played by waiters, schoolboys and the staff of the Ringmer Building Works. The only real disappointment at the time was that the King and Queen, who were due to attend a performance, had to cancel owing to the death of the Queen's mother. She was therefore denied the unusual experience of seeing a great opera centred round Glamis, the castle in which she herself had been born.

Don Pasquale was a tearing success, but the audience laughed so much at Stabile and the incomparable Baccaloni that the singers were often drowned. However, it was a fault on the right side, and there was a particularly striking tribute to Audrey from Francis Toye in the *Morning Post*. He said that her performance reflected 'an immense amount of hard work and of striving after the highest ideals', and that he 'did not think that anywhere else a singer with the privileges enjoyed by Miss Mildmay at Glyndebourne would have been at such pains to improve and develop her technical resources'. It was through this ability to lead by example that she helped to get Glyndebourne off to such a flying start, which those in charge were determined to maintain. And on a point of management, she shrewdly made it a rule that only producers, conductors and music staff should stay in the house during the season. If some singers had done so, it would have created a division between those who did and those who did not, which would have been generally unhelpful in view of the vulnerability and insecurity of singers, often where it would be least expected. It is doubtful whether anyone without Audrey's personal stage experience would have seen the importance of this point.

Altogether the season was regarded as Busch's greatest triumph ever, not only in the Mozart operas, where it was expected as a matter of course, but in introducing two very different works totally unfamiliar to English ears. *The Times* printed a lengthy personal tribute to him which pointed out the 'indefinable characteristic of *élan* in *Don Pasquale*' and the fact that in *Macbeth* he made 'his audience perceive the greatness of an unequal [i.e. uneven] work'. This was also the first year when an entire Glyndebourne opera, *Figaro*, was broadcast by the BBC, as well as individual acts from each of the other four operas. But with two new productions, it was not surprising that there was a loss on the season of about £7,000.

Audrey, who had given up her part as Zerlina and shared that of Susanna with Irene Eisinger, gave some concerts in Budapest in December. On her way there she wrote to John saying: 'I am so happy this year with you and those two [children]. I've never spent a happier year in my life.' John wrote in reply: 'It's thrilling that you always land on your feet. You go to these foreign cities where we only have shadowy connections and there everybody entertains you and applauds you.' He added, on a more eccentric note: 'We have two rainwater heads dated 1761. We are altering them to 1764, the year Mozart was in England.'

No doubt chiefly for reasons of economy, the programme for 1939 was identical with that for the year before. Plans had tentatively been made for Glyndebourne Opera to visit both Lucerne and New York, but they came to nothing. There were also what now seem to be some rather far-fetched ideas about Covent Garden. Back in April 1938 John had written to Audrey in Rome:

> If Beecham has another failure this year, I am convinced we shall be running Covent Garden next year. Rudi has had a talk with Bruce Ottley today. . . . The idea is say 30 performances at Cov. Gdn. 3 Rings = 12. 6 performances of 3 others = 18. Total 30. And say 30 performances here. Total 60 spread over 12 weeks.

This extravagant speculation came to nought, although the idea resurfaced during and just after the war, and it is hard to know how seriously John was thinking.

Interestingly, the Prime Minister, Neville Chamberlain, found time to attend a performance of *Macbeth* at Glyndebourne in July 1939, and was warmly applauded by the audience. Soon afterwards, John was able to indulge his great love of teasing and confusion by coming on to the stage after the last night of the season, 15 July, and announcing that he had 'serious news'. War was only six weeks away and the audience feared the worst. In fact he was referring to the first defeat of Eton by Harrow at Lord's since 1908. Early in September, no fewer than 300 evacuee children arrived at Glyndebourne from a London suburb, and Bing was sent off to buy six dozen chamber-pots for them at Woolworth's. Later, the number of children was reduced to about a hundred, and remained around that level, with a staff of thirty-five to look after them.

The season planned for 1940 had consisted of *Carmen*, *Figaro*, *Die Zauberflöte*, *Don Giovanni* and *Macbeth*. It was cancelled, but in the first five months of the year Glyndebourne kept its flag flying and provided much-needed public entertainment, as well as work for unemployed artists, by touring the provinces with John Gay's *The Beggar's Opera*. While they were in Edinburgh, Audrey looked up at the castle and remarked prophetically to Bing that it would be a good place for a festival, 'the Salzburg of the North'. Michael Redgrave played Macheath, and Audrey, who played Polly Peachum, liked his 'rather Harris-tweed voice', even though it was untrained. The producer was John Gielgud, but by the time the tour ended, at the Haymarket Theatre in London a week before Dunkirk, Audrey (and no doubt the rest of the cast) was not sorry it was over.

All thoughts of opera at Glyndebourne itself were abandoned till after the war, and tentative ideas for setting up 'Glyndebourne Towers' at Williamsburg, Virginia, and even an opera house at Niagara Falls, never materialized. But after much heart-searching, on 19 July 1940 Audrey took the children to Canada, where she herself had been brought up. John was left in melancholy solitude, at first writing constantly to Audrey, and regaling her with morale-boosting stories which circulated in those desperate months. One of the best concerned a British sailor, captured by the Germans and interrogated in a typically thorough fashion. When asked what the letters HMS on his cap stood for, he replied: 'Oh, those are the buggers we're after. Hitler, Mussolini and

Stalin.' John also busied himself with plans to form a 'National Council of Music', to cure 'the bungling amateur approach to musical performance in England'. He succeeded in enlisting many of the principal musicians in the country, Sir Adrian Boult (whom he much admired), Dr Malcolm Sargent, Dr Vaughan Williams, Miss Myra Hess and Professor Edward Dent, even though the latter had originally poured cold water on Glyndebourne and the idea of 'attempting Mozart in a Sussex hay-field'. But the plan for a National Council eventually ran into the sand.

John's experience over six seasons at Glyndebourne had provided him with much to offer, but without Audrey at his side there was little hope that he would offer it in a way that would be acceptable. He was depressed by the lack of ideals in public life and of any sign that the post-war world would be better than what had gone before. He even had another grandiose scheme, this time for buying Covent Garden, with vast contributions from the BBC, Rank Films and the City, but this, too, quickly collapsed. He also had hopes of persuading the BBC to take a more positive and challenging attitude with its programmes, and wrote characteristically in one of his letters to Audrey: 'The danger to the BBC is mediocrity. They must lead, not follow. They must not pursue popularity. Popularity should come from respect and from pride in the mind of the Public.' He managed to obtain a job for Bing with the John Lewis Partnership and Bing's parents were found accommodation in Lewes. Bing records meeting some soldiers on a weekend walk with John, accompanied by one of John's famous dynasty of pugs, still going strong to this day. This one had been named Bimperl after a dog of Mozart's. John, with his customary geniality, asked them how they liked Sussex and, pointing to Glyndebourne in the distance, informed them: 'That's Mozart's house over there'; and pointing to Bimperl, he added: 'And that's Mozart's dog.'

Probably through his friendship with Sir Alan Lascelles, John had been

Audrey Mildmay as Polly in The Beggar's Opera, *which toured
the country in 1940*

41

invited by King George VI to advise on the purchase of German wines, which had flowed freely at Glyndebourne. He commented characteristically: 'I find that German wines do not taste equally well in all places. Glyndebourne seems to be good. Tapley is bad. It is therefore conceivable that Balmoral or Sandringham might be unfortunate. I suppose one can only find this out by trial.' In any event, the war put a stop to the import of German wine, to Buckingham Palace or anywhere else. But vast stocks had been accumulated at Glyndebourne, and John had built a new cellar for them under a field opposite the house. He was convinced that the German wines would start to deteriorate if kept for more than ten years, and also that the total stock was far in excess of what would be required after the war, even if the opera were to be revived – which actually sometimes seemed unlikely. Thinking aloud in a moment of despondency in 1942, he wrote to Audrey of the possibility of pulling down the opera house (on which unfair tax liabilities had arisen), which cannot have done much for her own morale. Instead, he decided on a massive sale at Restell's, the leading wine auction house. In the course of three days at the end of January 1942 this raised the immense sum of £18,851 12s. 9d., which John triumphantly informed Audrey 'is all for you and the children'. No fewer than 1,200 dozen bottles of hock and moselle were sold, at record prices, and smaller lots of other wine and spirits, including 85 dozen bottles of port from Tapley. The best riesling, Forster Ungeheuer, fetched the astonishing price of 610 shillings a dozen, £2 10s. 0d. a bottle, at a time when few prices were over 10s. a bottle. Twenty-two bottles of yellow chartreuse fetched £5 13s. 4d. each, and four bottles of something described as 'Cognac du Roi' (Louis XVIII, 1820) also fetched over £5 each.

Meanwhile, Audrey had no easy time in Canada. Money, from whatever source, was short and she had much less household help than she had been accustomed to. She gave concerts in Edmonton, Seattle and elsewhere, and when Beecham put on *Figaro* in Montreal he enlisted her and later cabled John that she had 'scored a brilliant and special success as Susanna, which I think will have fortunate results'. (They were, in fact, her last opera appearances.) A coolness developed with Busch as a result

'Phoebe', now senior member of the Christies' pugs,
painted by Derek Hill in 1989

of his putting on *Figaro* in New York and not offering Audrey the part which she had always played with such success. But as Bing later pointed out in a letter to Wilfrid Blunt, she was

> a delightful artist as long as she was surrounded by the love and care she received at Glyndebourne; she was not a great singer and I don't know whether at that time she could have stood up to the cold eyes and ears of New York and the competition that was then around.

No doubt Busch acted in what he regarded as her best interests as an artist by not exposing her to the risk of failure, but her need to sing for her supper – and for the children's suppers – was acute and it is not surprising that she took offence. She and the children eventually succeeded in returning to England, via Lisbon, in May 1944. She was very

43

exhausted and may well have been suffering already from the high blood pressure which, combined with other illnesses, was so sadly to shorten her life.

An interesting sidelight on Glyndebourne in the war is provided in a letter from Lady Violet Bonham Carter, who spent a weekend there in October 1942, partly to see whether a job could be found for Bing at the BBC, of which she was a Governor. She wrote to John afterwards in typically enthusiastic and high-flown style:

> It was a most delightful and exciting experience, seeing Glyndebourne at close quarters, getting to know you, developing a 'national conscience', drinking 'first folio' wine – And through it all ran the 'accompaniment' of those hundred happy children's voices – chirruping in the morning like birds on the tree – scuttling about the woods and downs and gardens in gay little coveys – *Never* have I seen anything so perfect in conception and execution as the life of that little community. Plato's Republic and Utopia are left far behind it. Mrs Wheeler [who was in charge] beats them hollow.

The fact that they were there at all was due to the invaluable negotiating skills of W. E. Edwards, who may well have saved Glyndebourne from a damaging military occupation such as was suffered at Firle Place, a house of much greater architectural distinction four miles away.

3

A SLOW REBIRTH

1945–1951

A good example of the wide range of the Christies' enterprise and sense of mission is provided by the fact that the first venture which Glyndebourne came to control after the war was unconnected with opera, for which the money was simply not available. The Children's Theatre, founded in April 1944 under the chairmanship of Dr J. J. Mallon, Warden of Toynbee Hall, came under the management of Glyndebourne a year later, when John and Audrey both joined its council and helped it financially, and Bing took over its administration. Its aim, well ahead of its time, was to introduce children to the living theatre through full stage performances of classical and contemporary plays. The LCC sponsored various performances in London, and local education authorities supported provincial tours. But neither the Ministry of Education nor CEMA, the Council for the Encouragement of Music and the Arts – mockingly referred to by John as the Council for the Encouragement of Mediocre Artists – could provide money, with the exception of a single grant of £3,000 by CEMA in 1948. The producer, John Allen, eventually resigned when the LCC wanted him to put on three plays of which he disapproved. Soon afterwards the company closed down, but it had given more than a thousand performances which had been attended by over half a million children, to their great enjoyment. It cannot, therefore, be regarded as a failure, and it represents another unexpected feather in Glyndebourne's cap.

In the absence of immediate prospects for opera, Glyndebourne joined in another purely theatrical venture called the Company of Four, along with H. M. Tennent Ltd, Cambridge Arts Theatre and Tyrone Guthrie. They took over the Lyric Theatre, Hammersmith, in the summer of 1945 for a season of works by serious modern playwrights, including Cocteau, O'Casey, Saroyan and Thornton Wilder. But with unfamiliar plays and young, little-known actors, this was a losing proposition which did not greatly interest John, and Glyndebourne's involvement came to an end.

John's plan, resurrected from 1938, that Glyndebourne should run Covent Garden under Bing, was never a starter, chiefly because those in charge of that establishment were unwilling to be eclipsed by John. But the first rekindling of opera was fanned by Beecham, who, like John, had been debarred from Covent Garden by the new owners, Boosey & Hawkes, the music publishers. Such was Beecham's indignation that he offered to conduct *Carmen*, *Figaro* and *Die Zauberflöte* at Glyndebourne, free, for the 1946 season. Unfortunately, however, this particular co-operation failed to come off, largely because Beecham (who was very far from being Busch) was not prepared to train the young, unknown singers wanted by John, through the long weeks of rehearsal. Another, bigger problem was finance. John had regarded the huge sums he had spent on the opera before the war as an investment, inevitable in the creation of Glyndebourne as an institution. After the war he was still a very rich man in terms of capital assets, but with income tax and super tax at annihilating levels, disposable income was simply not available; and in the last resort he was not willing to make large inroads into the family properties in order to finance the survival of the opera.

The next plan, which actually came to fruition, was to put on *The Rape of Lucretia*, which Benjamin Britten was composing after his great success with *Peter Grimes* at Sadler's Wells in 1945. It had a major contralto part for the sublime Kathleen Ferrier, at that time a pupil of Roy Henderson, the latter having starred in many of the pre-war Mozart

The world première of Britten's The Rape of Lucretia *was given at Glyndebourne in July 1946, despite John Christie's antipathy to the work. Kathleen Ferrier was exceptional in the title role*

productions at Glyndebourne. Its world première was given at Glyndebourne on 12 July 1946; but the subsequent tour of five weeks in the provinces, followed by four in London and one in Holland, drew poor audiences.

The Rape of Lucretia was not a Glyndebourne production in the pre-war sense. It had a guarantee of £3,000 from CEMA, and another from John himself, who was 'startled' by the losses incurred on tour. There were two separate casts, playing on alternate nights, conducted respectively by Reginald Goodall and the Swiss Ernest Ansermet, whose English was even more erratic than that of Busch. He found Benjamin Britten humourless, and said that what he needed was 'a little joke then and now. Yes, very, sometimes.' And on another occasion, he attacked an unfortunate player who had offended him with the following words:

'Don't spoke! Don't spoke! If you didn't like it, you left!' The next year, the company who had performed *Lucretia* were to form the nucleus of the English Opera Group (EOG), and decamped (if that is the right word) to Aldeburgh, where an extremely successful festival was established, centred on Britten himself and Peter Pears – who had, incidentally, sung in the chorus at Glyndebourne before the war. (They tried, and failed, to persuade Moran Caplat, a nephew of John's estate manager who was now Bing's assistant, to abandon Glyndebourne and throw in his lot with them. Caplat had had a good war in the Navy, narrowly escaping death in February 1942 when the submarine on which he was serving was sunk. The captain and several others were drowned, but Caplat was one of twenty-three survivors who were taken prisoner by an Italian frigate.) The two festivals are so different as to lack valid points of comparison, and very few artists have performed at both, a notable exception being the world-class tenor Robert Tear. His Glyndebourne debut only came thirty-two years after he had first sung at Aldeburgh, and his sense of the atmosphere of both places is striking. In a recent essay he stated that: 'just as I felt Aldeburgh to be fully of uneasy vibrations and hidden malice, so this place [Glyndebourne] is good.' What he found at Glyndebourne had been a 'feeling of unforced benevolence', partly arising from its physical context, and freedom from the noises and distractions of the cities where all other major opera houses are to be found. 'Never', he added, 'have I worked with a chorus filled with such evident goodness . . . young, full of hope, and as yet uncorrupted by cynicism.' He also points to an interesting contrast between Britten on the one hand, and Haydn, Mozart, Verdi, Tippett and Janáček on the other. These five devoted their last great works to universal themes of joy, love, natural pleasure in humanity, and the whole spectrum of the human spirit. Britten, however, even though he had composed *Albert Herring* and *A Midsummer Night's Dream* in very different vein, reverted to darker themes in *Death in Venice*, which centres around sexual obsession, and the guilt and collapse it induces.

John disliked *The Rape of Lucretia* quite unreasonably. He complained with typical exaggeration that there was 'no music in it'; he took against the sets and the costumes (though according to Eric Crozier he later came to think better of the music). But above all, he took against Britten and his budding entourage, who understandably felt a mutual loyalty to each other which put them at odds with the 'happy family' atmosphere so brilliantly, and to a great extent unconsciously, created by Audrey at Glyndebourne before the war. It has to be mentioned, too, that John found homosexuality in general distasteful. Anne Wood, of the English Opera Group, pointed to the contrast between the German/international nature of the old Glyndebourne and the new 'young, very English, immensely creative group, which was out to establish a whole new era of English opera and music', releasing the creative energies of many others as well as themselves. It is also fair to add that Britten was possessive of his group, and disliked giving any degree of authority to anyone else. He considered that Bing was condescending and Bing, in turn, felt isolated especially on the tour in Holland. Clearly, Glyndebourne was not cut out to host a visiting company.

Nevertheless, Britten and Eric Crozier, who had been described in a letter from Bing to Ebert as 'the only really promising young British opera producer', still thought that their best hopes lay in a liaison with Glyndebourne again in 1947. Audrey, with her boundless goodwill, was prepared to consider this, but Bing was deeply suspicious, and felt that the 'Britten brigade' needed Glyndebourne much more than Glyndebourne needed them. In the event, English Opera Group did put on a revival of *The Rape of Lucretia* at Glyndebourne, together with the première of *Albert Herring* produced by Frederick Ashton and designed by John Piper, to which the audience responded with great enjoyment, laughing loud and long at all the episodes that were intended to be funny. John Christie disliked this, greeted members of the audience with the words 'This isn't our sort of thing, you know', and dismissed it as 'a very vulgar audience'. Whatever *Albert Herring*'s merits, it was indeed a far cry from Edwardian Eton where so many of his tastes and attitudes had been formed. Such personal antipathy is perhaps not surprising, especially when one remembers that he had been through the nightmare of trench warfare in 1915, and that Britten had spent the second war in

Kathleen Ferrier's rendition of the role of Orfeo in Gluck's opera in 1947 ranks among the highlights of Glyndebourne's history, though there were reservations about the production

safety and comfort in America. Temperamentally they were poles apart.

There was also a production, mounted by Glyndebourne rather than EOG: nine performances of Gluck's *Orfeo*, sung with the original Italian libretto, but complete with later additions to the score, and with the title role sung by Kathleen Ferrier. Curiously enough, she was never happy appearing in opera, and much preferred the concert platform. She turned down an invitation to sing *Orfeo* again (though she sang it in her last performances at Covent Garden) and also rejected the part of Ulrica in Glyndebourne's *Un ballo in maschera* at Edinburgh in 1949, confiding to a friend: 'I think I'm lousy on stage. . . I fall upstairs, downstairs, even over my own feet.' All the same, her performance at Glyndebourne was magnificent, and many who heard it were moved to tears. Her performance can now be heard on CD, and ranks among the highlights of Glyndebourne's history. In other respects, though, the production had a bad critical reception, especially the conducting of Fritz Stiedry and, even more so, the ballet scenes, which were described in words never before used of Glyndebourne: 'tedious', 'deplorable', and 'awful'. The audiences, however, starved of opera in general and of Glyndebourne in particular, loved it. In spite of weaknesses elsewhere, the production was a historic occasion and an encouraging sign that Glyndebourne, given the money, could still deliver.

Rudolf Bing still hankered admirably after the idea of an international music festival, *à la* Salzburg, in a British city. But where? Manchester, Liverpool and Bristol were too big and would swallow it up. York, Lincoln, Chester and others were too poorly supplied with theatres, halls and hotels. But Edinburgh, where Glyndebourne had taken *The Beggar's Opera* in 1940, was a real possibility. A magnificent setting, a proud sense of being a capital city, a theatre which – at a rather tight pinch – could hold opera, plenty of hotels and boarding-houses, and also plenty of trains, essential in the seemingly endless days of petrol rationing. The *History of the Edinburgh Festival* states that the Arts Council was 'circumvented', without saying how, and Maynard Keynes, its first Chairman, died soon afterwards. Typically, John later asserted that Keynes had 'tried to stop the Edinburgh Festival'. After it had become a huge success, the Arts Council certainly claimed to have supported it.

Fortunately, the head of the Scottish Section of the British Council, Harry Harvey-Wood, knew all about Salzburg and Glyndebourne. Bing hit it off with him to such an extent that Harvey-Wood offered to assemble a small committee of what would nowadays be called the Great and the Good of Edinburgh. It included the editor of the *Scotsman*; Lady Rosebery, a strong character who was both a good pianist and a friend of the Queen; the playwright James Bridie; and John Cameron, later a Law Lord. To them Bing stated his case with characteristic energy, clearheadedness and tact. Having satisfying them, Bing accompanied them to call on the Lord Provost, Sir John Falconer, who, though not himself a

KING'S THEATRE
EDINBURGH

Howard & Wyndham Ltd.   Chairman & Managing Director: A. Stewart Cruikshank.

THE EDINBURGH FESTIVAL SOCIETY LTD.
In association with the Arts Council of Great Britain and the City Corporation of Edinburgh
PRESENTS

GLYNDEBOURNE OPERA
ARTISTIC DIRECTOR: CARL EBERT
EVENINGS AT 7 O'CLOCK
VERDI
MACBETH

AUGUST 25th, 27th, 29th   SEPTEMBER 2nd, 4th, 6th, 8th, 10th, 12th

MOZART
LE NOZZE DI FIGARO

AUGUST 26th, 28th, 30th   SEPT. 1st, 3rd, 5th, 9th, 11th, 13th

CONDUCTOR: PRODUCER:
GEORGE SZELL   CARL EBERT

MARGHERITA GRANDI ★ ELEANOR STEBER ★ VIRGINIA MACWATTERS

JARMILA NOVOTNA   ★   CATHERINE LAWSON   ★   VERA TERRY

BARBARA TRENT   ★   FRANCESCO VALENTINO   ★   ITALO TAJO

JOHN BROWNLEE ★ OWEN BRANNIGAN ★ WALTER MIDGLEY

BRUCE FLEGG ★ ANDREW McKINLEY

THE SCOTTISH ORCHESTRA
THE GLYNDEBOURNE FESTIVAL CHORUS

Stalls 40/-, 30/-, 17/6. Pit Stalls 12/6. Grand Circle 40/-, 25/-, 17/6. Upper Circle 12/6, 9/-
Gallery 3/-. Boxes: Grand Tier Circle £6, Mid Tier Circle £3-10-0
BOX OFFICE TELEPHONE: EDINBURGH 51027
INPRINT ABB 2638

*Playbill advertising the two operas given in first season
of the Edinburgh Festival*

music-lover, soon saw the merits of the idea. With most of the opera houses in Germany, Austria and, to a lesser extent, Italy out of action, the competition in Europe would be negligible for the foreseeable future; and lovers of theatre and music could reasonably be expected to come to Edinburgh in considerable numbers, and *spend their money there*, if offered programmes of the quality that Bing could muster. (Indeed, a later Lord Provost estimated that the Festival brought £1 million into Edinburgh in three weeks.) Bing made the occasional faux pas by at first referring to the Scots as the English, and by advising that the Festival should open with 'High Mass in the Cathedral'. Nevertheless, John got on extremely well with Falconer, who became a tremendous ally of the Festival. In its first year, it engaged such great stars as Artur Schnabel, Joseph Szigeti, William Primrose and Pierre Fournier, who also played together as a quartet. Lotte Lehmann gave a *Lieder* recital accompanied by Bruno Walter, who also conducted Kathleen Ferrier and Peter Pears in Mahler's *Das Lied von der Erde* and was reunited, after a long separation, with the Vienna Philharmonic for several Edinburgh concerts.

Between 28 August and 13 September, Glyndebourne put on their own productions of *Macbeth* and *Figaro*, in which Italo Tajo was a sensation in the title role. Both the original conductors, Tullio Serafin and Georg Szell respectively, cried off, Szell at very short notice in mid-rehearsals, having already signed a contract and on what seemed very inadequate grounds. Bing never forgave Szell, but succeeded in replacing the original conductors with Walter Susskind for *Figaro* and Berthold Goldschmidt for *Macbeth*. In the latter, George Christie made his operatic debut, at the age of twelve, as Fleance. Never had such a galaxy of stars been gathered together in Britain; and the audiences, largely deprived of such entertainment on anything like this level during the war, were enormously enthusiastic.

Relations between Glyndebourne and Edinburgh were complex. The arrangement was that Glyndebourne would act as 'organizing centre', supplying the management skills and experience of Bing and his assistants Ian Hunter and Moran Caplat, but would not be liable for any formation expenses at Edinburgh or for any losses suffered on Glyndebourne productions put on at Edinburgh. What Glyndebourne needed was, first, a way of satisfying its creative urges, and an opportunity to get its wheels turning again without risking large sums of money; and secondly, in particular, it wanted to extend its Sussex season, and thus its potential for earnings, as far as Edinburgh in the months of August and September. But Edinburgh did not believe that audiences would come from the south of England in late summer to hear what they could more easily have heard at Glyndebourne itself in June. For this reason, and because funds were not available, there were no performances at Glyndebourne, in advance of the Edinburgh season, in 1948 and 1949. In both these years *Così* was put on at Edinburgh, conducted by Vittorio Gui with 'an effect of near perfection', and described by one American reviewer as having 'danced away with all the honours' of the whole Festival. The Bulgarian Donna Anna, Ljuba Welitsch, was also outstanding, with Richard Lewis as Don Ottavio, in the *Don Giovanni* of 1948. In 1949, the other opera was Verdi's *Un ballo in maschera*, modelled on a production put on by Ebert (and conducted by Busch) in Berlin in 1932. To understand the relative importance of opera in Germany and England, it is worth recalling that this production had caused such a sensation that a large section of the *Frankfurter Illustrierte* magazine was devoted to describing it. Happily, in Edinburgh *Un ballo* was at least as great a revelation to British audiences as Glyndebourne's *Macbeth* had been in 1939.

Speaking of Glyndebourne's special contribution, Ian Wallace, a wonderfully articulate source of information, whose father had been MP for Kirkcaldy, recalled later how these operas had brought glamour and excitement to the grey chill of Edinburgh. Of the old stars, Stabile, Brownlee, Grandi, Eisinger and David Franklin all shone out again, and the newcomers included Richard Lewis and Sena Jurinac, both of whom were to take their places among the great Glyndebourne favourites of the 1950s. Some idea of the generosity of the company's spirit is provided by the fact that Alda Noni and Paolo Silveri spent an afternoon singing to patients in the wards of the City Hospital, while Ian Wallace, who had himself spent two years in hospital with spinal tuberculosis, performed with the ukulele in the Royal Infirmary. Two other hospitals

The 1947 production of Macbeth, *given at the Edinburgh Festival: Owen Brannigan as Banquo and George Christie in his operatic debut as Fleance*

were entertained in similar fashion.

Nor was there a complete musical silence at Glyndebourne itself. In 1948 Beecham, who had been provided with a house on the Glyndebourne estate in Ringmer, conducted a series of all-Mozart weekend concerts in the opera house, and in the following year the series included works by Haydn, Schubert, Schumann and Brahms. Also in 1948, Glyndebourne took part in the Bath Assembly, which was trying to re-establish itself after the war. That year, the Assembly could claim to be 'directed artistically by Glyndebourne': there were nine performances of Children's Theatre and two by the London Philharmonic Orchestra as well as six of *Die Entführung*, in English, with Richard Lewis, John

Kentish and Owen Brannigan in the cast. The costumes and scenery were all made at Glyndebourne. The opera was the centrepiece of what was to become, a few years later, a much longer and thoroughly successful festival first under the artistic direction of Yehudi Menuhin, then of Michael Tippett, and, perhaps best of all, for ten years under William Glock. But in 1948 John, who also made two foraging expeditions to America about this time, despaired of further co-operation at Bath: he claimed (not unjustly, at that time) that getting anything done there was like trying to persuade 'a very old dog to get out of its basket'.

Rudolf Bing had now become Artistic Director of Edinburgh, as well as General Manager of whatever took place at Glyndebourne. Often pulled in conflicting directions by the demands of each, he solved the problem to his own satisfaction, if not to either of theirs, by accepting an invitation to take charge of the Metropolitan Opera in New York, while retaining an advisory role at Edinburgh. The Christies were understandably hurt by Bing's departure after all they had done for him, without perhaps always remembering how much he had done for them. They ignored the fact that the Festival had yet to be re-established at Glyndebourne itself, and that Bing, with all the *Angst* of a former refugee, had his own career to consider. In reply to the two sad and embarrassed letters from Bing lamenting their evident resentment, they showed their true and typical generosity by sending him the following telegram:

> Warm congratulations from two rather sad Glyndebourne hearts. Wish you ever increasing success and happiness and may you carry that large organisation forward to the great heights which its country's wealth and your capacity should achieve.

On the other hand, it should be remembered that Bing said of himself: 'Remember, under this cold exterior there beats a heart of stone.' But he remained available with advice for Moran Caplat, who now took over as General Manager of the opera. In May 1950, when the first proper post-war season at Glyndebourne itself was about to open, Bing warned Caplat that Ebert, who in fact was to go on directing at Glyndebourne for another ten years, was already difficult to handle. Bing wrote, irritably but understandably, that:

> He *really* doesn't know what he wants, and just loves to destroy what he has got so that he can then improvise all over again. He just must not be allowed to do that. Between you and me he just *must* feel more important than he actually is now, for he has become *un peu gaga* and at times seems hopelessly old-fashioned.
>
> Please brace yourself with infinite diplomacy, tact and patience. Machiavelli and Metternich will appear poor beginners by the time you have brought this off.

This was typical Bing, and to what extent his harsh words were deserved is a subjective question. In the end the answer would vary extensively from production to production; and over the years, many of the singers remained in awe of 'the Professor', and were deeply grateful for his guidance. But Bing's theme was to be echoed, with variations, by more than one general manager at Glyndebourne in the years that followed, with reference to other gifted but, not surprisingly, self-centred producers. Such observations underline the complexity of putting on an opera at all, with its huge range of vital components. Conductors, singers, orchestra, designer, wardrobe, lighting: all play essential parts. If there is not a single, co-ordinating commander-in-chief, their efforts are likely to lack the dramatic and musical unity on which the Christies, Ebert and Busch had laid such emphasis. If, on the other hand, there is such a person, sooner or later he will almost certainly be resented, as Caplat himself was to discover. It would be possible to give many more examples, both at Glyndebourne and elsewhere over the years – notably perhaps at Salzburg, under Karajan – of disagreements and indignant rumblings beneath a surface that always seems so smooth and harmonious to the fortunate audience when a production is eventually performed. But for anyone except those directly involved, the inevitable outbursts of bickering and ruffled feathers, the grudging compromises and general resentment become tedious, and will only rarely be mentioned.

While an experienced administrator like Bing could find fault with Ebert, many of the singers tell a very different story. Thetis Blacker, a member of the chorus in the 1950s, recalled later that to work under Ebert was the experience of a lifetime, particularly so, perhaps, for a relative beginner. To her he was a heroic, almost superhuman figure, who could conjure out of singers performances of which they had never imagined they were capable. Ian Wallace, too, regarded the extent of his guidance as 'magical'. Having been an actor himself, Ebert would suggest facial expressions and gestures which greatly increased the confidence of singers, and his powers of observation and memory for detail were astonishing. Any mistakes were quickly eliminated before they could become part of a routine. Wallace adds: 'By the first night everything had been done to make it easy for you'; and, as a result: 'Glyndebourne spoils you rotten for working anywhere else.' Hence the whole cast were determined to do their best out of love for opera and for Glyndebourne itself. None of them regarded working there as 'just another job'. Other singers have testified to Ebert's rare power to bring out unsuspected reserves of talent, and few, if any, other opera houses can ever have built up such a fruitful *esprit de corps*.

Janet Baker, however, had reservations. She sang in the chorus in 1956 and 1957, some years before her great triumphs as a soloist. At that stage, she was happy to accept the Glyndebourne system without reservation, but felt that Ebert's severity could sometimes be destructive. Yet she states that, as a singer starting out, she gained enormously through hearing what he actually said to the principals in rehearsals, and how they learned under his direction. She profited by their lessons; and the benefit was to remain with her throughout her life. The European understanding and appreciation of opera to be found at Glyndebourne provided an extra dimension for English singers, which at that time they could hardly have acquired anywhere else. On the other hand, she mentions an example of his severity 'having wrecked a singer's self-confidence', and John Christie, when in the mood, would excitedly urge

John Christie in 1950, addressing the company from the stage

people to come and witness an Ebert rage when one broke out.

At a time when prospects of opera at Glyndebourne itself were still very hazy, the 1950 season was only made possible by a guarantee from John Spedan Lewis of the John Lewis Partnership, who shared a number of ideals with John, though very different in temperament. He had already found employment for Bing at Peter Jones during the war, and had also helped Glyndebourne in other ways. He now gave a guarantee of £12,500 against loss, and the season went ahead. There may have been a subtle element of arm-twisting in the way in which this came about. Lewis is on record as saying that:

> My wife came to me and said that Audrey says they're giving it all up; they're going to retire to Devon and Glyndebourne will be sold. John confirmed that he saw no way of avoiding it, sadder still because Glyndebourne had never been sold in 700 years. But, he said, 'We can't charge more; people wouldn't pay.'

In *Così* Sena Jurinac moved on to the part of Fiordiligi, having sung Dorabella at Edinburgh the year before, and Geraint Evans made the first of many successful appearances, sharing the part of Guglielmo. The range of his voice was particularly remarkable, and he recalled later that at his first audition he had sung an aria from *Simon Boccanegra*, descending from the alternative top note to bottom G. Beecham, who was present at the audition, disconcerted Evans by calling out loudly from the back of the hall: 'What the hell does he think he is? A tenor or a bass?' And on another occasion, when he had followed Ebert's instructions almost too faithfully, Ebert commented 'Very good, Geraint. But now be Geraint Evans, not Carl Ebert.' This was particularly apt, because Ebert had, perhaps to a unique degree, the gift of inspiring singers to create their own interpretations of a role, once they had seen how he saw it himself. In the 1950 season, *Figaro* and the 1912 version of Strauss's *Ariadne auf Naxos* were taken to Edinburgh, the latter designed by Oliver Messel, whose meticulous research and professionalism matched the trouble taken by the musicians. (Rolf Gérard's sets for *Figaro* and *Così* were, however, quite heavily criticized.) In *Ariadne*, Miles Malleson played Jourdain in his adaptation of Molière's *Le bourgeois gentilhomme* which formed the first act. It was the first and last Glyndebourne opera to be conducted by Beecham, though there had been many plans for collaboration in the past.

Moran Caplat, who was by now firmly installed as Bing's successor, performed the first of many valuable services to Glyndebourne by persuading Busch to return in 1950. Although the task was made easier because the rift had been before Caplat's time, the reconciliation was nevertheless a notable achievement. It was good to have him back, although two months before Busch's sudden death in September 1951 Caplat wrote in a private letter to Audrey that he had become 'old, tired, still a better conductor than most, but he is slipping'.

Slipping or not, Busch's contribution up to the war had been incalculable. It was he who had introduced Ebert to Glyndebourne, and had got him to agree that the conductor's role was 60 per cent of the total, to the producer's 40 per cent. 'In opera,' he said, 'the heartbeat of the performance must come from the pit.' At the time, nobody contradicted him, but it is probably true to say that nowadays the producer's share has increased to about 85 per cent. His energy and stamina in his heyday were astonishing, and he would play piano duets for hours after dinner at the end of a day of intensive rehearsal. Like Ebert, he also had a good sense of humour and on the rare occasions when there was a violent disagreement between the two of them, John would quickly leave the room and fetch a bowl of ice, which he would place between the warring parties. According to Spike Hughes, no quarrel ever survived this intervention. Laughter would follow, and the work would proceed. And in a passing tribute four years after Busch's death, as well as commending his other gifts, John praised his 'honest efficiency ... No time, no money were wasted.'

There had, however been some criticism by John of Ebert, which made Ebert hesitant at one point about abandoning the many other sources of work he now enjoyed, to come back to Glyndebourne. Caplat, too, commented that Jock Gough, now the chief stage technician who, for many years, had been able to do no wrong in John's eyes,

> gets more impossible every day. He complains that his men are no good – but never tries to teach them or let them do anything themselves, and his continuous grumbling makes willing work impossible ... quite incapable of any sort of co-operation and sabotages the efforts of others in childish jealousy ... a very grave liability to the overall efficiency of the hands ... he wouldn't keep his job anywhere else but in many ways we should hate to lose him.

Evidently, the old guard could not be expected to last for ever, especially when those who were taking their places thought as they did.

Spedan Lewis's life-saving gesture had been for one year only. But for 1951 an even larger source of salvation had been tapped. John had been in touch with Sir Edward Bridges, the Permanent Secretary to the Treasury, ever since the middle of the war when he had been trying to set up the National Council of Music. Bridges, along with Kenneth Clark, had been one of John's most sympathetic listeners among the influential élite who had been approached. As Lord Bridges, he was later to become a trustee of Glyndebourne when he retired from the

Richard Lewis sang the title role of Idomeneo *at the first professional UK performance in 1951 by Glyndebourne and in six later revivals*

Treasury. He was supported by a Labour Minister, John Wilmot, who lived near Glyndebourne. Together they secured a special Treasury Grant for a season of four Mozart operas, successfully maintaining that the Festival of Britain in 1951 would be incomplete without a Festival of Mozart at Glyndebourne. This was the only public subsidy that the Glyndebourne Festival has ever received, although, much later, the Arts Council was to support Glyndebourne Touring Opera.

To avoid any danger of accusations about 'the mixture as before', the season opened with *Idomeneo*, the first professional performance of this opera in Britain, with Richard Lewis in the title role. Desmond Shawe-Taylor, writing in the July issue of *Opera* magazine, which was largely devoted to Glyndebourne, summed up the opera's quality by referring to Mozart's 'incomparable faculty for expressing the passion and emotions of characters that become altogether human, pathetic and convincing' in spite of having stepped out of the perhaps unfamiliar mythology of ancient Crete. It was also decided to follow Mozart's revised edition of 1786 when he rewrote the part of Idamante for a tenor in place of the original castrato, or, as would be the case nowadays, a counter-tenor. And for the first time, the continuo was played on a harpsichord (by John Pritchard), rather than the piano on which Busch had previously insisted. Audrey felt inspired to write to Bing in New York that this was 'one of the best things we have ever done ... something between utter serenity and tempestuous excitement'. Oliver Messel's sets were so highly thought of that a model of them has a place to this day in the Mozart Museum in Salzburg, among other landmarks of technical progress in the production of his operas. In *Così*, which was the first Glyndebourne opera to be televised, Sesto Bruscantini made his Glyndebourne debut as Don Alfonso, with Sena Jurinac (whom he later, and rather briefly, married) as Fiordiligi. Ominously, Busch was criticized for having suddenly become inflexible, 'a drill sergeant', in both *Figaro* and *Don Giovanni*, which were the other two operas given. Three months later he was dead, at the age of only sixty-one.

4
THE 1950s

If the death of Busch ends a chapter of Glyndebourne's musical history, it also coincided with developments on the financial side without which Glyndebourne could never have become – and remained – secure, and could not have survived with anything like its original character intact. John Lewis in 1950 and the Treasury in 1951, crucial though their support had been, had provided no basis for the future. But now a great ally appeared in the shape of N. T. Sekers (later Sir Miki Sekers), an opera-loving Hungarian who had shrewdly taken advantage of industrial grants from the Government to set up the West Cumberland Silk Mills at White-haven. In 1951 he had donated specially dyed fabrics to Glyndebourne for the costumes for *Don Giovanni*. But he did not stop there. Pondering on the handsome programme book, complete with colour advertisements, which had been produced for the Festival of Aix-en-Provence, he had the idea of organizing something similar for Glyndebourne. His ambitious target was to enlist forty advertisers, who would contribute a total of £20,000. The first year produced eighteen, but he had set the snowball rolling, and by 1964 the advertisers numbered only one short of the original target. The pioneer firms, to whom Glyndebourne owes much more than their individual contributions, included Yardley, Marshall & Snelgrove, Floris, Aristoc, W. & A. Gilbey, and The Gramophone

Miki Sekers, during an interval, in 1954

Company (now EMI), all of whom might regard the production of opera as more or less relevant to their business. But it also included S. G. Warburg, High Duty Alloys, and Abdulla, the first of a series of large-scale contributors from the tobacco industry. The mixture of generosity, energy and modesty expressed in Sekers's letters during the formation of the band of advertisers is exceptionally attractive, and does him great credit. Indeed, without his contribution, or something similar, it is difficult to see how Glyndebourne could have been put on its feet again as an independent institution. Together with Oliver Messel, he gave select lunches and drinks parties, where captains of industry were cajoled into adding their companies to the ranks of corporate membership, a privilege which was granted to the advertisers.

This was another of Messel's valuable contributions to Glyndebourne. From a modern perspective his designs, considered on their own, sometimes have a whiff of the chocolate box about them. But in Ebert's productions of Mozart and Rossini, they were exactly right for the time and were generally agreed to complement the music and further enrich the experience of the audience, who were emerging from over a decade of wartime privation and post-war austerity, when frivolous decor had become a thing of the past. His sets for *Il barbiere di Siviglia* in 1954 earned a round of applause of their own at every performance.

Sekers was joined by John Wilmot, the already mentioned Labour MP and former Minister who, as Lord Wilmot, later became Chairman of the Glyndebourne Festival Society, which was established in 1952. Its aim was to raise £25,000 a year by means of three kinds of membership: corporate, individual and associate, each carrying different degrees of benefit. By the opening of the 1952 season these categories consisted of 25, 65 and 716 members respectively. The first of the annual programme books was funded by the advertisers, with an appropriate cover designed

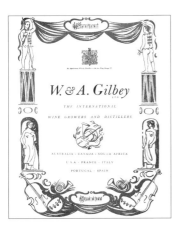

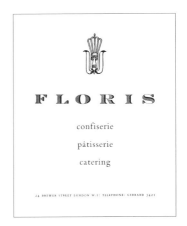

Some advertisements from the first programme book

by Oliver Messel, and a resounding re-statement by John of the philosophy, achievements and policy of Glyndebourne. There followed articles on the operas themselves by, among others, Desmond Shawe-Taylor, and Frank Howes of *The Times*, whose relationship with the Christies was very greatly to the advantage of Glyndebourne over the years – although towards the end of his life John complained obsessively and quite unreasonably to his old friend Sir William Haley, the editor, about what he considered the excessive space given in its columns to Covent Garden. On the whole, Fleet Street remained unruffled by these familiar outbursts, regarding them generously with something like affection.

Before the 1952 season, there was a special performance of *Idomeneo*, in memory of Fritz Busch, and a bronze death mask was unveiled in the covered way leading to the opera house (now relocated on the foyer wall outside the new house). The conductor was John Pritchard, who had gained experience working under Busch at Edinburgh, and was to play an increasing role, though the management were cautious about entrusting too much to him too soon. New energy, vitality and sheer fun were introduced by the production of the first of a series of works by Rossini, then little known in England except for the occasional *Barber of Seville*. *La Cenerentola* had been put on, though not conducted, by Beecham at Covent Garden in 1934; and Vittorio Gui, who now con-ducted it at Glyndebourne, had established an important reputation in Italy before the war for his part in the general Rossini revival there, though his range extended far beyond Italian music. In his youth he had been a friend of Strauss as well as of Puccini and Debussy, and he had been the chief and most authoritative exponent of the works of Brahms in Italy. He had also composed *Fantasia Bianca*, a symphonic poem which was in some ways the forerunner of Disney's *Fantasia* thirty years later. He was a great musician, with extensive enthusiasms. Up to this point, the inspiration of Glyndebourne had been German, especially in its thoroughness and eternally patient attention to detail. But Busch had relied more than once on information from Gui about suitable singers who were emerging in Italy, and whose promise blossomed into mature quality under the Glyndebourne rehearsal system. With Gui, the Mediterranean sun came out. The Spanish soprano Marina de Gabarain sang Angelina both in 1952 and in the revivals at Glyndebourne and Edinburgh in the following year. The critics were less enthusiastic about her than about her 'ugly sisters', Alda Noni and Fernanda Cadoni, but this of course did not deter John from introducing her to a foreign ambassador who was his guest at one performance as 'The Queen of Spain'. (There was also for many years a bearded viola player in the orchestra whom John invariably introduced as Sir Thomas Beecham.) And Ian Wallace had such a success as Don Magnifico that he was invited by Gui to sing the part in Rome. Gui also conducted *Macbeth* and *Così* and Ebert confirmed his versatility in all four operas, each so strikingly different.

There was, however, one growing cloud on the horizon. Audrey's health had been steadily deteriorating. Though she bravely concealed it, she had been suffering from crippling migraines for several years, probably as a result of high blood pressure, for which, at the time, there were no sure remedies. She underwent two operations on her spine in 1952, and the year before had been unable to go to Edinburgh. At Glyndebourne she spent many days in bed, only getting up for the evening performances and the endless round of entertaining existing and potential benefactors and supporters, from which she never flinched. She was also bedridden for several weeks at a family-owned hotel at Instow, near Tapley. As well as increasing kidney trouble, in the autumn of 1952 her blood pressure mounted still higher, until she became blind in one eye, and began to lose the sight of the other. Much of the time she felt desperately ill, but in the better intervals she still took as keen an interest as ever in what was going on. Moran Caplat took endless trouble to keep her informed in a gentle and affectionate fashion, and her secretary Margaret Bellamy was wonderfully thoughtful and imaginative. In the previous November and again in February, Caplat wrote to Ebert that she seemed 'much better' but the end came at last on 31 May 1953. In accordance with her stated wish the season opened, as planned, only a week later.

Since she herself was a professional, it was to her rather than to John that people often brought their complaints, their troubles and their fears, in the confidence that they would be fully understood, and if at all possible remedied. The deeply moving tributes to her in the 1954 programme book, as well as the dozens of personal letters of sympathy, all bear witness to her tact and fairness as well as to her exceptional kindness of heart, though it never diminished her sense of standards and her power of communicating them. And who else would have had a half-bottle of champagne put on the dressing-table for each principal singer on every first night? Even though they were not consumed until after the performance, the effect on morale was considerable. Earlier, she even had circular tables installed in the canteen, so that nobody could sit at the head of the table and rule the roost. Consequently the humblest stage-hand might find Carl Ebert or Sena Jurinac sitting down beside

Preparing a dressing room before a performance, 1953. Audrey would always send champagne to the principals on a first night, a custom continued to this day

him, and different branches of the staff were able to make friends easily in the atmosphere she created, as indeed they do to this day. It is worth stressing the importance of this aspect of her achievement. In order to teach and maintain the standards that the Christies set themselves, it was essential to create a climate that would attract promising, and sometimes established, singers to Glyndebourne, even for less pay than elsewhere.

In 1950 Audrey had given her own version of the Glyndebourne philosophy, which had put such a special stamp on the productions:

> In opera the music comes first. It is not a drama with music, but a drama through music. . . . Drama it is and must be, otherwise surely the composer would have chosen another medium, cantata or oratorio. But since he has chosen to make an opera then one must serve the dramatic side with equal faithfulness. Singers must portray characters as well dramatically as musically. Glyndebourne, the place, seems to inspire all to express the original dream which they set out to reveal. Elation in quest for perfection.

At her memorial service, Bishop Bell, the famous Bishop of Chichester, referred to her 'natural sympathy, which went out to any in trouble, any stricken soul, or anyone who was shy or awkward or in difficulty', and her friend Mrs Edwin Fisher wrote that:

> After her two grave operations she told me how she would fight against taking the drugs which were given her to relieve the great pain she had to endure; how she would count the hours until the next dose was due and then say 'Not yet; I'll bear it a little longer.' I think she was one of the bravest people I have ever known.

But as far as Glyndebourne is concerned, John Christie himself must have the last words, taken from the short message that he had printed and sent out in answer to the innumerable letters of sympathy which poured in. They are very characteristic, not only of his vision but also of his complete lack of self-consciousness:

> Time may give us wings and bring us nearer together. We must grow these wings and grow them consciously. . . . Audrey has given us our purpose. Our purpose was born from Audrey's life, and from her and with her knowledge and guidance. The purpose is a gem of fine quality and has many facets. . . . Audrey lived to see Everest conquered. We cannot, we will not let her down.

Indeed, she was not let down. Their joint creation had acquired an irresistible force which overcame the immovable tragedy of her early death.

Edinburgh had invited the Hamburg Opera to appear there in 1952 instead of Glyndebourne and Caplat wrote rather acidly to Ebert that: 'they have now decided that Edinburgh is to be a World Fair of art rather than a creative festival . . . it has been moving that way ever since it was realised that out of festival time Edinburgh and Scotland were utterly uncreative themselves'. However hotly this would have been denied, it is not difficult to understand Caplat's attitude. The Hamburg Opera had a considerable popular success, even though Caplat thought it 'lacked the sparkle and excitement that they were used to getting from us'. Their performances marked his first acquaintance with Günther Rennert, an ex-pupil of Ebert's, who directed some of the Hamburg productions and was later to become Head of Production at Glyndebourne. Caplat thought that he 'still had a long way to go', but that Ebert could be 'quite proud of his success so far'. The announcement that Hamburg was to replace Glyndebourne had caused violent and gratifying indignation in Scotland, and furious letters appeared in Scottish newspapers. Somewhat abashed, the Edinburgh management asked Glyndebourne back in 1953. It is worth noting that Gui had so much enjoyed conducting Glyndebourne operas at Edinburgh in 1948 and 1949 that he wrote as follows to Caplat, who had struck up excellent relations with him and was more than once a guest at his house in Italy.

Gui's form of English was idiosyncratic, but he was easily understood:

> I look forward very serious to take again the direction of the operas in the Christies' theatre, that I consider the only really artistic initiative today in Europe. I know, moreover, that the collaboration between Charles Ebert and myself can give results as it should be impossible to rejoin anywhere. Therefore the question of money is of scarce importance for me, and I am satisfied with your proposals that I accept without discussion.

It is impossible to exaggerate just how rare it is for the general manager of an opera company to hear the sentiments expressed in that

Carl Ebert, John Christie and Moran Caplat in 1953

last sentence; and it is worth at this stage summarizing Glyndebourne's financial position. The total costs for the year, net of box office receipts, were £25,740. The net contribution from the Glyndebourne Festival Society in its first year of existence was £3,200 and, thanks to the advertisers, a further £4,750 came in from the new programme book. There were obvious grounds for hoping that these contributions would increase over the years, as indeed they did, but at the end of 1952 there was still a deficit of nearly £18,000 to be found by John. The tax position for rich individuals was to improve under the Conservative Government that had taken office in 1951, but not with immediate effect.

One way of helping to safeguard the future would have been to turn Glyndebourne into a charitable trust. John had first had ideas about this during the war, but no progress had been made during the years of uncertainty. Audrey had always had strong reservations. She feared the day might come when her son George, who had always been given to understand that he would take over in due course, might find himself only one of a number of people in control, and that the special character of Glyndebourne, which she had played such a vital part in creating, might be diluted or destroyed by others. She greatly appreciated the comparison made by Miki Sekers between the way in which the Wagner family had maintained Bayreuth and her own hopes for the future of Glyndebourne. In one of the last letters that we have, she wrote, on 4 February 1953, telling him, prophetically, that she did not want

> to hamper the growth of Glyndebourne by sticking to too old traditions – as D'Oyly Carte has done for Gilbert & Sullivan – but year by year to give it fresh 'fertilisation', yet always replenishing and improving the original idea . . . *and* if George is capable of improving on what we have started, his initiative may not be frustrated or hampered.

How abundantly her hopes were to be fulfilled! The Trust was not finally set up until after her death, but she had the satisfaction of knowing that it would be in the form that she wanted. On 31 May 1954 the announcement of its formation stated that: 'the Trustees had made an agreement with Mr Christie that he and his colleagues, who have brought the Festival to its present high level of distinction, shall continue to be responsible for its direction and administration'. It was a big concession, even bigger than John's own pact with Busch and Ebert twenty years earlier; and it was the first performing arts organization in this country to have been turned into a charitable trust.

The list of trustees attests to the fact that, however intransigent John might be at times, Glyndebourne's position was now such that men and women of the highest calibre answered his call. The first Chairman was Sir Wilfrid Eady, another Treasury man, who had devised the Eady Plan to come to the aid of the British Film industry; he was also a trustee of the Old Vic, and had come to live outside Lewes. Also from the Board of the Old Vic (and the BBC) was Lady Violet Bonham Carter, who had been so impressed by the 'war nursery' on her wartime weekend at Glyndebourne, and whose half-brother, the famous director Anthony Asquith, made a semi-documentary film about Glyndebourne the following year, entitled *On Such a Night*. (It was revived, as a period piece, on French television in 1996, evidence of the unfading charm of his treatment of the subject.) Sir Mark Turner and Sir Geoffrey Gibbs, both bankers who had had valuable experience in the Ministry of Economic Warfare, also joined, together with Gerald Coke, who was the Chairman of Rio Tinto, and a noted collector of Handel manuscripts. The Trust also included two Sussex neighbours, Lord Duncannon and Lady Reading, both of whom had served in varied and distinguished public causes; the admirable Scottish accountant A. B. Barrie; John's solicitor, Col. C.H.N. Adams; and finally Miki Sekers and Lord Wilmot, whose invaluable support has already been described.

The 1953 season had included two radical departures. First, the British première of Stravinsky's *The Rake's Progress* was put on in Edinburgh, and subsequently revived in Sussex four times. The original choice as a designer had been John Piper, but he was not a great admirer of Hogarth, though he respected him. Nor did he think much of the Auden–

Osbert Lancaster's witty designs for costumes in the Brothel scene of
The Rake's Progress *(1953)*

Kallmann libretto. Altogether he considered the opera (which had first been performed only a year earlier) too much of a mongrel, and was not convinced that it was a first-class piece of work – though there are of course many other operas of equally mixed origins. Fortunately for countless opera-goers, however, both Osbert Lancaster and, in 1975, David Hockney, in their different ways produced designs which were original and startlingly effective. The other novelty was Gluck's *Alceste*, sung with the original French libretto. The sets were designed by Hugh Casson, and his decision to make use of the full depth of the stage, right back to the rear wall, had a very favourable effect on the acoustics. John's rooted prejudice against the language was partly overcome by his reflection that Gluck, like Mozart, was obliged to compose operas in whatever language was required by the commission. Spike Hughes mentions that apart from Magda László, who was Hungarian, the rest of the cast were English-speaking, and their accents ranged from Sussex to Scotland – and even, in the case of John Cameron, to Australia. This again raised the ever-insoluble question of whether operas should be put on in their original language or in translation. Philip Hope-Wallace, a distinguished critic though not over-friendly to Glyndebourne – Osbert Lancaster rather unkindly nicknamed him Abandon Hope-Wallace – has pointed out with some justice the drawback of having Australians and Welshmen exchanging jokes in eighteenth-century Italian, and predictably getting little or no audience reaction. This state of affairs sometimes led even as great a producer as Ebert to reinforce the wit of a passage with excessive visual counterpoint, and what Hope-Wallace called 'a fatal over-insistence, in comedy, as if the audience would go to sleep if the stage were not in perpetual movement'. And, of course, when the ensembles and solos reached such a consistent level of excellence, any faults grated all the more by contrast, which explained the view, quite often expressed, that the great Ebert was sometimes less great in the comic operas than when dealing with serious or tragic situations.

Before the introduction of supertitles in the 1980s, there were inevitably drawbacks to productions in the original language. But when such endless trouble is taken to perfect the productions, it is not unreasonable to expect the audience to do some homework by familiarizing themselves in advance, to whatever extent they can, with at least the outline of an opera's story. John had decided from the outset that audiences should be urged to take the trouble to wear evening dress as a gesture of respect for the trouble taken in the production, and to make every evening at Glyndebourne a special occasion. If this created a danger of social smartness for its own sake, that was a price worth paying. (Elisabeth Söderström has commented that at no major opera house in the world – though Bayreuth is probably an exception – is more than half the audience there for purely musical reasons, and that in all probability this has always been so.) And if they can take the trouble to dress up, they can also take the trouble to learn something about the opera in advance if they want to appreciate it to anything like the full. Better that, surely, than trying to force an often clumsy and unworthy

Ebert and Lancaster at a costume parade for The Rake's Progress, *1953*

On the opening night of Die Entführung *in 1953, the spoken role of Pasha Selim was taken by Carl Ebert*

translation into the structure of the music, with words that may be inadequately articulated – though it is not necessary to go as far as the American critic H. L. Mencken, who observed that: 'Opera in English is, in the main, about as sensible as baseball in Italian.'

The 1953 season was the longest yet, with thirty-seven performances at Glyndebourne and, starting only a month later, another eighteen at Edinburgh. *La Cenerentola* was put on with exactly the same cast as the year before – the first time this had happened – and on the first night of *Die Entführung* Ebert himself took the spoken role of the Pasha Selim owing to the non-appearance of the well-known film actor Anton Walbrook. Another drama consisted of an all-theatrical collision, luckily not serious, when a car containing Bruscantini, Jurinac, Oncina and Helmut Krebs crashed into one driven by Rodney Millington, owner of the theatrical directory *Spotlight*. *Die Entführung* was televised, to the complete approval of most of the press including the *News of the World* and *Daily Worker*. Only *The People* proved that the philistines were still alive and kicking when it protested that two and a half hours of *Die Entführung*, even once a year, 'rudely ignored the masses who are the overwhelming majority'.

The next year saw the official transfer of the house and garden and the opera house to the Trust, described earlier. During the previous winter the theatre had been enlarged to accommodate a further 125 seats. This was done by widening the proscenium opening by about six feet, and by rebuilding the balcony which contained about a third of the new total of 718 seats. For the first time Glyndebourne put on a well-loved perennial, *Il barbiere di Siviglia*. Elsewhere, it is often carelessly staged, in the comfortable near-certainty that, given even a reasonable level of singing, it will succeed, though even Rossini himself once said: 'My *Barber* is a bright farce, but *Figaro* is the finest possible masterpiece of musical comedy.' At Glyndebourne, of course, there was the usual intensely careful preparation; and Gui, who later conducted other Rossini works at Glyndebourne, was regarded by many as the greatest-ever conductor of his music. Caplat's memoirs contain a telling anecdote about the need to keep the opera in its original two–act form and to cope with the scene change at the end of the first scene. Messel's solution was to design it with the corner of the house centre-stage, with streets in forced perspective leading steeply away on either side. At the appropriate moment, the chorus took hold of the house and opened it out, in the manner of a doll's house, revealing a two-storeyed interior. Every night, this transformation won a round of applause. Ebert, confirming Gui's reservations about his fitness to direct a sparkling Italian comedy, grumbled bitterly about the practical difficulties of grouping the characters in a set with such a steep perspective, although he had earlier approved the models. Messel turned on the soothing charm: 'Carly darling, it's going to be *beautiful!*' Two days later, Caplat overheard Ebert walking past his office window and explaining proudly to a visitor in the garden about his brilliant conception of the doll's house and how well dear Oliver had carried it out. 'Of such is theatre made.'

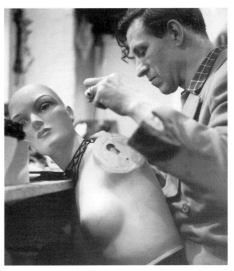

Graziella Sciutti and Juan Oncina being fitted with their costumes for the 1954 La Cenerentola *by designer Oliver Messel*

Property master Harry Kellard at work, 1953

As for the singing, it depended, as so often, on which paper you read. Hope-Wallace said that none of it was 'individually very remarkable', while *The Times* described it as 'almost uniformly excellent'. Both however agreed that Oliver Messel's sets were a little too fantastic for any sense of reality to survive, though the *Sunday Times* found them 'ingenious and enchanting'. (Reviews, which are generally based on a single early performance, usually vary, and not always as a result of ignorance or prejudice. Janet Baker has pointed out that the pressure of a first night, with its special frisson, can easily delay the development of a finely balanced production. Most people who see a production see it only once, and 'can only therefore understand a small fraction of its actual life'. Yet the differences between reviews are quite often interesting to the general public, if not to the management or the cast, and can help their readers to form clearer independent conclusions; in a history of Glyndebourne, however, there can only be room to quote the smallest of samples, especially as one is often reminded of Kenneth

Tynan's happy dictum that a critic is a man who knows the way, but can't drive the car.)

Alceste was revived, and both Richard Lewis and Magda László were judged to have improved on their performances of the year before. As a curtain-raiser to the 1916 revised version of *Ariadne auf Naxos* there was a characteristic Glyndebourne innovation in putting on Busoni's *L'Arlecchino*, composed in Switzerland, also in 1916, and directed by Carl Ebert's son Peter. This was the first performance of any of Busoni's operas in England, and while *L'Arlecchino* was admired, *Ariadne* was so much better established that the juxtaposition seemed a little unfair on Busoni. John Pritchard's conducting of both works was a significant early milestone in his career, whereas that of Georg Solti in *Don Giovanni* was, oddly, much less successful, and was considered excessively tense. Back in Edinburgh, Rossini's *Le comte Ory* was, if possible, even more of a success than *Il barbiere* had been at Glyndebourne. The *Glasgow Herald* explained helpfully that the name part was 'an early *Don Giovanni* from the time of the Crusades', and the Hungarian Sari Barabas, together with Bruscantini, Wallace and Oncina, shone in music which makes considerable demands on the singers. The joint efforts of Ebert, Gui and Messel coalesced into a splendid whole, and indeed, Ernest Newman's view was that this had been the greatest triumph of Ebert's whole career.

As if this were not enough, after a total of fifty-four performances in the United Kingdom, the company appeared by invitation in two performances of *Cenerentola* at the Berlin Festival at the end of September, reviewed under the perfectly comprehensible headline 'Perfekter Rossini aus England'. On both nights there were over thirty curtain calls, and the audience would not leave until the house lights were switched off. Later in the year, this production was issued as the first long-playing record of a complete Glyndebourne opera, once again making the standards of Glyndebourne known to a wider world. If one had to choose, in chronological order, three outstanding achievements by Glyndebourne in the recording field, the pre-war Mozart productions would be the first, Gui's Rossini series in the 1950s the second, and Haitink's 1980s Mozart series the third.

The 1954 season was also notable for two personal awards to John. He was made a Companion of Honour in the New Year's Honours List, and he was the first Englishman ever to be awarded the Mozart Medal of the Vienna Mozart Society. Typically, and successfully, he asked that it should also be awarded posthumously to Audrey.

In 1955 Glyndebourne celebrated its twenty-first birthday, though not in terms of seasons, because of the dark years in the 1940s. There was appropriately a new production of *Figaro* – Gui's first at Glyndebourne – with Ebert himself as the only link with the production of four years earlier. Apart from Sena Jurinac's Countess, the main parts were played by Italians; the audience was dazzled and amused, but perhaps not moved as it had been by Busch and his casts in the past. *Le comte Ory* was introduced to Glyndebourne itself with great success, *Il barbiere* was repeated (and televised without complaint), and *The Rake's Progress* was revived for its third consecutive year. Gui, now aged seventy, was advised by his doctor not to go to Edinburgh, and *Falstaff* was conducted there by Carlo Maria Giulini, *Il barbiere* by Alberto Erede, and *La forza del destino* by Pritchard.

It was announced that with no fewer than six Mozart operas to be prepared in the following year, the bicentenary of the composer's birth, Glyndebourne would not have time to offer anything new at Edinburgh, and the Hamburg Opera was accordingly invited to appear again. The fact is that, having successfully re-established itself at home, Glyndebourne no longer needed Edinburgh, and the complications involved in taking its new productions there were considerable, especially in the cramped space of the King's Theatre. Equally, Edinburgh had now established a momentum of its own, and had no difficulty in attracting a wide range of international companies in order to vary what it had to offer. Back in 1947, everything had been different. Nevertheless, when the end came, it was a parting of friends, and there was a brief sadness in the air. The Mozart anniversary season was a huge success, and *Die Zauberflöte* was revived in a new production, rather surprisingly for the first time since 1937. As always with this opera, casting problems loomed large, but Mattiwilda Dobbs succeeded admirably as the Queen of

Night, and, gratifyingly, was considered to have improved on her previous performance of the role at Covent Garden. Back in 1953, Jani Strasser had thought her the best Zerbinetta (in *Ariadne*) that he had ever heard. In *Figaro* Joan Sutherland, later to have a dazzling career in the *bel canto* parts in Donizetti and Bellini, was a success, at any rate vocally, as the Countess, sharing the role with Elisabeth Grümmer. Oliver Messel's sets, as well as their sheer visual quality, were praised by Andrew Porter for 'imposing nothing on the music, and seeming to spring from it . . . reflecting and decorating Mozart instead of trying to interpret him'. Those producers who, years later, insisted on labouring the class message of *Figaro*, thereby replacing Mozart's gossamer with denim, could have learnt much from the whole production.

Another feature of the 1956 season was that, instead of Edinburgh, the company were invited to appear for a fortnight in Liverpool in September, with very few cast changes from the Festival in the three Mozart operas performed. They were warmly received, and were implored, unsuccessfully for many years, to return. The sea air inspired the old submariner Moran Caplat with the idea of acquiring an aircraft carrier, and giving operatic performances at suitable anchorages around the world. It was an attractive plan, but the requisite vessel was never found, and the prospect of putting on, say, *Otello* in Venice or *Khovantschina* in St Petersburg sadly never materialized.

The voluminous and ever-patient correspondence between Caplat at Glyndebourne and Ebert in Germany and America between 1952 and 1960, in the days before international telephone calls and faxes became commonplace, is very revealing. Often the results were negative, but they show how much persistence and tact was required for a first-class cast to be assembled. Singers who said they would be available often turned out not to be, and, less often, vice versa. Those who had already established a reputation usually had engagements elsewhere, and the more they had the less time could they spare for Glyndebourne's sacred rehearsal schedules – quite apart from the much higher fees they could command elsewhere. For example, Elisabeth Schwarzkopf might well have appeared at Glyndebourne in 1953 had she not been waylaid by

Walter Legge (whom she married that year) for recording sessions with EMI, which one might have thought could have been postponed. But the time needed for recordings is relatively short and the artists' fees are high, so it is understandable that singers who are asked to record should give priority to doing so. But in general, Glyndebourne now concentrated more on the young and promising singers whom it could afford to pay, and who could make themselves available for the periods of preparation. It is also noticeable from this correspondence that although they were to work together with magnificent results in the Rossini and Mozart productions, Ebert sometimes had considerable reservations about Gui's attitudes and suggestions. He accused him, early on, of thinking in terms of 'Italian, and only Italian, provincial festivals', and of not understanding 'the aim and task of Glyndebourne'. This was largely unfair, but it was a foretaste of the disagreements that were eventually to lead to Ebert's departure from Glyndebourne at the end of the decade.

After the 1956 season, John had a prostate operation, and in the winter a second and more serious heart attack. The sight in his remaining good eye began to deteriorate, and by the time of his death in 1962, he had become almost blind. Unable to shave, he grew a beard in the last year of his life, which came as a shock to those who saw him sitting in the foyer almost to the very end. Although he had played a decreasing part in the running of Glyndebourne ever since Audrey's death, he still liked to make his views known, if not in the trenchant manner of earlier days. For a time, the gap he left was unfillable, especially for those who had been coming to the operas for a long time. And the way in which he himself personified Glyndebourne had been well summed up by his old admirer Neville Cardus in a review of *Falstaff* two years earlier:

> When all is said and written of performances at Glyndebourne, the place is the thing – the creation of one man and in its way as much of a work of art as anything presented there. At every performance – when audiences are roaring their bravos – it is John Christie who should have priority of appearance, over everybody else, in response to curtain calls.

Mercifully, his last years were greatly brightened by the marriage of his son George to Mary Nicholson in 1958, and by the birth of their son Hector in 1961. As time went on, Mary came to play a vital role as wife, mother, hostess and trustee of Glyndebourne Arts Trust. Indeed, Glyndebourne was, in a different way, almost as lucky in having her help in continuing and developing its traditions as it had been in having had Audrey Mildmay to create them. Mary's charm and ever-open friendliness, together with a practical energy and a resilience after frequent gruelling marathons, are as remarkable as her husband's. Her brisk cheerfulness, whatever the obstacles to be overcome, always made people feel better for having been in her company, and, together with her other qualities, will never be forgotten by the many hundreds of people who came into contact with her at Glyndebourne over the years. George had been gaining valuable experience of finance for culture by working at the Gulbenkian Foundation and took over as Chairman of Glyndebourne Productions in 1956, not long after his marriage, and still only aged twenty-four. John remained on the Board as President, but after an initial period of settling in, George took an increasing part in planning for the musical future.

The 1957 season was notable for the first showing at Glyndebourne of the production by Ebert of *Falstaff* that had been put on at Edinburgh two years earlier. The designs were by Osbert Lancaster, very much in his element, though Ebert's treatment sometimes seemed over-insistent and heavy-handed. Less popular was Rossini's *L'italiana in Algeri* but the fault seems to have lain not so much with the production or the cast as with the first-night audience, whose lack of enthusiasm, in spite of Gui's unfailing gifts, somehow penetrated the bones of Peter Ebert's production, which never fully recovered. In fact it stands out as one of those rare failures which to this day remains hard to explain. *Ariadne* was notable for the Glyndebourne debut, as the Composer, of Elisabeth Söderström, who was to become a great favourite particularly in the Strauss repertory in the succeeding years. In *Die Entführung* Messel once again received praise unprecedented for a designer of sets. Eric Newton summed it up by declaring that Messel 'had a gift far beyond pastiche . . .

not only is the stage a delight to the eye but the music has more meaning for the ear'. What designer could ask for more? Another triumph was the televising of *Le comte Ory*: the Head of Music Productions at the BBC calculated that the audience which saw it amounted to the equivalent of full houses at Glyndebourne throughout the year for fifteen years.

In 1958, Edinburgh decided that it could still not afford Glyndebourne. However, the company was invited to take part in an international season at the Théâtre Sarah-Bernhardt in Paris, where two performances each of *Falstaff* and *Le comte Ory* were given. Back in February, Gui had not been optimistic. He had written to Caplat:

> I am afraid about the French . . . since I know this people, their superficiality, their distraction, their ignorance of everything that is not happening in Paris . . . and, over all, their credulity what permit the clever people to let believe everything [sic] . . . . I am not clever!, But in spite of my old age, I am not yet resigned to accept, without reaction, the wrong and the injustice.

He was not far off the mark. The French were indeed characteristically incurious at first about a foreign composer, even when the subject of his work was as French as could be. *Le comte Ory* had not been heard in Paris for thirty years. At an invited preview the audience sat on their hands – no laughs, no encouragement – but the opening night was a great success, though the later performances were only half full, a weird experience for a Glyndebourne cast. When it came to *Falstaff*, the French critics, chauvinistic as ever, were bewildered to find that an opera based on Shakespeare, with music by an Italian, a German producer, an Italian conductor, an English designer, and singers from Spain, Wales, Italy, Mexico and Switzerland as well as England, could together form such a perfect ensemble. But to give them their due, they generously hailed it as '*un Falstaff exemplaire*', and encouraged their readers 'for the honour of France and Parisian taste', not to miss it: '*Quelle leçon, quelle leçon de mise en scène – nous a donné le Festival de Glyndebourne!'*

It was indeed an exceptionally strong cast. Geraint Evans, supported by Fernanda Cadoni, Ilva Ligabue, Oralia Dominguez, Graziella Sciutti, Juan Oncina and Mario Borriello, had improved on his already good performance of the year before, and Gui told one of the critics that Evans was as good as any Falstaff he had known except Stabile. John stayed in the British Embassy for a few days, in uncertain health and not on his best behaviour, disappearing at inconvenient moments, according to his hostess, and loudly proclaiming his dislike of the French in the theatre foyer.

Back at Glyndebourne, the season opened only eleven days after the return from Paris, but chiefly with revivals of high-class productions. In

Relaxing in the old Green Room before a performance of Falstaff *(1958)*

Figaro, Graziella Sciutti had a great success as Susanna, and stood up bravely to Ebert, who, she later recalled, 'wanted my vision to be his'. However, after her triumphant first night, he embraced her and said simply: 'You won.' She added that he had given her great confidence in what she was doing, and very good advice about how to direct her career. The only novelty was *Il segreto di Susanna*, a forty-minute frolic by Wolf-Ferrari which was greatly enjoyed as a new curtain-raiser to *Ariadne*. John, in response to a critical reviewer, said that he had never seen such exact timing in his life; and that for Michel Roux, as the suspicious husband, 'beautiful singing tone would have been unsuitable. He produced the sound of an angry Frenchman [perhaps still ringing in John's ears] marvellously.' Always willing to admit what he himself found wrong, he declared Helga Pilarczyk, as the Composer in *Ariadne*, 'intolerable', and did not know why David Franklin 'had gone off so much'. But his fault-finding could occasionally be quite unreasonable. He was always critical of every new Susanna in *Figaro*, lest they should be thought to compete with what Audrey Mildmay had achieved in the role. On one occasion, when someone praised a new Susanna to him, he replied: 'Yes, she's learnt a lot since she's been here, and she's not as bad as she was, but *basically* it's a hideous voice.'

In a letter about the rehearsal stage which was being built, the acoustician Hope Bagenal had written: 'You know that I will do anything I can for you because through you the Muses function in these islands. Therefore you come into the category of *misterium tremendum*.' John had been called many things in his life, but there is no record, even at Eton, of anyone else being inspired to describe him in Latin. More appropriately, he was given an Honorary Doctorate of Music at Oxford, and on the day when it was awarded the editor of *The Times*, Sir William Haley, who had already congratulated him, sent him a telegram 'with best wishes for a happy day'.

John Christie with Lady Jebb, at the French Embassy in Paris, May 1958
(also captured by photographer Jane Bown, left)

The Presentation of the Rose: Anneliese Rothenberger and Elisabeth Söderström in Glyndebourne's first Rosenkavalier *(1959)*

Ebert, on the other hand, had been re-elected President of the International Theatre Institute, and in addition to all his professorial duties in California he agreed to produce *Macbeth* for Bing in New York in January 1959. He had been sharing much of the rehearsal work at Glyndebourne with his son Peter who, like most sons of illustrious but ageing fathers in the same line of business, often had a difficult time. For example, he did not feel able to take over independent responsibility for *Cenerentola* in 1959, feeling he could not improve, nor would he wish to change, his father's production. In 1958, his father had also caused great consternation by announcing on 23 April that he would not be arriving at Glyndebourne until 17 May, and that Peter could take all but the last rehearsals in Paris. This was cutting it fine, by any standards, and Caplat wrote to him: 'The news of your late arrival is a great blow. It is all the more depressing because this seems to happen every year and makes all our planning doubly difficult and frustrating. ... I beg of you to move Heaven and Earth to go back to your original promise.' Ebert replied indignantly that: 'If your letter did not bear your signature I would hardly believe it was you who wrote it. Reproaches and – unfounded – accusations does not sound like you.' But he revealed for the first time that he had signed a contract with the Berlin Opera four years earlier, under which he would only be free each year for Glyndebourne from 17 May for a period not exceeding seven weeks. These details had not been known to Caplat before. But philosophically – or perhaps to indicate how well Glyndebourne could manage – he reported to Ebert before the dress rehearsals of *Ariadne* and *Il segreto di Susanna* that: 'John Pritchard is doing very good work, and his *Ory* performances have been really excellent.'

The big excitement in the twenty-fifth anniversary season in 1959 was the first performance at Glyndebourne of *Der Rosenkavalier*. The chief obstacle was the limited size of the orchestra pit, but when Busch had conducted it at Dresden before the war, Strauss himself had agreed to a reduction in the string section in order to fit the players into the space available in a small theatre. Busch had been discussing the possibility of reviving this production at Glyndebourne not long before his death in 1951, so the idea was not new. The orchestra was reduced from its original ninety-four to sixty-six, though the composer had agreed to as few as fifty-one. When the public announcement about Glyndebourne's silver jubilee was made, it included the news that Ebert was to retire as Artistic Director and principal producer. The Berlin Opera House was to be rebuilt and would claim a lot of his attention, so it seemed an appropriate moment for the break to come, not least since Ebert was now seventy-two.

The season opened on 28 May, twenty-five years to the day after the first performance of all, but this time with *Rosenkavalier* rather than *Figaro*. John made a speech which was supposed to be a tribute to Ebert, neatly culminating with the presentation to him of a silver rose bowl. After twenty-five minutes of denunciation of Covent Garden, the Arts Council and other organizations whose representatives were his guests that evening, he still had not mentioned either Ebert or the presentation; but thanks to a helpful prompt by Caplat, Ebert eventually got his rose bowl. The cast was superlative: Régine Crespin as the Feldmarschallin, Söderström as Oktavian, and Anneliese Rothenberger as Sophie. Ebert had complained bitterly about the fact there had been no full discussion of the sets between himself and Messel, going so far as to declare: 'Glyndebourne will never find a producer of real standing if the laughable system of the predominance of the designer over anything else is not broken.' Caplat replied, with great tact, that he 'should not have to act as a buffer between you and the designer but only as the man who gets things made and pays for them'. John Cox, who produced *Rosenkavalier* in 1980, said later that Ebert's production was 'impossible to live up to and difficult to escape from'. There were, however, adverse comments about the fierce impact even of 'a slimmed-down orchestra in the small auditorium,' and while Crespin, Söderström and Rothenberger were praised to the skies, Oskar Czerwenka as Ochs was criticized for being a bucolic boor without any redeeming shred of nobility, which was certainly my own impression at the time. (At Covent Garden that summer, there was also another production of *Rosenkavalier*, in which the singing was satisfactory without being special, but Rudolf Kempe's conducting was described as having a broader sweep than Leopold Ludwig's at Glyndebourne.) One of Glyndebourne's 1959 performances of *La Cenerentola* was attended by the Queen Mother, who also went to *Porgy and Bess* in 1986, and in 1997 paid another visit, at the age of ninety-six, to hear *Manon Lescaut*, at the end of which she talked at length to many of those involved in the production.

The other work performed for the first time at Glyndebourne in 1959 was *Fidelio*, which Busch had always wanted but Ebert had always rejected. It was the first production there by Günther Rennert, who had been head of the Berlin Opera during the war, and of the Hamburg Opera from 1946 to 1955, and was much approved of by his old mentor Ebert. Douglas Craig, who had been assistant general manager under Caplat since 1956, and stage director before that, has described Rennert as an 'automaton for concentration', and a drill sergeant, and mentions that at an early rehearsal he took three hours over the first twelve pages of *Fidelio*. He also had the habit of selecting a whipping-boy in the cast,

who was blamed for never getting anything quite right. Casts at Glyndebourne soon knew what to expect, and occasional artists claimed to feel
more like prisoners than participants, and made irreverent jokes about
life at 'Glynditz'.

Rennert was never happy except when in complete, almost dictatorial
control, but he accepted the Glyndebourne ethos from the start, and
won great respect there; and although even busier than Ebert with work
elsewhere, he worked at Glyndebourne until he was offered the presti-
gious position of Intendant at Munich in 1967. His *Fidelio* was one of his
most successful productions, and a personal triumph for Gré Brouwenstijn, who was described by *The Times* as 'the greatest Leonore of our
post-war time'; while Rennert's relations with her offstage were recognized as being as significant to them both as they were in the opera itself.
Another way in which he differed from Ebert was that he only worked
in conjunction with people's intelligence, and was inclined to fly into
rages if that intelligence was not forthcoming. In *Fidelio*, when infuriated
by a break made by the conductor in a three-hour rehearsal, he rushed
away to work off his anger on a piano. In spite of Rennert's displays of
temperament, Pritchard for one established good relations with him; and
there were others at Glyndebourne who liked him as well as respecting
and admiring his considerable talents, notably his sense of pace and structure, and his theatrical imagination – not least in his work with the
designer Ita Maximovna.

Ebert, on the other hand, though also a formidable personality, was
capable of being friendly and very helpful to newcomers, and directed by
acting out the parts himself, thus giving the artists the confidence to
create their own interpretations. (Having been a stateless refugee himself,
he had political sympathies with certain operas.) At the end of 1959
Ebert, who was by then a professor in the opera department of the University of Southern California, and once again busy in Berlin, retired
from his official position at Glyndebourne, though he was to return to
direct individual operas. In February 1960 he was awarded an Honorary
CBE in recognition of his work in Britain. The title of Artistic Director
was abolished on his retirement: Gui and Rennert were appointed artis-

tic counsellors, the former as Head of Music and the latter as Head of Production.

John had in the past not been interested in public recognition of his own achievements. He was, however, delighted by two awards that came to him: something called the Great Silver Honorary Medal for services rendered to the Austrian Republic; and the German Bundes-verdienstkreuz. Writing to thank Konrad Adenauer, the German President, for this award he added significantly: 'Our work here was undertaken ... because it was necessary to bring to this country what was normal on the Continent and yet hardly existed here. This, thanks to two Germans, Busch and Ebert, and to the genius of my wife, has been successful.' The decoration itself included a miniature version for evening wear, as well as the medal itself. Very characteristically, John commented: 'How appropriate: one for me, and one for the pug.' These two honours in the jubilee year were exceptions to what had become a semi-retirement for him. Besides his heart attacks, he later also suc-cumbed to jaundice, but he still briefly acknowledged the usual letters of praise for Glyndebourne with something of his old panache, and also concerned himself with building up a reserve fund against possible new requirements for the future, since generally speaking the opera season was now for several reasons paying its way. His twilight years were greatly helped by the loyal and sympathetic friendship of Rhona Byron, a neighbour and a director of Glyndebourne Productions who, as Wilfrid Blunt put it, 'was always at hand when he could no longer bear his own company'. After George's marriage she was also an invaluable help to his wife Mary in the tricky business of fitting into a complex and eccentric atmosphere.

The great novelty for 1960 was Bellini's *I puritani*, performed in England for the first time since 1887. It was conducted by Gui and pro-duced by his stepson Gianfranco Enriquez, a man of brilliant ideas but as far removed in temperament from Rennert as chalk from cheese. Undisciplined, unpredictable, unreliable in his attendance at rehearsals, he nevertheless created some of the outstanding Glyndebourne produc-tions of the decade. In Rome, he was at one time imprisoned for failing

1. *The new theatre and old Organ Room from the garden, a harmonious combination of contrasting architectural styles*

2. *The 1955* Le nozze di Figaro, *designed by Oliver Messel.*
Sena Jurinac, as the Countess, was especially memorable

3. *In his 1973* Figaro, *Peter Hall insisted that the opera be given with none of the customary cuts.*
Few who saw this production had ever witnessed such admirable concentration on the essence of the opera,
'the shadows of human sadness cast by the sunlight of comedy'

4. *Carl Ebert's 1950s production of* Don Giovanni *was designed by John Piper, the first of many distinguished artists to design for Glyndebourne*

5. *Peter Hall's chilling 1977* Don Giovanni *was admirably complemented by John Bury's dark and strikingly original sets*

6. *In 1994 Deborah Warner shocked a few but stimulated many with her 'mad, volatile and dangerous' depiction of* Don Giovanni. *The production was criticized for not regarding the opera as* dramma giocoso

7. In 1963, Franco Enriquez's production of Die Zauberflöte *was celebrated for 'cheerfully accepting its humble, fairy-tale origins' and allowing 'simplicity and charm to flower into magic'*

8. In 1978 David Hockney's design for the opening scene of John Cox's production of Die Zauberflöte *quoted directly from Paolo Uccello's* St George and the Dragon

9. *In his iconoclastic 1990 production of* The Magic Flute, *set in an imaginary Los Angeles landscape, Peter Sellars replaced the opera's spoken dialogue with subtitles. Audiences and critics were fiercely divided*

10. *Trevor Nunn's acclaimed 1983 operatic debut,* Idomeneo, *was informed by his fascination for Shakespeare's last plays, in which love triumphs over seemingly insuperable obstacles*

11. *Humour and psychological insights characterized Peter Hall's 1978* Così fan tutte. *His advice to the cast: 'Keep in mind that Mozart was in love with two women, and married just one!'*

12. *As Dido in* Dido and Aeneas *(1966), the young Janet Baker gave one of the most moving performances of the early post-war years at Glyndebourne*

13. *In the 1967 season Cavalli's* L'Ormindo *received its first public performance since 1644. The realization by Raymond Leppard was universally acclaimed, as was Ann Howells as Erisbe*

14. *Peter Hall's triumphant debut at Glyndebourne, Cavalli's baroque fantasy* La Calisto, *was especially memorable for Janet Baker's portrayal of both Diana and Jove, and for John Bury's spectacular reinvention of seventeenth-century stage pictures*

15. *Dubbed 'Monteverdi's Flying Circus' because of John Bury's ingenious stage effects, Peter Hall's 1972 production of* Il ritorno d'Ulisse in patria *was praised for 'a style of acting which is neither pastiche nor standard operatic'*

16. *Another Hall/Bury collaboration, the 1984* L'incoronazione di Poppea *featured an 'unnervingly sure and subtle' Maria Ewing in the title role and more spectacular stage effects*

17. *The Organ Room at Glyndebourne was John Christie's first addition to the original house in 1920. He had bought the organ firm of Hill, Norman & Beard and installed an instrument. By the 1930s his interest had waned and it was removed, leaving only its magnificent façade. The room continues to be used as a foyer*

to pay the agreed maintenance to his estranged wife; but he was let out every evening to attend to his duties in the theatre. For the 1960 programme book Gui himself composed an elegant, rather high-flown, but much needed article on Bellini, whose operas were then, apart from *Norma*, largely unknown to the average member of the audience. 'Amid the blooms of this miraculous garden, and beneath the shade of these ancient trees we bring the sad, melodic inspiration of Bellini.' He mentioned that Chopin, on his deathbed, had asked to be buried near Bellini, and also that Stravinsky, apparently with so little in common with him, had declared provocatively that:

> Beethoven left to the world riches due partly to his lack of melodic gifts, but Bellini scattered widely a tireless profusion of magnificent melodies . . . Beethoven's work seemed the fruit of obstinate effort. Bellini received the gift of melody without troubling to ask for it, as if Heaven had said, 'I bestow on you the very gift that Beethoven lacked.'

Even though Beethoven was, as everyone knows, capable of wonderful melodic invention, it was a striking tribute to Bellini.

In *I puritani*, Joan Sutherland's brilliance and balance in the long, infinitely testing arias came as a revelation, and few in the audience had ever heard the like. The reviews from the Continent were a reminder that Glyndebourne was international not only in its performers but also in its critical coverage. From Brussels, the exotic headline *Glyndebourne in al zijn glorie* was readily intelligible, while Claude Rostand, a leading French critic, compared Sutherland tellingly with Callas for having '*une voix moins puissante mais infiniment plus égale, plus parfaite, plus pure . . . justesse impeccable, style sans concessions et sans vulgarités*'.

Less happy, however, was the state of the Royal Philharmonic Orchestra. An interesting letter has survived from Gui to John Christie, dated 18 May, commenting that they were no longer of the same standard as the year before, and that: '*Fidelio*, with these horns as I have this year, should be no possible next year.' Something may well have been done, since only twelve days later Neville Cardus, writing of *Falstaff* in *The Guardian*, commented that: 'the playing of the RPO was truly fine, with the precision that is three parts of wit' – further evidence that, with reviews, even by the greatest experts, you never can tell.

Meanwhile two complications had cropped up, worth mentioning as typical examples of the endless casting and timing problems which are the bane of the management's life. First, Geraint Evans was offered the glorious chance, crucial to his career, of singing Figaro for Karajan at La Scala, which involved shortening the rehearsal schedule for *Falstaff* at Glyndebourne. In the circumstances, and after much heart-searching, Caplat consented, and Gui gave his magnanimous approval. Secondly, Gui felt that he himself was indispensable for the launching of the 1960 Maggio Musicale season in the brand new theatre in Florence. Earlier, he had thought it quite impossible that the theatre would be ready in time for him to need to postpone his arrival at Glyndebourne by several weeks, and indeed, to miss the first two operas there – and all this only a few months after he had been given a three-year contract at Glyndebourne as Artistic Counsellor with special conducting commitments. Even these two particularly acute problems were surmounted in the end, and audiences of course remained blissfully unaware of these managerial trials. Similar scheduling clashes had to be solved, year in, year out, by Moran Caplat; and his patience, tact and coolness over three decades deserve special tribute.

In 1960 Bruscantini was back at Glyndebourne as Ford in *Falstaff*, and *Der Rosenkavalier* was revived, with exceptional praise from Neville Cardus for Régine Crespin's Feldmarschallin: 'a most poignant tenderness and sensibility . . . as memorable as Lotte Lehmann'. There was a new production of *Don Giovanni*, conducted by John Pritchard in place of Gui, with a hugely successful debut as Zerlina by Mirella Freni who was to become a world-class star. *La Cenerentola* and *Die Zauberflöte* were revived: the latter was to have been conducted by Beecham, who however fell ill, and died in the following March. Disappointingly, his replacement Colin Davis, widely regarded as a very promising young conductor, was accused by critics of having adopted a ponderous and sluggish approach to his task.

Having failed to find the necessary money to engage Glyndebourne since 1955, Edinburgh now bowed under a storm of criticism for the absence of the company. In August 1960 *Falstaff* and *I puritani* were taken there, together with an odd but imaginative triple bill: *Il segreto di Susanna*, revived from two years earlier, but with Bruscantini replacing Michel Roux as the angry Frenchman; *Arlecchino*, revived from 1954, again conducted by Pritchard but with Ian Wallace as the only survivor from the earlier cast; and *La voix humaine*, composed by Poulenc two years before, from a so-called 'lyric tragedy' by Cocteau, who produced and designed it. This last work consists of a one-sided telephone conversation between a woman and her invisible lover who has rung up to say that he is going to marry someone else the very next day. There was much praise for Denise Duval, the sole member of the cast, who admitted in an interview the difficulty of doing twenty-two different things at once, all by herself, in a marathon scene lasting forty-five minutes. Cocteau refused her request for a prompt box, but the problem was solved by linking the prompter to the telephone which was constantly in her hand. *La voix humaine* was an enterprising departure from anything that Glyndebourne had ever considered doing before.

It had been an adventurous and largely successful season. But in the next few years, for a variety of reasons, well informed suggestions began to be made that more painstaking talent-sifting was now required at Glyndebourne in the Mozart operas, several singers being no longer equal to the composer's style, while others had barely scraped acquaintance with it. Whatever the justice of these complaints, now that the immediate post-war period of reconstruction and consolidation was over, there is no doubt that competition from other opera houses was hotting up, and Glyndebourne's casting problems were steadily to increase.

5

HESITATION AND RECOVERY

1961–1981

It is worth summarizing at this stage the unique characteristics of Glyndebourne which placed it in a class of its own in the operatic world, before describing how its special quality began to falter; and how it was later successfully reasserted.

First was its aesthetic independence. Its commitment to the highest artistic standards had created a rock-solid allegiance among the members, both corporate and individual, of the Glyndebourne Festival Society, which gave them the confidence to attend, and often enjoy, productions which they would probably never have thought of hearing anywhere else. This loyalty was to become of crucial importance when the great rebuilding gamble was embarked on, with complete success, nearly thirty years later. Secondly, there was Glyndebourne's determination to discover unfamiliar works, both old and new, to prevent the repertory from becoming a museum, albeit full of the glories of the past; and its commitment to promoting performers at the outset of their careers, who could contribute to the atmosphere and would want to return regularly to Glyndebourne, because of the uniquely attractive working conditions and the sheer value of the experience they would gain. Over the years these had included Sena Jurinac, Sesto Bruscantini, Ian Wallace, Richard Lewis, and Elisabeth Söderström; and both before and after this time, other great names were to emerge from the chorus, starting for example with Peter Pears, Italo Tajo and Erich Kunz before the war, and later, Janet Baker, Anne Howells, Ryland Davies, Thomas Allen, Philip Langridge and Richard Van Allan. (The career of the last-named must be unique, since he had served as a policeman and then as a coal-miner, in order to pay his way through a teachers' training college, before discovering the potential of his voice.) These were the defining characteristics that prevailed around the time of John Christie's death in 1962, and the gradual emergence of a largely new regime.

The 1960s were to include a number of productions to rank with the very best: Rennert's *Fidelio*; the *Pelléas et Mélisande* of Ebert and Gui with designs by Beni Montresor; the introduction of Monteverdi and Cavalli to the Festival; the collaborations between Enriquez and the designer Luzzati; Janet Baker's *Dido* and Elisabeth Söderström in *Capriccio* and *Yevgeny Onyegin*. But the departure of Ebert and the retirement of Gui, quite apart from the death of John Christie himself, left gaps which were far from easy to fill. Inevitably, Moran Caplat was obliged to take the reins more firmly into his hands, to try to resolve all the conflicts inherent within a multi-faceted operation like Glyndebourne.

By 1965 Harold Rosenthal, the editor of *Opera* magazine, while wholeheartedly wishing Glyndebourne well for the future, had the feeling that the powers of Rennert and Pritchard as heads of production and music respectively, had been eroded, and that 'a great international festival, if it is to maintain standards, must have really firm, even dictatorial musical and artistic direction'; that this had 'been lacking in recent seasons', and that he earnestly hoped it would re-emerge (as indeed it later did).

Judged by these criteria, the flair of the 1950s appeared to be fading, partly because of the shortage of available and affordable singers of great promise from overseas. This was partly solved by the emergence from the Glyndebourne chorus of a series of top-class performers including those just mentioned. As regards the selection of works to be performed, the admirable Desmond Shawe-Taylor wrote a piece in the *Sunday*

Sena Jurinac as Fiordiligi (1951)

Joan Sutherland as the Countess and Michel Roux as the
Count in Figaro *(1956)*

Teresa Berganza as Cherubino (1958)

GOLDEN VOICES OF THE 1950S AND 1960S

Magda László as Poppea (1962)

Luciano Pavarotti as Idamante (1964)

Ileana Cotrubas as Mélisande (1969)

Sesto Bruscantini as Leporello (1960)

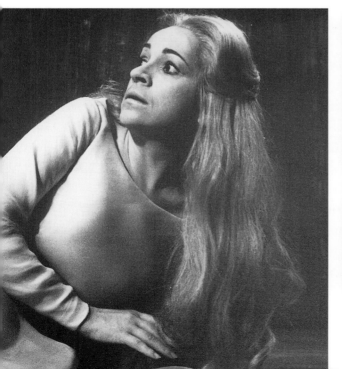

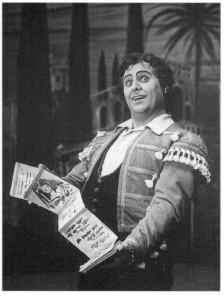

Franco Zeffirelli looks at the set model for his L'elisir d'amore *(1961)*

Times on 'Glyndebourne and the Future', suggesting four operas ideally suited to its special character: *Pelléas et Mélisande*, *L'incoronazione di Poppea*, *Capriccio* and Rossini's *La pietra del paragone*. His good judgement, not to mention the breadth of his enthusiasms, was rewarded by the fact that the first two were put on in 1962, *Capriccio* in 1963, and the Rossini in 1964, each being revived at least once subsequently. But it was not simply a question of following his recommendations: Ebert and Gui were already determined to stage *Pelléas*; *Poppea*, despite the incomplete nature of the score, was an opera which the gifted musician Raymond Leppard, supported by Caplat, was eager to do; and as for *Capriccio* and *La pietra*, Rennert and Pritchard already had them in mind.

The 1961 season opened with the unveiling by Lady Violet Bonham Carter of a bronze bust of John Christie by Oscar Nemon, to mark his retirement as Chairman. She observed that it was 'a little larger than life,

Luigi Alva as Nemorino, Mirella Freni as Adina and Enzo Sordello as Belcore in the 1962 revival of L'elisir

but the subject's personality had outgrown that of normal men'. Even in the last two years of his life, John's insatiable love of extending and improving had been active every winter, and the theatre's capacity had now been increased to a total of 768 seats. The bust was originally placed outside the Green Room, and has now come to rest outside the end wall of the Organ Room, on a shelf supported by two pugs, gazing up in wonder (and, surely, admiration) at the new opera house a few yards away.

An important newcomer to Glyndebourne that year was Franco Zeffirelli, who produced and designed Donizetti's *L'elisir d'amore*. Most people found the ensemble enchanting, but a few felt that 'the overcrowding of the stage' – which Ebert would never have devised – had been excessive, and that altogether there was too much rather precious, fidgety activity on stage. But another serious critic felt that, although the production and designs were 'sure to be sniffed at by the tetchy and over-fastidious', he 'could imagine no greater compliment'. Zeffirelli also echoed Gui's own criticism of over-earnest, Germanic treatments of light-hearted Italian comic opera. His stated aim in *L'elisir* was for 'spontaneity, even improvisation', however carefully rehearsed. He had worked with each of the principals before, and was convinced that 'each was about the best for interpreting my wishes in this opera'. But perhaps the production was short on finesse and good singing, even though the Peruvian Luigi Alva was universally singled out for praise as Nemorino. Martin Isepp, Strasser's indispensible successor as Head of Music Staff, recalls that after an exhausting day's work on the new production, Zeffirelli, who was already a world-famous name, would be quite happy to work on the creation of new costumes in the wardrobe department in the evenings, with the wife of the conductor Carlo Felice Cillario also lending a hand. If there was something of a house-party element in the atmosphere at Glyndebourne, it was definitely the hardest-working house-party in history.

In sharp contrast was the British première of *Elegy for Young Lovers* by Hans Werner Henze, with a libretto by W. H. Auden and Chester Kallman. (Elisabeth Söderström later recalled that the work was sometimes cheerfully referred to as 'Allergy for Old Buggers', which also says something about the prevailing atmosphere.) The librettists had the misfortune to come across John in the garden and to be asked who they were. When they explained, and told him what they had written, he is alleged to have replied: 'Oh dear! You shouldn't have, really you shouldn't,' and to have stumped off disconsolately back to the house. Later, he commented to Ivor Green, then assistant chief technician and head of the department since 1985: 'If you see the score anywhere, burn it.' Be that as it may, booing was heard on the first night for the first time at Glyndebourne, and both audiences and critics found it hard to be seriously interested in the central character, a megalomaniac poet who carried little credibility as a genius, but appeared to be pseudishly exploiting to the full the trappings of his reputation. (In addition to being far from well physically, the composer had the misfortune to overhear a member of the audience lamenting, in the interval: 'We must warn poor Gwendoline!') The situation was further complicated because Henze had intended the poet to come across as a truly great man, whereas Auden and Kallman wanted to show him up as a poseur and an exploiter. It was hardly a recipe for success. Relations between Rennert, who produced it, and Auden were disastrous. Both regarded themselves as outright leaders in their particular field, and neither was willing to compromise. The opera was never revived at Glyndebourne, and Rennert did little for the morale of the cast by announcing that one of the scenes was actually unplayable (*unspielbar*).

The four revivals of that season included *Il barbiere di Siviglia*, and *Don Giovanni*. After the Festival, the latter was given in a concert performance, with a splendid cast, at the Proms. Operatic extracts had often been given at the Proms before, but this was the first occasion, and a notable one, when a whole concert had been devoted to the complete performance of a single opera, to an audience many of whom were probably not regular opera-goers. Like other Glyndebourne coups (see Appendix 2), their example was later followed by other opera companies. Obviously, considerable adaptation was necessary in order to

Auden, Chester Kallman and Hans Werner-Henze discuss their new opera,
Elegy for Young Lovers, *with Moran Caplat*

make a success of a semi-staged form of presentation, and the credit for this was largely due to Moran Caplat. Another cause for celebration that season was that, a few weeks earlier, on 10 July, George and Mary Christie's first son was born. He was christened Hector Thomas Cleveland in Ringmer Church.

The next year, 1962, saw the last return of Ebert to Glyndebourne, to produce *Pelléas et Mélisande* in the centenary year of the birth of its composer. Gui, who in his youth had known Debussy well, was the conductor, and the sublime sets were designed by Beni Montresor, and reproduced very effectively on the cover of the programme book. Spike Hughes has aptly commented that *Pelléas* is not only 'different' from any other known opera but also 'difficult': 'its whole mood is dark, misty and elusive, and unless it is performed superlatively well it can be one of the most powerful soporifics in the repertoire'. Debussy himself had been very specific about his aims in *Pelléas*. He had fallen under the spell of Wagner, like so many of his generation, but rather than imitate him he aspired to creating a new dramatic form, in which music begins at the point 'at which speech is powerless in expression . . . emerging from a shadow into which, at times, it should return. The action should never be held up, it should be continuous and uninterrupted.' There could be no better exposition of what goes on in *Pelléas*, and unfamiliar though the opera was to most of the audiences, the Glyndebourne production was deeply and widely admired, with Denise Duval outstanding as Mélisande. A bold and brilliant departure from the German and Italian traditions of Glyndebourne, this subtle, elusive work was also a splendid antidote to the danger of staleness. Three years before reading Maeterlinck's play on which the opera is based, Debussy had declared: 'I dream of a libretto which does not condemn me to perpetrating long, heavy acts, which offers me constantly changing scenes, varied both in place and in atmosphere, where the characters do not argue but submit to life and to fate.' *Pelléas* embodied that dream; and more than one knowledgeable critic considered that this was also one of the finest of all Ebert's productions since Glyndebourne began.

The other novelty of that year could hardly have been more different.

Like several other works already mentioned *L'incoronazione di Poppea* had never been staged before in a fully professional production in Britain. Monteverdi had in fact been disregarded, at least on the operatic stage, for decades, even centuries – though Nadia Boulanger's pre-war recordings were treasured by those lucky enough to possess them. He is almost as good an example of the merry-go-round of musical fashion as Bach (who in 1789 only received two lines, as an organist, in Dr Burney's famous *History of Music*). Composed when Monteverdi was seventy-five, *Poppea* is an unusually amoral opera, with virtue unmercifully defeated at the end. Temporal power and sexual passion are what the opera is about, and they are expressed, perhaps for the first time in opera, at a vivid personal level, with the result that, in this milestone production, the realism and intensity of the characters – even Nero – and their actions left their mark indelibly on many of those who saw it, though to all but a few the music came as a complete revelation.

One of the dramatic strengths of the opera is the success with which the composer and librettist portray contradictory elements of real-life emotions, and express the freshness and beauty of passion, with no regard for conventional standards of right and wrong. Nero and Poppea hardly touched each other, yet the emotional intensity, thanks to the sensuality of Magda László, who was back at Glyndebourne after eight years, was overwhelming, and all who took part were caught up in the atmosphere of excitement. Yet even at this pitch of exaltation, opera casts being what they are, outbursts of the broadest humour are not unknown. Lucano, Nero's companion in corruption, is at one point handed a flower. One evening its stamen had been replaced by an object of such vivid obscenity that even as experienced a performer as Hugues Cuenod came close to forgetting his lines.

In arranging *Poppea* for modern performance, Leppard, who had exhumed it from a library in Venice, faced a tricky problem. If it were based purely on scholarship, and on the original form of the work, its recreation would have been a desiccated falsification of the composer's intentions. (In seventeenth-century Venetian operas, only the bass line and the vocal lines were provided by the composer, and everything else was filled in by the performers.) But if colour and climax swamped authenticity, it would have been derided by the purists. In so far as this circle can be squared, Leppard was widely praised for having squared it. The programme book described the work as a 'new version realized by Raymond Leppard', and the debt the audience owed him was incalculable. Initially, Pritchard conducted, with Leppard at the harpsichord, but at the first revival Leppard conducted as well as playing the continuo. He was later accused of taking liberties (by musicologists who could never have created anything so effective themselves) but at the time his vision of the work was hailed as imaginative and successful, though minor details of Rennert's production were criticized. So well received was *Poppea* that, like *The Rake's Progress*, it was put on in three consecutive years. Once again Glyndebourne had shown the way, and Monteverdi's works later took off worldwide. Leppard realized another of them for Glyndebourne and two more of his operas in Santa Fé, which were later exploited elsewhere as well. The only disappointment lay in the over-rectangular sets of Hugh Casson, curiously unsuited to a truly baroque opera.

By 1963 Gui was seventy-eight. He conducted the revival of *Pelléas*, but had to withdraw from *Fidelio*, which was taken over by Bryan Balkwill, though six of the original principals, including Brouwenstijn, were to repeat their roles. Gui however conducted a new production of *Die Zauberflöte* directed by his step-son Enriquez with original and inventive designs by Emanuele Luzzati. It was this combination that inspired Desmond Shawe-Taylor to observe, several years later, that: 'The happiest productions [of *Die Zauberflöte*] cheerfully accept its humble, fairy-tale origins, make it look as pretty as possible, and allow simplicity and charm to flower into magic or occasional sublimity, on the wings of Mozart's incomparable music.' Also revived was *The Rake's Progress*, for which a surprising number of seats remained unsold (the work was not revived again until 1975). The impact of *Poppea* at the Proms was espe-

John Christie, a few months before his death in July 1962

cially powerful since the music was also quite new to that audience. (Indeed, it was referred to in a Nottingham newspaper as *The Coronation of the Pope*.) The tally of seven operas put a considerable strain on the management: rehearsals overlapped, accommodation for so many performers was another headache, and the schedule itself had become clogged. The season was also the last in which the Royal Philharmonic Orchestra appeared at Glyndebourne. The partnership had lasted sixteen years, but because of the orchestra's financial difficulties many of its members felt unable to guarantee their reappearance in the following year. The contract was therefore terminated, but the orchestra was granted compensation of £7,500, a heavy blow to Glyndebourne's own finances. The replacement was the London Philharmonic Orchestra, of which John Pritchard (who had now been working at Glyndebourne for over a decade) had just been appointed principal conductor. He provided a valuable element of continuity, and helped to solve the teething troubles which arise when an orchestra first plays in the pit rather than on the concert platform. The new relationship has survived happily ever since.

John Christie died on 4 July 1962, and on the following night the audience stood, heads bowed, in his memory. Enough has already been said about his strengths and weaknesses, but it was largely *because* he so often disregarded the opinions of others – maddening though this may often have been at the time – that he was able to achieve more for opera in Britain than anyone. Freddie Stockdale, in his recent book *Emperors of Song*, coined the unforgettable phrase 'rhinocerine nonchalance' for the way in which John forced his way through obstacles which would have defeated anyone else. Further, in his respect for the professionalism of Ebert and Busch at the beginning, and through the persuasiveness with which he involved Edinburgh after the war, and his recruiting of Miki Sekers to raise funds in the 1950s, he showed an astonishing and wonderfully effective versatility. His memorial service took the form of a performance of the Mozart Requiem in Westminster Abbey on 3 September, given by the Glyndebourne Festival Chorus and the Royal Philharmonic Orchestra and conducted most appropriately by Gui. As John's biographer Wilfrid Blunt put it: 'Not many men live their lives

Gerald Coke chairs a trustees' meeting in the dining room at Glyndebourne (1960)

for an ideal; fewer live to see their ideals realized, and fewer still die in the knowledge that what they have fought for will outlive them.'

His son George was left in ultimate control, though he had far more sense than to exert it without tireless consultation with those directly responsible for the successes of the past. Of all those who discreetly guided him in his early days, none was more helpful than Gerald Coke, who, in addition to chairing several public companies, was now Chairman of the Glyndebourne Arts Trust. George has inherited all his father's unshakeable determination and single-mindedness. Like him, he would sometimes makes sweeping statements, as a tease to keep people on their toes and to provoke argument. Together with his enjoyment of life, and a sense of fun he constantly shares with others, he has powers of concentration and, above all, a stamina which often bewilders those who have to try and match it. Equally striking are his diplomatic gifts, of which his father never felt the need, and a talent for raising money which deserves a place in the *Guinness Book of Records* (particularly in connection with the rebuilding of the opera house). Furthermore, unless

Capriccio *rehearsal, 1963: Pritchard and Rennert with cast. On left is Jani Strasser's assistant, Brian Dickie, who became Director General in 1981*

Ebert and Gui with Hans Wilbrink and Denise Duval, Pelléas et Mélisande *rehearsal (1963)*

or until they fall down on it, he is prepared to trust people to get on with the job, once they are appointed. He stressed in the 1963 programme book that the general policy must be, and would be, to develop the old traditions rather than follow them religiously and risk turning Glyndebourne into 'a museum with performances'. Dangers would be faced, long-shots would be taken, mistakes would sometimes be made; but in spite of any obstacles that might lie ahead, Glyndebourne was to move firmly forward.

Another of the old guard to be lost was the veteran Jock Gough, improviser of so much on the stage at Glyndebourne since the very first season. He had ended up with the resounding title of chief theatre technician and director of scenic construction, having stood up to his devoted employer as no one else would have dreamed of doing, and indeed threatening in all seriousness to resign two or three times a year. He had suffered frostbite in the severe winter of 1962–3, and then had a bad fall on the stage before the 1963 season opened. On his retirement, another link with the early days was broken, and the stage crew of eight were no longer expected to be on call seven days a week.

The 1964 season proved a bumpy ride. First, *Macbeth* was on the programme again, and with it the casting problems from which it seems to be inseparable, above all in the role of Lady Macbeth, but the Greek baritone Kostas Paskalis shone as Macbeth in the Enriquez/Luzzati production. In the revival of *Idomeneo*, Idamante was played by one Luciano Pavarotti, who had been booked when still unknown. It is gratifying to record that, years later, he recalled of his only appearance at Glyndebourne: 'What I learned there was to sing *piano* – from Jani Strasser.' Of all the Glyndebourne discoveries who afterwards soared into the stratosphere of popularity, he and Joan Sutherland are perhaps the best examples. Mention must also be made of the excellent performance of Gundula Janowitz, who made her first appearance in Britain as Ilia, having sung Pamina under John Pritchard at Aix the previous year, and of that stalwart Glyndebourne tenor, Richard Lewis. But the chief contretemps of the season arose when Gui declined to appear. The object of Gui's deep disapproval was Rossini's *La pietra del paragone*, an opera he

113

had recommended to Glyndebourne three years earlier. However, he had been appalled at the version concocted by Rennert and his collaborator, Paul Friedrich. 'Rossini', he stated,

> cannot be well interpreted by the German people; even our old Ebert, indubitably a great producer, was not at all at his best with *Cenerentola* and the *Barbiere*. The sense of humour, the comicity (*comicità*) of our great Rossini, must never be *caricatura* – the style of our great genius, a Mediterranean genius, is immensely far from the comicity of the German races.

Gui eventually relented, and conducted some performances of *Die Zauberflöte*. Guided by the fact that Schikaneder, the librettist, cast himself as Papageno, Enriquez made this part the focal point of his production, with Heinz Blankenburg playing the role impressively. Theatrical magic abounded, and the exacting Desmond Shawe-Taylor, in the *Sunday Times*, found the result 'uncommonly ingenious, imaginative, original and delightful'.

Gui relented again in the following year, his eightieth, and was on his way to England as usual by car, when his wife was taken ill and their journey held up. But eventually, for his final appearances at Glyndebourne, he conducted later performances of *Figaro* and of *Il matrimonio segreto*, a very worthwhile addition to the repertory. Its composer, Cimarosa, stands half-way between Mozart and Rossini; and it is noteworthy that when Rossini first became famous, Stendhal, later his biographer, commented: 'One's impression on listening to *The Barber of Seville* is always that of listening to a new edition . . . of some score by Cimarosa that one has heard, and loved, long ago.' Gui survived another ten years, dying at the age of ninety in 1975.

Another novelty in 1965 was Donizetti's *Anna Bolena*, for which Gui would have had little enthusiasm. In his idiosyncratic way, he had even been heard to dismiss Donizetti as, musically, 'a middle-class composer'. Unheard in England for seventy-three years, it had been almost equally neglected in Italy until a historic performance at La Scala in 1957 with

Callas and Giulietta Simionato. At Glyndebourne the Turkish soprano Leyla Gencer, a wonderful singer but sometimes a prey to disastrous nerves, took the name part; and Juan Oncina, who had starred in all Gui's Rossini revivals and in other major roles at Glyndebourne, returned after an absence of four years.

Earlier plans for the season had to be changed for reasons of the usual kind. Mirella Freni was to have appeared in *La traviata*, but the time-table would have required her to sing one of Verdi's most difficult roles thirteen times in 26 days. Peter Brook was to have produced *Don Giovanni*, only to find that other commitments made it impossible. In the end, *Der Rosenkavalier* was revived, with the first appearance in England of Montserrat Caballé – who arrived at Glyndebourne not knowing the part of the Feldmarschallin at all. She was 'indisposed' during the first week of rehearsals, and learned the notes of the role in six days with the help of Gerald Gover and Martin Isepp of the music staff. (Isepp, incidentally, recalled later that this experience was so awful that he could never bear to listen to Caballé again.) As usual, most of the audience was unaware of this crisis and there were some excellent reviews. Caballé also sang some performances of the Countess in *Figaro* that year, though with less success, but at once became unaffordable by Glyndebourne and never sang there again until the gala concert before the demolition of the opera house, nearly thirty years later. Even Gui's conducting was thought to have lacked sparkle and tension – understandably in view of his age and health problems. What with three different countesses, three counts and two conductors, the production caused an unusual number of headaches for the management.

It had been an altogether difficult year, not least because there was simply too much going on. In his end-of-season address George Christie announced much-needed changes in order to consolidate for the future. The season was to be cut from thirteen weeks to nine and from six productions to four, with twenty fewer performances. In those days plans did not have to be made four or five years in advance, as they have today. But to reduce the scale of operations so sharply only ten months before the beginning of the next season was such a drastic measure, and drew so much attention, that it was mentioned on the leader page of *The Times*.

The following year, 1966, a seemingly unlikely double bill was presented. Both Purcell's *Dido and Aeneas* and Ravel's *L'heure espagnole* were new to Glyndebourne (and, together with Busoni's *Arlecchino*, had been recorded after the 1965 season for BBC Television, which substantially defrayed the cost of staging them the next year). The stylistic contrast between the two operas did not, in fact, jar – no doubt partly on account of the generous supper interval separating them. Janet Baker as Dido gave a performance universally regarded as one of the most moving in all the post-war years at Glyndebourne.

Another novelty that year was Massenet's *Werther*, in a production by Michael Redgrave. Not only the opera, but also the composer, the producer, the designer of costume and scenery, and the singers in the four principal parts, were new to Glyndebourne. (It was only, incidentally, through a muddle on the part of his French agent that Plácido Domingo was not auditioned for the part of Werther.) But the experiment was a considerable success, and the production was revived in 1969. The other offering turned out to be perhaps the most disastrous production ever staged at Glyndebourne, Handel's *Jephtha*, an oratorio adapted by Rennert and well received in Germany, originally in 1957. Here, it was described by critics as 'dull', 'plodding', 'lethargic' and even 'vandalized', criticisms unheard since the unsuccessful ballet scenes in *Orfeo* in 1947. It was to be thirty years before another Handel oratorio was put on at Glyndebourne; though Peter Sellars's truly remarkable staging of *Theodora*, in 1996, was well worth waiting for.

Rennert remained as Artistic Counsellor in 1967, but was only responsible for one more production, namely Cavalli's *L'Ormindo*, before taking up the job of Intendant at Munich Opera. The memory of *Jephtha* made his departure easier to bear, but his gifts as a director and his ruthless pursuit of quality far outweighed his bullying habits and his lapses in conveying the requisite lightness in Italian comedies. To some extent too, his years at Glyndebourne mellowed him, and visitors from Germany who had known him in action there were often surprised by his comparative tractability in Sussex. And his underlying goodwill is demonstrated by the fact that after his departure to Munich he would send a letter, not just of good wishes, but of involved concern for the success of each new season, which would be received in time for the opening night.

Gui's retirement had brought John Pritchard to the role of Music Counsellor, the first Englishman to have been in ultimate control of music at Glyndebourne. His authority grew, and he was given the title of Music Director in 1969, and remained in the post until 1977, when he was appointed chief conductor at the Cologne Opera. At the outset of his permanent appointment, however, Caplat was careful to avoid the difficulties that had been caused by the absences of Ebert and Enriquez – indeed, Pritchard's contract as a conductor back in 1959 was reinforced by a covering letter saying that: 'in no circumstances can we agree to your release from any of the orchestral rehearsals or performances as set out in the schedule'. For the immense trouble that Pritchard took in those years, the help that he gave to many singers and his supreme sensitivity, Glyndebourne owes him a great debt, as George Christie handsomely acknowledged in the 1971 programme book. He later summed it up when he said that Pritchard 'had the ability to paint any landscape, modern or baroque, be it a Rossini lightweight or a Verdi heavyweight . . .'; and as well as his celebrated interpretations of Mozart, he also conducted with great success operas by Debussy, Massenet and Strauss. He had worked at Glyndebourne every year since 1951, when, on the recommendation of Roy Henderson (who had of course sung in the first season of all), he had worked as a coach, and had also assisted Busch at Edinburgh. Later, he had been principal conductor of the Liverpool Philharmonic and then the London Philharmonic Orchestra. In 1962 his services to music had earned him the CBE, and in 1964 he prepared an interesting paper on the problems facing Glyndebourne in its new circumstances, in the particular context of the departure of Ebert and the impending retirement of Gui. He had already conducted many Glyndebourne productions, and his experience of the current problems, his keenness to help solve them and his general devotion to the place were all highly developed. Without excepting himself from criticism, he felt that: 'We are too slow, too divided, too NICE, too late, too choosy, too cliquey, and much too diffuse in our system of inter-consultation.' It was a long way from the majestic utterances of Gui, or the forceful decisions of Ebert. Team spirit had always been emphasized at Glyndebourne, but a wider consensus had now developed. To cope with the greatly increased competition for the services of top-class singers, he suggested creating a category of six 'Special Division Artists', who would be paid up to £200 per performance (compared with the previous maximum of £120), for up to ten performances, and given contracts for two years, with an option on a third.

The idea was to establish a distinctive nucleus for the company, though probably not at the same level as in the 1950s when Jurinac, Bruscantini, Oncina, Evans, Lewis, Lorengar, Noni, Cadoni and Wallace were available, in a much less competitive market, year after year. Pritchard felt that there was also a need for an experienced producer to handle revivals, and one whose stagecraft would give singers confidence, early in their careers. Finally, he insisted that it is *vocal* excellence that draws audiences, and fine voices are more important than expensive sets and extravagant costumes. (It is, of course, a personal view: Mahler, when Director of the Vienna Opera, claimed that he chose singers for their ability as actors, not for their voices.) All this was certainly helpful in giving a new sense of direction after the wobbles mentioned above.

Pritchard had started from humble circumstances, had made his way in the bleak, post-war world and had grown increasingly enamoured of the good things of life which success had now brought him, including a fine Elizabethan house in Sussex, Carter's Corner, previously owned by Lord Hailsham. He was a lavish host, inclined to be over-tolerant to hangers-on eager for the champagne and suppers that he often provided. As time went by, his self-indulgence increased, and a certain laziness developed, alternating with restless bursts of energy. He also feared loneliness. He was easily distracted, easily hurt, easily bored; and although he was later knighted, the fact that he was not asked to record for any of the major companies reduced his impact on stay-at-home music-lovers. Yet in the opinion of Ileana Cotrubas, who sang under him to great acclaim in *Pelléas* in 1969 and *Figaro* in 1973, he was 'one of the finest musicians in our profession'. A superb conductor of Mozart, he was also amazingly quick to grasp the quality of contemporary music and he could master an exceptionally complex piece by Stockhausen, for example, with a speed that bewildered his colleagues. Another of his talents was that instead of finding it necessary to collaborate with the director from the outset, he could arrive in mid-rehearsal and mysteriously pick up the whole mood and atmosphere which the director was seeking to convey, and conjure it up from the pit. Nothing, moreover, could exceed his courage in the last months of life, when, mortally ill with a combination of thrombosis in a leg and cancer of the chest, he conducted the last night of the Proms and then rushed off for *Idomeneo* in San Francisco. Like many great artists he was prone to dark moods, and in his case the chief cure for them was to plunge into a programme of intense work, and to use his gifts of sympathy, innate musicianship and kindness to help singers to give of their best.

Following the cutback in the Festival programme in 1966, a pattern had been established for the next few years, and was announced by George in his end-of-season speech. Each year there would be one revival and three new productions: one Mozart opera, one nineteenth-century work, and the third to be either a pre-Mozart piece or else a twentieth-century one. George had already described the reasons behind the new formula in an article which was published in *Opera* magazine in May of that year:

> We have found in the past year or so that, with the introduction of two new productions each year, the repertory was not building up as fast as we would like, nor being kept sufficiently fresh and up-to-date to provide a season of six operas, of which four were customarily revivals from our repertory. There is a danger, where we rely too heavily on revivals – especially in the case of productions dating from fairly far back – that they lose their sheen.

clockwise from top left

Elisabeth Söderström as Christine in
Intermezzo *(1974)*

Thomas Allen as Don Giovanni *(1977)*

Carol Vaness as Electra in
Idomeneo *(1983)*

Janet Baker as Orfeo in
Orfeo ed Euridice *(1982)*

Felicity Lott as GTO's Fiordiligi *(1978)*

He added another objective:

> to provide greater interest and attraction for those who work at
> Glyndebourne ... the market for good artists will continue to
> become increasingly competitive. ... An increasing number of
> Festivals have come into being, and critical appreciation ...
> demands better standards. In consequence, singers of specially
> high quality are more and more in demand, and more and
> more difficult to engage, particularly for Glyndebourne where
> we need them for a fairly long period of intensive rehearsals
> followed by twelve or so performances. ... By increasing the
> proportion of new productions, we should on the whole be
> offering a greater amount of stimulating work, containing more
> novelty, interest and inspiration. Singers attach a good deal of
> importance to the training aspect of our work, particularly with
> roles which they have not previously sung ... and for which
> we engage them for new productions.

There were thus three new productions in 1967 (the year, incidentally, in which Moran Caplat was awarded the CBE in the New Year's
Honours). The first was *La bohème*, from which something truly remarkable was expected in order to justify staging so endlessly familiar a work.
But it was not to be. Michael Redgrave's production was bathetic by
comparison with his *Werther*. He made the mistake of following too
faithfully the historical detail of the mediocre novel on which the opera
is based, and, surprisingly for such an experienced stage director, he
failed to fit the action satisfyingly to the music, even ignoring Puccini's
own careful stage directions. His health was already beginning to suffer,
and the cast was unexceptional. There was also trouble with Luzzati's
sets for a new *Don Giovanni*, and though the costumes and decor were as
original and striking as ever, there were anomalies in the Enriquez
production, which was considered 'interesting' rather than entirely
successful. But experiment was in the air, for which as always there
might be a price to be paid. Cavalli's *L'Ormindo* was even more obscure

than other recent 'discoveries', not having apparently been performed in public since its first appearance in Venice in 1644. Desmond Shawe-Taylor put it in a nutshell when he wrote in the *Sunday Times* that: 'Raymond Leppard will doubtless be accused by purists of having composed the opera himself. If so, he has made a remarkably fine job of it.' And Andrew Porter declared that it was one of the most exciting things that Glyndebourne had ever done. The music, of course unfamiliar, was sometimes inventive and entertaining, and at other times purely beautiful. The part of Erisbe was a personal triumph for Anne Howells, who had been recruited so late in the day that her name did not even appear in the programme. Even some heavy-handed 'comic' effects by Rennert failed to spoil the general ensemble.

Unfortunately, throughout these years, the BBC showed a distinct lack of enthusiasm towards Glyndebourne. *Falstaff* had been televized in 1960, *L'elisir d'amore* in 1962, *Die Zauberflöte* in 1964, the triple bill in 1965, and *Don Giovanni*, shorn of its overture, in 1967. But there was no longer an annual television broadcast as before. In a letter from David Attenborough, dated 27 November 1967, he argues, rather unconvincingly, that the BBC were going to concentrate first on studio productions at Wood Lane (which, as they should have known, are infinitely more expensive than televising ready-made stage productions), and secondly, on 'a major international event with international artists' (which is, of course, exactly what new productions at Glyndebourne are). The BBC decided not to revisit Glyndebourne in either 1968 or 1969, and Attenborough's excuses added insult to injury, though it must be admitted that a minority of the recent performances had at least been uneven, if not altogether poor. It did, however, leave the way clear for Southern Television to establish relations with Glyndebourne, which they did in 1969 with a documentary, directed by Wendy Toye, under the rather arch title of 'A Goodly Manor for a Song'. The programme followed the various stages in the production of *Così*, from first rehearsal to first night, including the building and painting of scenery and the making of wigs and costumes. Subsequently, Southern Television's various transmissions from Glyndebourne were compared very

Così rehearsal, 1969: Jani Strasser with Anne Howells and his assistant Nicholas Snowman, who is Glyndebourne's current General Director

favourably with the BBC's later tendency to show operas 'in terms of television'.

For some time George had mentally been making plans for a new enterprise, for which he is far from claiming anything like sole credit. Creating Glyndebourne Touring Opera, or GTO as it became known, was obviously going to be hard work, but the two main incentives were both powerful. First was the fact that the chorus at Glyndebourne, unlike anywhere else, was recruited afresh every year, with about a third of the total comprising new members emerging from the colleges of music. Many of them had a chance to understudy the main roles, but of

Pritchard and Strasser at Così *rehearsal with Enriquez and cast, 1969*

course very few ever actually replaced their principals. These aspiring soloists therefore generally moved on to other engagements elsewhere, and their training and experience were lost to Glyndebourne, sometimes for ever. A determination to capitalize on this valuable resource was therefore one good reason for setting up the touring company – at a time, moreover, when a weak pound was making foreign singers more and more expensive. Another objective was to reach out to a much wider audience and thus defuse the dreary accusations of élitism (in those days only just acquiring currency as a term of general abuse for something of high quality) or at least of an exclusiveness which, for obvious reasons, was inevitable at Glyndebourne itself – though television has more recently had a considerable impact in making such excellence accessible to the general public.

Taking opera to the regions was a thoroughly democratic plan, and much in keeping with John Christie's original general aim to 'make a better world'. The viability of the venture depended on its qualifying for Arts Council support, but as the Council's first offer only amounted to £15,000, the launch was put off from 1967 to 1968, by which time George's old employers at the Gulbenkian Foundation had also agreed to put up £30,000, over three years. Some regional sponsorship was forthcoming from companies in or near the cities visited – which in the first year alone included Newcastle-upon-Tyne, Liverpool, Manchester, Sheffield and Oxford. (Since that time, a wide variety of other cities has been added to GTO's touring circuit.) The 26-year-old administrator of GTO, Brian Dickie, gained experience in running it which later earned him the position of General Administrator of the Festival itself. Harold Rosenthal, with his exceptional knowledge of opera, considered both GTO's *Don Giovanni* and its *L'elisir d'amore* more enjoyable at Liverpool than they had been in Sussex the year before, and this was by no means an exceptional reaction to GTO productions. When the touring company celebrated its twenty-fifth birthday, Rodney Milnes pointed out that operas about young people, such as *La bohème*, *Yevgeny Onyegin* and *Così fan tutte*, benefit from being sung by young people, provided they have been through the meticulous system of preparation that is sacrosanct at Glyndebourne. And right from the beginning, a company capable of sending out singers of the quality of Norma Burrowes, Jill Gomez, John Wakefield, Richard Van Allan and Ryland Davies, not to mention Ian Wallace as Doctor Dulcamara, could certainly never be regarded as a 'second eleven', as is sometimes inferred from the term 'touring company'. GTO broadened Glyndebourne's work, for performers almost as much as for audiences, and soon became an integral element of Glyndebourne itself, especially when it began to perform there for a short season before setting off on tour. It also helped to keep the performers at Glyndebourne young at heart, optimistic and eager to learn – though at the other end of the scale it is also true that Hugues

Cuenod, who first sang at Glyndebourne in 1954, appeared in *Figaro* as Don Curzio during its golden jubilee, thirty years later, at the age of eighty-two, and as M. Taupe, the prompter in *Capriccio*, in 1986 and 1987, by which time he was eighty-four. When the production was again revived three years later, he turned down the part, but attended one of the performances, after which a special presentation was made to him. Throughout his long career, he had established the astonishing record of only missing two years at Glyndebourne between 1954 and 1977.

In GTO's first four years, the tours were made before the Festival season, in March and April, with rehearsals beginning in a very cold opera house in mid-winter. The first year, there was still so much snow in the Pennines that the truck transporting the sets and lighting equipment from Newcastle to Liverpool was delayed overnight and only reached the theatre about an hour before the audience. Mercifully all went well, the press made much of the company's victory over the elements, and the crisis was turned to Glyndebourne's advantage.

In 1967, the year when GTO was postponed, a more far-flung tour was undertaken by the Festival company in Scandinavia, thanks to the initiative of Norman McKenna, the Manager of ICI in Scandinavia. Two operas were taken, the *Don Giovanni* production of that same year, and a revival of *Il matrimonio segreto*, and there were performances of each at Oslo, Drottningholm, Gothenburg and Copenhagen, where Fritz Busch had first worked on leaving Germany, and where his memory was still revered. Caplat was quite undaunted by all the extra work involved in taking the company abroad, and bravely considered that spreading Glyndebourne's fame overseas more than justified the extra trouble. Complications arose over the theatres, because they were all so different from those at home, and from one another; but these obstacles were largely overcome, certainly in the eyes of the critics. However, no tour on that scale was ever attempted again, and most of those who took part breathed sighs of relief when it was safely over (having incidentally shown a surplus of £1,840).

For the 1968 Festival, the novelty was *Yevgeny Onyegin*, produced, perhaps fortunately, by Michael Hadjimischev (whose father had been Bulgarian Ambassador in London before the war, and who spoke perfect

English) instead of Michael Redgrave, who had been the original choice but was already committed elsewhere. Elisabeth Söderström, herself half-Russian, had a brilliant success with her portrayal of Tatyana, and, as Lensky, the excellent Polish tenor of Wiesław Ochman added a further authentically Slavonic nuance to the production.

The 1970 season was the first at Glyndebourne for Peter Hall, whose productions over the next seventeen years have been hailed as landmarks in its history. His first production was *La Calisto*, by Cavalli, who had been a pupil of Monteverdi. (Raymond Leppard, who again completed the score, has compared the Cavalli and Monteverdi relationship to the influence of Beethoven on Schubert.) Like *L'Ormindo*, *La Calisto* had not been performed for over three centuries. The production was memorable. To anyone unfamiliar with Ovid's *Metamorphoses* the story was not only new, but hard to swallow even by operatic standards. The nymph Calisto is seduced by Jupiter, and turned first into a bear and finally into a constellation in the sky; in the meantime, other sexual cavortings revolve in a baroque fantasy around this improbable pair. After four years' absence, Janet Baker returned triumphantly in the dual roles of Diana and of Jove impersonating her. One aspect of Hall's sheer talent as a producer is generously summed up in a letter to him from Janet Baker, in which she said that she had 'emerged from *Calisto*, a different person and a better performer. . . . You give me such a wonderful sense of freedom; your sense of creating, moment by moment, is the most exciting way of working I have ever seen.'

Hall had first been invited, at the age of twenty-two, by Caplat and Ebert to work as an assistant director back in 1954, and again in the next year, but having also been asked to manage the Arts Theatre in London, had had to turn Glyndebourne down. Caplat now explained to him that he did not go in for separate budgets for each opera, which simply encouraged producers to spend all the money, and then to ask for more. Instead, there was at Glyndebourne a total budget for the year, and Caplat used his own judgement in allotting expenditure where he considered it most worthwhile, with the proviso that, if scenery or props were ordered, they had to be used. (It must, however, be admitted that this system did not make for tight budgetary control, which was only instigated when Brian Dickie took over from Caplat in 1981.) Designers and producers therefore examined models with some care before real money was spent, and consequently far less of it was wasted than elsewhere.

Rossini's *Il turco in Italia*, the next 1970 novelty, starred Graziella Sciutti as Fiorilla, and Paolo Montarsolo as Selim. But it was marred by a lack of coherence, which arose from the fact that the sets by Luzzati had been designed for a production by Enriquez, from which the latter backed out at the last minute, to be replaced by John Cox. That same season, however, there was also *The Rising of the Moon*, the first opera to be commissioned by Glyndebourne. The composer was Nicholas Maw, who described it in the programme book as an operatic comedy rather than a comic opera. He analysed the requirements and problems of this genre as follows: 'The dramatic and musical ingredients must be made

La Calisto *was Peter Hall's first production for Glyndebourne (1970). Here he discusses technical matters with John Bury, Moran Caplat, June Dandridge (Production Manager) and Raymond Leppard*

sufficiently simple, while remaining both recognizable and memorable. There must be a real dramatic conflict, as in a serious work, but it must still be funny as well. It should also include some good tunes. Finally, the personalities of the characters should be explored through the music, so that they become real and therefore interesting.' On reflection, these ingredients may not be very surprising, but it was helpful of the composer to state his aims so clearly, and he was certainly rewarded by the audience's reactions. Unfortunately, this work has not become part of the repertories of other British companies, which it certainly deserves to be, though it has been performed abroad. It was revived the following year, with some improvements, particularly in reducing the weight of the orchestration so that the singers, and their words, were more audible.

In the 1971 programme book, George traced the way in which historically the prima donna, with all the connotations involved, had for many years ruled the roost. (Adelina Patti, who retired in 1906, had commanded a fee of £1,000 a performance, with a clause in her contract stating that she was not to be required for rehearsals.) In later years the prima donna's celebrated status was largely upstaged by that of conductors such as Beecham and Toscanini, who in their turn conceded their supremacy to producers. Cautious optimism was in the air once more. There was to be a return, though not quite at once, to what John Christie had called 'Test Match Opera', an excellence rating which may have amused true Brits but which must have puzzled Americans and Germans. It was in 1972 that the good intentions that had been formulated over the last few years came to fruition.

The biggest excitement of that season was Peter Hall's *Il ritorno d'Ulisse in patria*, another re-creation of Monteverdi by Raymond Leppard. Hall was especially praised by one of the more penetrating reviewers for having created 'a style of acting which is neither pastiche baroque nor standard operatic; it is just acting, it works, and it is extremely difficult to achieve'. The ingenuity of John Bury's effects, with Jove, Neptune and Minerva advancing and receding, descending from the skies, and reascending when their divine pronouncements were finished, was most impressive, and the aerial effects inspired Anne

Howells, who sang Minerva, to refer to this remarkable production as 'Monteverdi's Flying Circus', reflecting the name of an immensely popular television programme of the time. Ivor Green, then an assistant technician and now the resourceful and much-liked master carpenter, recalls that of all the productions that he was involved in, this was the one that put the biggest strain on the stage crew. Janet Baker's performance as Penelope was as moving as ever. The soliloquy with which this character opens the opera, her grief and anxiety occasionally mixed with anger, but finally resolving with unique courage, lasts a full quarter of an hour: it is a formidable responsibility, and Janet Baker's performance, which can still be savoured on video, was a major triumph. She later also paid generous tribute to the sheer quality of the sound produced by the orchestra under Leppard. The most exciting scene for the audience, and the most alarming for the cast, was when Benjamin Luxon, as Ulysses, began firing real arrows, with devastating effect, at the parasitic suitors who had been besieging the unfortunate Penelope. The scene was so carefully choreographed, and rehearsed, that in spite of the danger no one was ever wounded in the two seasons that the opera was given.

Comparisons were inevitably made between this opera and Gluck's *Orfeo*, which happened to be on at Covent Garden at the same time. They were strongly in Glyndebourne's favour. And, in general, Glyndebourne's achievement in putting these seventeenth-century works back into the repertory is something of which it can be even prouder than of almost any other of its miscellaneous triumphs over the years. Without Glyndebourne and Raymond Leppard, the incomplete scores of Monteverdi and Cavalli could have lain gathering dust in Venetian libraries for a great deal longer. To have these sleeping beauties springing to life was an enriching, thrilling and absolutely novel experience. Nor was the enthusiasm for it exclusively home-grown. The review of *Il ritorno* in *Le Monde* ended with the following generous sentence: '*Quand la grâce, le goût, le lyrisme et la vérité se rejoignent ainsi, on est en droit de crier au miracle – un miracle plus fréquent à Glyndebourne qu'ailleurs.*'

Since Pritchard was now often working in San Francisco, and John Cox in New York, they were able to introduce a number of emerging

American singers to Glyndebourne (where, as usual, they furthered their careers before becoming too expensive). Of great importance for continued financial stability was the agreement reached in that year with Southern Television to make regular recordings of two operas a year for three years at Glyndebourne, including all the Mozart works put on. Piecemeal BBC recordings in the past had been a great deal better than nothing, but the new deal obviously gave better scope for more ambitious forward planning. And in the next year, 1973, the Peter Stuyvesant Foundation renewed a covenant of £5,000 for another seven years, at that time the biggest single commercial sponsorship of Glyndebourne.

But possibly the most important innovation of 1972, for the long term, was the first appearance in the Glyndebourne pit of Bernard Haitink. He was chief conductor of the London Philharmonic Orchestra, but till now it had played at Glyndebourne without him. Born in 1929, he had only twice conducted an opera before, *Der fliegende Holländer* and *Don Carlos*: two works far removed from the Glyndebourne repertory. *Die Entführung* was thus his first Mozart opera. Coming to it fresh, his conducting was described by *Opera* magazine as a 'full-bodied, full-blooded interpretation based on perfectly judged tempos, refinement of detail, and taut rhythms'. Southern Television recorded this work and also *Macbeth*, and there was special praise for both the television director and producer, David Heather and Humphrey Burton, who gave viewers the feeling that they were joining the audience, so that the camera was, in Spike Hughes's words, 'the servant, occasionally the interpreter, but never the boss'. And the result gave 'the feel and excitement of a real theatrical performance'. Haitink's success with *Die Entführung* led him to feel that the ideal balance for a conductor's career might be two-thirds orchestral work and one-third opera. He once told Brian Nicholson, one of the Glyndebourne trustees, that when a concert was over, it was over for ever. But at each performance of an opera, he found something new in it, and it was thanks to Glyndebourne that his career in opera blossomed to such great effect. He also attached exceptional importance to the work of the chorus master, and has commented in an interview that to find the ideal person for this role 'is much more difficult than finding a music director. They're a very scarce commodity, I think there are only three in the world.'

It was in 1973 that Martin Isepp took over from Jani Strasser as Head of Music Staff, having served on it since 1957 as an accompanist, a harpsichord player and music coach, in addition to important work elsewhere. By the time he left Glyndebourne, Isepp had further developed, in his own way, the excellence of the ensemble element in the operas, a discipline which occupies a kind of hinterland between the work of the director and the conductor and is of very great importance for the actual quality of a performance. Isepp's musicianship also qualified him to accompany many great singers on the concert platform, including Janet Baker, Elisabeth Söderström, Elisabeth Schwarzkopf and

Bernard Haitink, rehearsing Die Entführung, *his operatic debut at Glyndebourne (1972)*

John Shirley-Quirk. Apart from his contribution to the actual productions, his work at Glyndebourne over the years was an immense help to
many singers at those crucial moments in their careers when they started
to develop the potential they had already shown.

The same year featured Peter Hall's first Mozart opera, *Figaro*, with
John Pritchard conducting, and was notable for the special harmony
developing between the two men. Figaro's servant-and-master relationship with the Count had a significance that was beautifully pitched and
never exaggerated by Hall. It was also the first production in living
memory to make no cuts in the text, so that subtle points that are often
missed were properly made. And although this had also been insisted on
by Ebert, the recitatives, crucial in a plot as complex as *Figaro*'s, were
treated within the cadences of normal speech, instead of being gabbled
in order to reach the next aria as soon as possible. Another virtue of
going back so respectfully to the original libretto was that endless stage

Peter Hall's much-praised Figaro *(1973) in rehearsal:*
Ileana Cotrubas, Benjamin Luxon, Hall and Knut Skram

directions that had taken root over the years could be disregarded, so that the comic effects came where the music called for them, instead of where a long series of conductors and singers had decided to stick them in, for reasons of their own rather than Mozart's. Characteristically, Hall set out to establish, with the cast, just who the characters in the opera were, instead of clamping them into some prefabricated socio-political pattern. Few of those who saw this production had ever witnessed such admirable concentration on the essence of this opera, 'the shadows of human sadness cast by the sunlight of comedy', which cause the audience to laugh and cry simultaneously more often than in any other opera, and possibly, than in any other work for the stage. Among the cast Frederica von Stade as Cherubino, and both Elizabeth Harwood and Kiri Te Kanawa (in her Glyndebourne debut) who shared the role of the Countess, were exceptional, as was the strikingly intelligent and beautifully sung performance of Ileana Cotrubas as Susanna. Spike Hughes

Kiri Te Kanawa as the Countess and Benjamin Luxon as the Count (1973)

incidentally contributed a fascinating article to the programme book of that year on Beaumarchais, creator of the story, and only those members of the audience who were exceptionally well informed already would have failed to learn something from it to increase their existing appreciation. Hughes, who had been familiar with *Figaro* for fifty-five years, declared that Hall's production was the one that he had enjoyed the most; and the German musical journal *Orpheus* gave it an award for the best production of opera mounted outside Germany in that year.

Hall was at this point available only for one production a year at Glyndebourne, and he now decided to embark on Mozart's operas in the order in which they were written. He too wrote a piece in the programme book expressing a commitment and an intensity of purpose that often brushed aside other people's priorities. He wanted audiences to be 'provokers and participators with the production . . . giving and taking with the risk of rejection and misunderstanding', as if in a new love affair. A sense of communication with the cast should also link the individual members of the audience together, so that in the interval, and at the end, complete strangers should feel stimulated to share their experiences. Like Ebert before him, he had come to feel that opera is 'the most potent form of theatre', and audiences should never be allowed to sit back, complacently accepting the absurdities which few operas are entirely without.

Hall went on to say that he had 'seen brilliant productions where the drama was of a higher standard than the music. . . . The effect was ludicrous; like a stick without a rocket. But opera would be healthier if the drama regularly reached comparable standards to those set by the musicians.' In a later article he was to add: 'I think you have to journey to the words through the music.' Whether consciously or not, this was an echo and a reaffirmation of what Ebert and Audrey Mildmay had striven for in the early days, and had been so painstakingly achieved. Hall also describes (in an essay in *Glyndebourne: A Celebration*) how Mozart's

*Frederica von Stade as Cherubino and
Ileana Cotrubas as Susanna (1973)*

operas, and the way in which they were originally performed, are so perfectly suited to the scale of the old opera house at Glyndebourne, and again raises the question of which comes first, the music or the drama. His answer is: 'Opera should make a perfect circle, the drama making the music and the music making the drama'; or as Cyril Connolly once put it, 'the words fitting the music like ormolu on kingwood' in the best eighteenth-century French furniture. Since his Mozart productions, not even the most egoistic or contrary critic has openly disagreed with Hall. Interestingly, he has explained that he loves working with singers, who are 'less intellectually pretentious than actors. They talk less and do more'; and the music 'allows a revelation of character which is richer and freer than words alone'. But he qualified this by saying that this depends on the closest partnership between director and conductor throughout the preparation of the work. On another occasion, he added with a smile that singers also 'do what they're told. They're used to a conductor waving a stick at them. But actors will argue about anything.' Elsewhere, he has commented that if he had to define a Glyndebourne singer, it was one 'humble enough to work hard, and re-study the part, and be corrected musically; eager enough to ask new questions; and pre- pared to work very hard for very little money for very long hours. That all sounds terribly idealistic, but it is in fact true – it's what singers do at Glyndebourne.' He has also stressed that in spite of the rational case for translating operas into English, he feels '*profound unease when the words that are sung have a different sound to those that inspired the composer*'. The Glyndebourne philosophy could not be more lucidly expressed, and its confirmation by a man of the theatre so sensitive to nuance, and so infi- nitely difficult to satisfy, could not be more significant. If this raises the productions to a higher level than the one at which they will afford the maximum popular enjoyment, then that is the price that has to be paid in the permanent quest for excellence.

In an interview in *Opera* magazine with Max Loppert of the *Financial Times*, Hall summed up his powerful reaction to the old accusations of Glyndebourne only providing for minority audiences, not all of whom really cared about opera:

I don't think it does. I really don't, and if I did I wouldn't work there. I think it represents standards, and a search for scrutinizing works, often with new talent, and nurturing new talent. I think the audiences at Glyndebourne are no more deadbeat than they are at any other opera house of that kind. I think the idea of Glyndebourne as a reprehensible, élitist place needs challenging, because it publishes itself very widely, and that's not sufficiently understood. I mean, I know that if I do a production at Glyndebourne, it will be seen by about 12–13,000 people in the Festival. All right, that's not very many, but we start small. It will then be given a Promenade concert, it will be broadcast, it will tour to five or six regional centres, and it will end up on commercial television. Usually all that happens within six months of the first night. So you reach millions. I think that's a smart way of recognizing that to create opera properly you have to think small – I don't mean physically small, but with great care – and then publish on a wide scale.

In another interview on his return from directing the *Ring* cycle at Bayreuth in 1983, he deprecated the habit of excessive 'reinterpretation' of operas by directors:

You have to be a very, very major creative genius to take hold of another genius's work and reinterpret it. And most of us are not creative geniuses – we are interpretative craftsmen, and we ought to try and interpret to the best of our ability what the piece means ... and not to indulge our own fantasies. ... I used to do Shakespeare in a very polemical way; in recent years I've tried not to. ... If you can say [about a production] 'I did that because I honestly believe that is the way to make the meaning of the work speak to the audience of today', then whether you succeed or fail your motives are correct.

Strauss's *Capriccio* was also revived in 1973, having been successfully transplanted into the 1920s in a production by John Cox, with much-praised designs by Martin Battersby, an acknowledged authority on the period. By bringing it nearer our own times, this made the story, including its stilted libretto, more immediate and interesting for the audiences; but in naming it as one of his three or four favourite operas, the conductor Andrew Davis admitted that you either loved it or found it extremely boring. (It explores the eternal question of whether the words, and the drama, are more important than the music, or vice versa.) And, to fulfil the commitment to regularly staging a contemporary work, there was a production of *The Visit of the Old Lady*, composed by the Austrian Gottfried von Einem from a play by Dürrenmatt, and given in English at the composer's own suggestion. It contained plenty of action to satisfy the audience: a real Ford car on stage, a train that roared through a station, and a revolving stage. But there were many complaints about the lack of musical distinction or continuity, the laboured satire, the general *longueurs*. The opera was not rated a success – though, as always, some found more in it than others, and it was revived in the following year. (The scenery, costumes and props, incidentally, were later sold to the Stockholm Opera for £6,000, and this was followed by many other sales in subsequent years: among them, the sets for *Die Entführung*, *Don Giovanni* and *La Cenerentola* were sold to Madrid, *Carmen* to Canada, *L'Ormindo* and *The Cunning Little Vixen* to Germany, and *Albert Herring* to Los Angeles.)

La Calisto was revived, with Louise, the daughter of George and Mary Christie, as the (silent) bear into which the nymph is transformed. She was eight years old, and thus began her operatic career four years earlier than her father had done on his debut as Fleance in *Macbeth* at Edinburgh in 1947. Finally, there was *Intermezzo*, a slice of the married life of Strauss and his wife, which might have been embarrassing had it not been for John Cox's success in universalizing the underlying comment on the vagaries of matrimony, and in making it extremely funny at the same time. This was sung in English, and the composer's libretto was consequently enjoyed to the full. Elisabeth Söderström was at her very

Martin Battersby's 1920s designs for
Intermezzo *(1973) were highly acclaimed*

best, and was described as 'one of the miracles of the contemporary stage'. The *Evening Standard* Award of the Year for Opera was given to Glyndebourne partly for this production, and partly for the exceptional standards achieved with young singers – and all without state aid.

A suggestion was made around this time that the company should visit America. Columbia Artists, who were to have promoted the trip, proposed a three-week tour playing in New York, Washington and either Philadelphia or Boston. Eventually, however, there were objections from the American unions to the Glyndebourne company's appearing in the Juilliard Theatre, and it was also likely that a different orchestra would have to be used in each city. Negotiations continued for many months, with the added possibility of an invitation to Ottawa, but ultimately nothing came of the plan. Nevertheless, the invitation abundantly confirmed Glyndebourne's reputation beyond Europe.

Britain was by now experiencing a period of ever-increasing inflation, initiated under the Conservative Government of 1970–4, and not remedied by Labour. Costs at Glyndebourne went up as never before, and further drastic measures were therefore required. A special finance committee was set up by the Glyndebourne Arts Trust in May 1975, under the Chairman of the trustees, Anthony Lloyd, QC, a close Sussex neighbour who was to make a significant contribution to the health of Glyndebourne. Its task was to find major sponsors, to the tune of £40,000, for the new productions for 1976 and 1977. The moving spirit of the committee was Sir Alex Alexander. In earlier years Miki Sekers had pioneered the task of attracting sponsorship and so made Glyndebourne's resurrection in the 1950s possible; now Alexander carried on the task on a most impressive scale. Of Czech origin, he had started life in Britain with almost nothing, and had made an enormously successful business career: he consequently suffered from few inhibitions and was not one to take 'no' for an answer when it came to putting heavy personal pressure on chairmen of large companies and extracting their support. And the more Glyndebourne's reputation grew, the more attractive it became – even if not on a financially quantifiable basis – to be associated with it. As for ticket prices, they had started (in the stalls) at two guineas in 1934, increased to three guineas in 1952, four in 1958, five in 1965, seven in 1971. By 1980 they had trebled to £21.50; by 1986 they had again doubled to £46; and doubled again to £90 by 1992 — all more or less in line with inflation (see Appendices 3 and 4.)

Support was also to be sought for the chorus, as a unique training ground for young singers. This cause, it was hoped, might appeal to a different category of potential benefactors from those who would underwrite the higher cost of sponsoring a single new production. Eleven commercial firms came in as sponsors in 1976, the first year of the chorus scheme. They paid a minimum of £1,000 each, and in several cases much more. A further eighteen companies made smaller but still generous contributions. The great importance of the chorus, in addition to its part in the various Festival productions themselves, is shown by the following figures: of the thirty-four members in 1976, eight had appeared as soloists with GTO the year before, and twenty-three under-studied major roles in the current Festival, two of them replacing the principal singers. A further nine also played minor roles in the Festival, and no fewer than fourteen would be singing major parts in the GTO tour of 1976 itself. Further, many of them were chosen to sing with the other major regional opera companies in Britain, a good recent example being Paul Nilon. The Worshipful Company of Musicians had also instituted the John Christie Award for the most promising young singer of the season: early recipients such as Ryland Davies and Richard Van Allan and their successors subsequently played a number of leading Festival roles with great success.

Finally, the new finance committee was asked to increase by fifty the number of corporate members, who then paid an annual subscription of £300, later increased in line with inflation. By January 1976, largely through the efforts of Alexander, and of George Christie himself, the committee had succeeded beyond the wildest hopes of the trustees. An additional £70,000 had been sought for 1976, but in fact £87,180 was raised. Better still, support for the chorus was to be on a continuing basis for several years. Additionally, there was a generous pledge from Imperial Tobacco towards a new production, by Peter Hall, of *Don Giovanni* in 1977; and W.D. & H.O. Wills later also contributed handsomely towards the general maintenance and upkeep of the buildings and gardens. By 1976 the Arts Council were to provide GTO with £160,000 under their touring scheme. There was also a windfall of $30,000 from the Corbett Foundation of Cincinnati, which was being wound up. This had to be spent on a piece of new equipment, and a Strand Electric lighting control board of sophisticated design was bought. Some seat prices, which had remained nearly static, were also raised, in line with inflation. This summarizes the truly remarkable way in which Glyndebourne responded to the financial problems of the times.

Of the 1975 Festival, the leading critic Rodney Milnes stated that every single item in the programme 'has to be seen by anyone remotely interested in opera'; and, given a deep pocket, this was good advice. He particularly praised the fact that nothing in it was either predictable or obvious. Janáček's *The Cunning Little Vixen*, hardly known in England, was produced by Jonathan Miller, who, unfortunately, did not feel at all at home at Glyndebourne, though enjoying the artistic context. Part of the opera's message is that man thinks only of himself whereas Nature largely ignores death and simply gets on with reproducing itself. Raymond Leppard took the leap from the seventeenth century to the twentieth in his stride, and the orchestral colours of Janáček were reckoned by Desmond Shawe-Taylor – a considerable connoisseur of the composer – to have shone with an unparalleled freshness and clarity. No whiff of either Beatrix Potter or Walt Disney was allowed to spoil things, and the stage handling of a large cast of characters, only half of them human, was beautifully calculated. But pleasing the critics is one thing, keeping audiences is another.

Although familiar from Ebert's 1953 production, with Osbert Lancaster's sets, *The Rake's Progress* of 1975 was a complete novelty to the eye, thanks to John Cox's production and David Hockney's original and striking designs. Like Lancaster's, these were all based on Hogarth's engravings, although expressed in Hockney's own personal style. But there was also a remarkable element of historical authenticity of which the critics were ignorant. In the Bedlam scene, where the inmates were placed in serried rows of small boxes, from which they would emerge to sing, and then sink out of sight, every item of design was derived from Hogarth's details. This was no mere designer's whim, but was based on the structure of Lincoln gaol in Hogarth's day. The work made a strong impression on audiences, many of whom were seeing it for the first time. Hockney, who was on the crest of the wave, communicated with the audience through an idiom which, for the majority, was eloquent and powerful. Stephen Spender, who was one of the artist's first patrons, considered that Hockney's vision 'had somehow achieved the miracle of completely absorbing the music, producing a true marriage of the arts'. (John Cox reflected later that his working arrangement with Hockney

Raymond Leppard and Jonathan Miller during a rehearsal of The Cunning Little Vixen *(1975)*

*David Hockney and John Cox discuss the set model for their 1975
collaboration on* The Rake's Progress

went deeper than is usual between director and designer; and Hockney came to feel that he was a full partner in the enterprise, expressing definite views about the character of the performances.)

Nevertheless, despite the excellence of the productions and the level of critical acclaim, parts of the programme had become somewhat too adventurous for the audiences of that time; bookings for *The Cunning Little Vixen* were so sluggish that two tickets were offered for the price of one. But the appetite of the public changes, and it was far more receptive to the innovations of Anthony Whitworth-Jones in the 1980s and 1990s, more so, as it happens, in the case of corporate members than of individuals. One reason for the formation of the finance committee had been the falling-off in box office bookings, a situation as unhealthy as it was unfamiliar. Nor was there, for a time, a waiting-list for corporate membership, and even the waiting period for individuals wanting to join the Festival Society had come down to about five years. Rumours spread, in the City and elsewhere, that all was not well with Glyndebourne, both financially and artistically.

By 1976, in addition to the remarkably successful efforts of the new finance committee to put this situation right, the Fred Kobler Trust, which had made *Intermezzo* possible in 1974, had donated another £20,000 for *Falstaff*, while the Corbett Foundation of Cincinnati added a further $50,000. Apart from the professional musicians who had contributed to Glyndebourne's continued success up to that time, the role of Gerald Coke had been unique. As Chairman of Rio Tinto, and a member of other boards, he had been for twenty-two years the perfect Chairman of the trustees. Now retiring from that office, he contributed to the programme book of that year a retrospective article, its paragraphs interleaved with strikingly apt quotations from the Mozart operas. As well as paying a fresh and first-hand tribute to Glyndebourne's creators he stressed the quality of continuity, under George, and the vital role played by Mary Christie, 'immeasurably greater than anyone who is not privileged to have inside information would realise'. He pointed out that for five months of the year (and another three nowadays) her home becomes a mixture of Green Room, packed dormitory and office, with her own desk overflowing in one corner; while her exceptional talent for making everyone feel welcome plays a great part in bringing out the best in them, and making them miss Glyndebourne sadly when they move elsewhere.

The 1976 production of *Falstaff* by Jean-Pierre Ponnelle has gone down as one against which others should be measured. Though Ponnelle was accused of being occasionally indifferent both to the score and the libretto, and to have had a few irrelevant ideas, Pritchard's conducting and the orchestra's playing were impeccable, and the American Donald Gramm in the name part had a major success. A designer himself, Ponnelle succeeded brilliantly with his sets, but with three new productions the stage crew had their most gruelling season ever: Ivor Green remembers at one point having hardly any sleep for three days. Almost incredibly, the pastoral backdrop was so realistic that some members of the audience thought that the back of the stage was open, and that what they could see was the real field behind the theatre. (The backdrop featured, among other bucolic details, a bull serving a cow; and in the following act a slightly different version showed this happy pair already attended by a calf.) The production was twice revived. A new production of *Pelléas* by René Terrasson, though wonderfully conducted by Haitink, never recaptured the triumph of Ebert, Gui and Montresor in 1962–3, and the essential dreamlike quality of the work was never evoked. *Capriccio* was revived, and induced the BBC back, after an absence of five years, to televize it.

The next year, 1977, was notable for Peter Hall's *Don Giovanni*. Concentrating as usual on the essential interplay of the characters, he gave a steely, chilling presentation of them, with glittering interpretations of Giovanni by Benjamin Luxon and of Donna Anna by Joan Carden, 'sung as perfectly as I ever hope to hear it', in the opinion of Rodney Milnes. John Bury's dark sets and designs were striking and original and a real departure from the smart eighteenth-century conventions accepted as appropriate in the past. Haitink took over as conductor from Pritchard half-way through the season, and was quoted by Caplat in December as saying that: 'every time he leaves the stage door at Covent Garden he feels glad that he is one day nearer Glyndebourne'. The production

Hockney's striking front cloth aptly re-created Hogarth's original etchings (1975)

Curtain call, GTO, 1975: Simon Rattle and cast

Hockney's costume designs for *The Rake's Progress (1975)*

moved to the National Theatre in August, the first time that Glyndebourne had performed in a London theatre since *The Beggar's Opera* in 1940. There was also a new production of *La voix humaine*, with Graziella Sciutti as director as well as sole member of the cast.

It was John Pritchard's last year as Music Director at Glyndebourne, where he had first conducted twenty-five years before. By now his work had come to suffer from intermittent bouts of slackness – even though his capacity for rising to the occasion when required was often astonishing. The conclusion was reached that he was not fulfilling his potential as Music Director of the Festival. But against this must be set his enormous helpfulness to singers as well as orchestral players, with whom he was immensely popular, and whom he so often inspired to surpass what they might otherwise have achieved. Perhaps partly for tax reasons, he moved on to a new challenge as chief conductor at the Cologne Opera House. The award of an honorary KBE to Bernard Haitink was pleasantly timed to coincide with his appointment as Music Director at Glyndebourne, and Peter Hall also received a knighthood.

Because of the expenditure of an astonishing £58,477 on re-cladding the fly-tower, redecoration and some re-seating in the auditorium, there was a deficit of £74,655 on the year. The loss was recouped partly from the Building Reserve that had been built up and partly from the Production Company's Contingency Reserve (which was effectively reduced by nearly half). A decision was reached by the trustees in November that the right balance between the box office and other revenue should be 65 per cent/35 per cent. Accordingly, ticket prices were to be gradually increased, the more expensive ones from £13.50 to £15.00 and £11.00 to £12.50, and the cheaper ones from £5.00 to £6.50. Fortunately the finance committee's efforts at fund-raising continued successfully, with the lion's share of credit still due to Sir Alex Alexander, who received notable help from Robin Warrender, the Chairman of Bain Dawes Insurance Brokers, and David Astor, the nephew and namesake of the editor of the *Observer*. Few written details of Alexander's triumphs have survived, most of them having been achieved on the telephone, or whenever opportunity arose with the chairmen and chief executives of companies he had selected as targets. Not only were his initial powers of persuading large companies to become sponsors unique, he also had an astonishing gift for making them feel that the level of support they had suggested was unsuitably modest, and that more was to be expected from firms of such national importance. His achievement was even wider-ranging than that of his predecessor Miki Sekers (though the latter's contribution, in its day, had also been indispensable). It would be impossible to overstate both these men's importance to the survival and continued development of the opera house.

Hall moved on in the following year to *Così*, and, as with his first two Mozart operas, stripped it of anything hackneyed or overstated, such as the exaggerated disguise of the officers and the outsize magnet. Working, as often before, with John Bury as designer, he revealed Mozart's examination of human nature which can so often leave the audience disturbed or confused, especially on the question as to which of the two romantic attachments is the more genuine, and at what stage. (Mozart also of course knew something about sisters, having himself been passionately in love with Aloysia Weber before marrying her sister Constanze.) As well as being a comic *tour de force*, sometimes teasing the characters themselves and sometimes the audience, Mozart's opera takes a distinctly serious turn when the sincerity of the characters is being tested and found wanting, when sham gives way to reality; yet despite the apparent contradictions he ultimately refuses to represent human feelings as simple and straightforward. All these elements were put into sharper focus than usual in this production. As well as singing gloriously, Maria Ewing was enchantingly funny as Dorabella, and won all hearts (including that of Peter Hall, who married her not long afterwards). His advice on *Così* included the following: 'Just keep in mind that Mozart was in love with two women, and married just one.' Hall considered that there was 'great grace, elegance and seriousness' about the performance, but 'the triumph was Haitink's. He makes a specific Glyndebourne sound, rich yet fastidious. Tempi notched up with a little more vigour, a little more wit.'

For whatever reason, 1978 was a bumper television year for Glynde-

bourne: Southern Television recorded three productions and the BBC two more. In 1979 Southern came back for *Fidelio* and Haydn's *La fedeltà premiata*, a first for this composer at Glyndebourne. (Appropriately the work had originally been commissioned for Eszterháza, the private opera house in its rural setting where the composer was based for twenty-four years.) The libretto is absurd but 'filled with incident and racy dialogue'. It was also put on at the Proms, where it was an even greater novelty than at Glyndebourne.

On a more sombre note, 1978 was also the year in which three of the greatest stalwarts of Glyndebourne died. Oliver Messel, Günther Rennert and Jani Strasser had all made an immense contribution to the opera there. Strasser (who, unlike the other two, has not so far been given his due in the story) had been principal coach until 1973, and innumerable singers, including Audrey Mildmay herself, have expressed their debt to him over a period of forty years. He had been Chief of Music Staff (though his title varied) from 1954, and though there were some who found his idiosyncrasies hard to take, his ability as a teacher had never been in question.

His talent for leading the music staff was exceptional; and he also had a remarkable gift for conveying to singers what conductors would want, so that by the time a conductor arrived at Glyndebourne the singers would already have reached a much more advanced stage of preparation for their roles than would, in other circumstances, have been possible. All this naturally strengthened his position in the Glyndebourne team, and consequently his conviction that he nearly always knew best, which occasionally led to friction. Over the years, he also became expert at casting, and familiar with a host of little-known singers all over Europe who might be suitable for Glyndebourne. His knowledge and expertise in this area reached such a level that Moran Caplat, on a casting expedition with George in Germany, decided to play a trick on Strasser. Inspired by the signal about seat-belts before their plane landed, he sent a

*Håkan Hagegård as Guglielmo and Maria Ewing as Dorabella
in Peter Hall's 1978* Così

telegram from the airport to Strasser at Glyndebourne, saying: 'Do you know Turkish soprano Fastense Atbelts? Would value your informed response.' By the time George and Moran reached their hotel, there was a reply from Strasser waiting for them which ran: 'Have heard good things of her. Please follow up.' He also took meticulous notes at rehearsals, on one occasion going so far as to present Kerstin Meyer with some final comments after the last performance of her role: 'Just in case you do the part again.'

In 1979 Peter Hall staged *Fidelio*, with Söderström as Leonore. She had taken her time before embarking on what is always a considerable challenge, but even more so for an intrinsically lyric rather than dramatic soprano, whose voice was not naturally suited to the role. But her experience, artistry and sheer intelligence combined to make her inter-pretation of the part one of great integrity, and it was praised to the skies. (She was delighted by a conversation which was overheard about her performance, and quickly passed on to her. One member of the audience, more at home on the football field than in the opera house, was overheard to say, 'I thought she looked like Kevin Keegan'; to which his companion replied, after some thought, 'Well, she *moves* like Kevin Keegan. . .'.) Hall successfully humanized the opera by laying particular emphasis on the domestic aspects of the story instead of following the more usual approach of concentrating on the general themes of repression and prison. Hall's version, as in other cases such as his 1973 *Figaro*, was a more personal one, with the characters developed as real human beings rather than symbols of political strife.

In that same year's revival of *Il ritorno d'Ulisse in patria*, Frederica von Stade had the unenviable lot of stepping into the shoes of Janet Baker as Penelope, and it was a personal triumph that her performance did not suffer by comparison with her predecessor; there were indeed those who thought it better still, and Hall commented that she was 'just as modest and dedicated as ever', and much like Janet Baker. This was Raymond Leppard's last opera at Glyndebourne before departing for Indianapolis, and in his book *Raymond Leppard on Music* he later summed up the essential elements that have made Glyndebourne what it is:

The care with which the management put together the initial group of people who will see the opera onto the stage as one piece, director, designer and conductor, making sure they are compatible and able to come to decisions about style and purpose in the production ... and the encouragement of young, talented singers who are likely to develop ... and become for a few years part of the company. This is a long established intent which has repaid a million times over the care and effort of seeking them out and looking after them once found.

This is a wonderful analysis of the Glyndebourne philosophy from one who had been largely responsible for some of the most original and innovative of its successes in the sixties and seventies, and who knew Glyndebourne from the inside but was also able to compare working conditions there with those in other leading opera houses. Nevertheless, he felt it was time to make a move into a wider world. The collaboration of Ebert with Busch and Gui, of Peter Hall with Pritchard and Haitink, Leppard and John Bury, of Enriquez with Luzzati, and later of Lehnhoff with Hoheisel; and the design work of Messel, Lancaster and Hockney with various directors and conductors, all working in conditions that simply did not exist elsewhere, with a constant stream of young singers developing and maturing, season after season: these were the artistic elements that went into Glyndebourne's numerous creative successes.

After the Festival four performances of *The Rake's Progress* were given in the Théâtre des Champs-Elysées in the Paris Festival d'Automne, and the reviews were as rapturous as those for *Falstaff* and *Le comte Ory* twenty-one years before. The French theatre's hunger for Glyndebourne is demonstrated by the fact that in an unguarded moment they admitted that the visit *must* take place 'whatever it costs'.

Prior to that, there had also been a significant innovation in the form of the Kent Schools' Festival at Glyndebourne, when over 4,000 secondary school-children came to a series of special performances. Their response was wonderful, and the County Education Authority, not unnaturally, requested an encore in 1981. Following their tour in England, GTO also gave three performances of *La fedeltà premiata* at Nancy, a gloriously ideal setting for eighteenth-century opera. Nancy, too, asked for a return visit, which took the form of four performances of *The Rake's Progress* there the next year.

By 1980, Hall was busy at the National Theatre and unavailable for Glyndebourne. John Cox collaborated with the 87-year-old French designer Erté on *Der Rosenkavalier*. Erté set the opera in the middle of the nineteenth century, a period in which he felt very much at home; but most people felt that this arbitrary updating from a century earlier was unjustified, as was the decision to hold the levée in Act I in another room, rather than the bedroom specified, and that, in general, 'you don't mess around with *Rosenkavalier*'. Nor did there seem to be much of Vienna about the sets, which in the first act were heavily padded, and had an adverse effect on the acoustics, as well as being described by one reviewer as 'a sort of milliner's bandbox'. Both the sets and costumes, instead of heightening the effect, as they should, were a distraction that severely damaged it. Nevertheless, another reviewer stated that Felicity Lott, as Oktavian, 'triumphs over any circumstances ... and leaves one at a loss for words'. She herself was also moved to tears, on stage, by Elizabeth Harwood's Feldmarschallin, and her heartrending interpretation of the emotional pain of growing old.

There were also distractions in a new production of *Die Entführung* by Peter Wood, with too much stage business during the overture, and live doves in a large gilded cage that echoed life in the seraglio. Their cooing competed with the Constanze of Valerie Masterson who was making her only appearance at the Festival. Other diversions included garden rakes being brandished, straw hats torn up, spectacles mislaid and potted plants waved about. Mozart's sublime score could have done without them, but what seems fussy and tiresome to some may often charm others: Peter Heyworth in the *Observer* found the production and all its inven-

The veteran French designer Erté discussing his set model for Der Rosenkavalier *with John Cox, Moran Caplat and June Dandridge (1980)*

Interval with Calman...

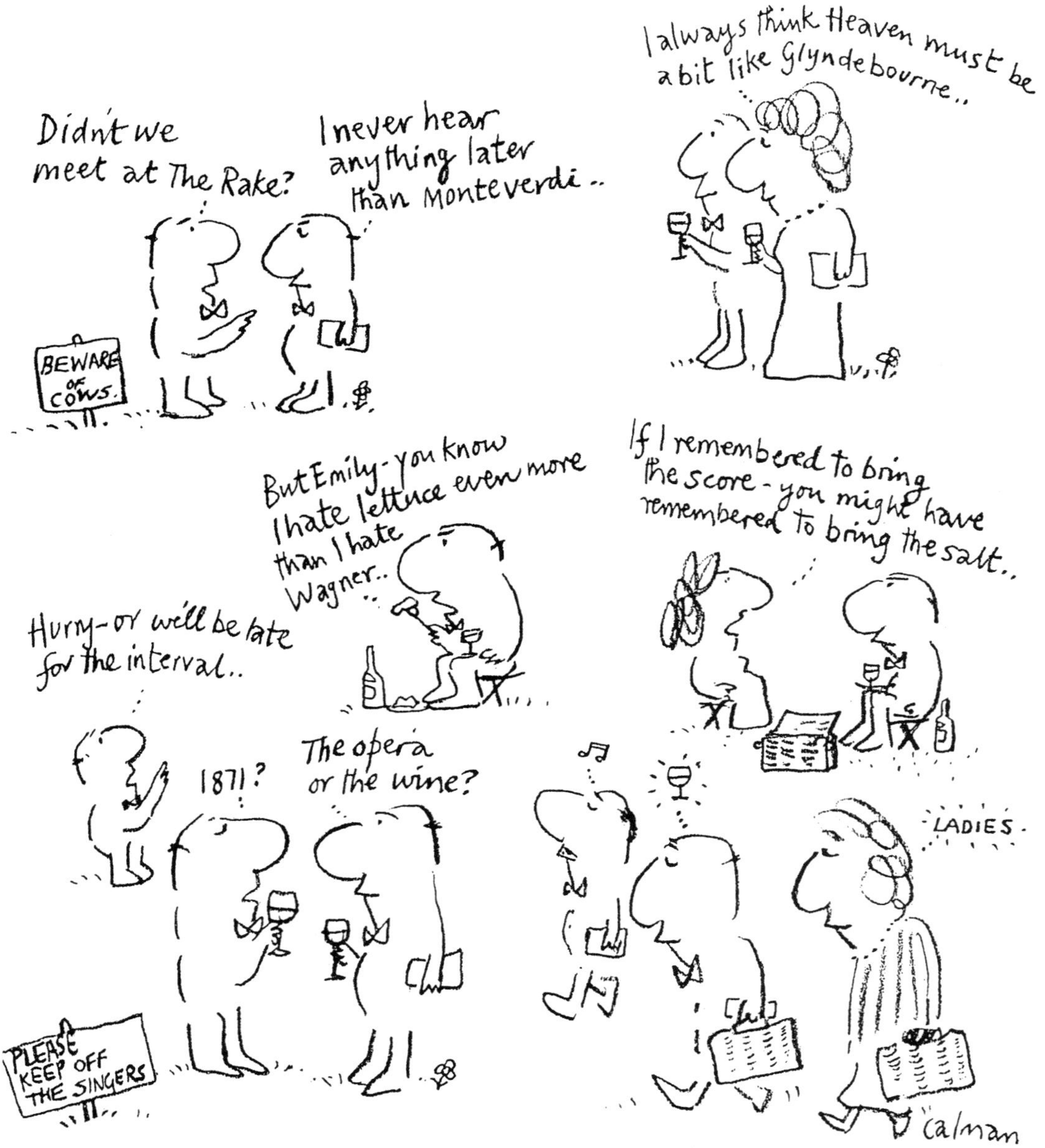

tive humour very much in the style of Hans Wurst – that is to say, of Austrian comedy in Mozart's day. Gustav Kuhn, the conductor, and Willard White as Osmin each scored a great success.

In 1980 Carl Ebert died. His contribution to the creation of Glyndebourne's methods and standards, and to maintaining them until his final departure in 1963, was unique: without him Glyndebourne could never have pursued the course that it did. He had begun his own career as an actor, then as a trainer of actors, and his success as Director of the Darmstadt Theatre after 1927, above all in establishing a closer co-operation with conductors and designers than had been at all usual before, had led to his appointment as head of the Berlin Opera in 1931. He had then bravely turned freelance, working at first in Switzerland, Austria and Italy, and later, during the war, in Turkey; and had only agreed to work on the first season at Glyndebourne because he could not believe there would be a second. It was ultimately thanks to him that John Cox (who had first worked as assistant to Ebert and Rennert in 1959) was able to claim, in an interview in *Opera* in 1978, that Glyndebourne was the only practical teaching opera company in the country. Geraint Evans recalled that Ebert always aimed at perfection, 'and was prepared to work and work until he brought out the very best in you'. Thus he helped innumerable singers to fulfil their maximum potential; while Ebert's faithfulness to the composer is summed up in his observation that 'It's not too hard to produce a Mozart opera – he wrote all his stage directions in the music,' – a point which more obtrusive producers have been known to miss. A fine bas-relief of him by John Skelton now occupies a richly deserved position on the foyer wall of the new opera house.

John Cox's own role covered everything that the audience sees, rather than hears. Strauss was Cox's particular speciality and Hockney and Battersby his most striking introductions as designers. In his foreword to the 1982 programme, George Christie also paid tribute to his 'perceptive and delicate response to the detail in the dramatic development of a work', for which there is special need in the case of a comparatively intimate house such as Glyndebourne. On his appointment, too, a conscious plan had been formulated to put on works not previously seen there. His qualities were pinpointed in an interview given by Elisabeth Söderström, who scored outstanding successes in his productions of *Intermezzo* and *Capriccio*. She explained that he was 'marvellous at helping you to make it natural and spontaneous'; that he 'missed no detail in a singer's performance, and could therefore help you that much more'. She also stated that his production of *Intermezzo*, in English, was the happiest of all her experiences at Glyndebourne, thanks to the exceptional response of the audiences all through, and to the opportunity she had of interpreting the qualities of Pauline Strauss, the composer's formidable wife and also the central figure in the opera.

In that same interview, she paid affectionate tribute to the general Glyndebourne atmosphere, commenting that when heated discussions broke out, and strong differences of opinion arose, these rarely developed into full-blown rows, 'because there was always someone to help you'. This may have been more a reflection of her own sunny disposition than anything else, but the fact that she saw it as she did testifies to the conditions that she found there – not least the unique opportunities for soothing and reviving walks over the downs. The only drawback that she could think of at Glyndebourne was the length of the supper interval, coming when the singers are well warmed up. But, she added, 'you learn to cope'. For the audiences, whether one picnics in the shelter of the yew hedges in the garden or on the banks of the pond, or chooses to eat in the dining-rooms, the supper is not only one of the incidental delights of the evening, it also refreshes and fortifies those who have made long journeys and whose powers of concentration may be flagging: applause, laughter and general enthusiasm is often at its peak in the first half-hour after the interval, which can itself be encouraging for the cast.

6

New Brooms

1981–1992

Moran Caplat retired in 1981. Of the great qualities which he exercised over the thirty-six years he spent at Glyndebourne, stamina, patience, tact and thoughtfulness are perhaps the chief among them. In the cheerful interview just quoted, Elisabeth Söderström paid a notable tribute to these qualities when she commented: 'Moran never told me what to do or what not to do: but I soon learnt.' No one could have been equally successful in every aspect of such a many-sided job; and if a shortcoming has to be mentioned, it may be that Caplat was less welcoming than he might have been to the press. Perhaps he could have defused some of their adverse comments, perhaps not. At any rate, he certainly showed discernment in his many expeditions to hear the unknown but promising singers who would blossom and flourish under the conditions available at Glyndebourne and would become the lifeblood of each new season. His imagination and talent in adapting a series of Festival operas for the Proms – entirely his own idea – have already been mentioned, but should never be forgotten. On his retirement at the age of sixty-five, he was appointed briefly to the Board of Glyndebourne Productions Ltd, and for a time continued as editor of the annual Festival programme book.

It was time for a new broom. This was found in the form of Brian

Dickie, who had been Administrator of GTO since its foundation and, before that, had worked for four years as assistant to Jani Strasser. His first work experience had been with Freshfields, the solicitors, and as a result he may have had a better idea of general commercial practice than his predecessor. He was also Director of the Wexford Festival from 1967 to 1973, which gave him a broader perspective from which to consider his task at Glyndebourne. His replacement in charge of GTO was Anthony Whitworth-Jones, whose previous experience had been with the London Sinfonietta, and whose commitment to contemporary music was, and remains, strong. This was to play an important part in the ever-present need to extend Glyndebourne's artistic boundaries beyond safe, familiar works.

Peter Hall's *Figaro* was revived in 1981 and dedicated to Ebert's memory, with Norma Burrowes much praised as Susanna; but the great sensation of the year was his magical staging of Britten's *A Midsummer Night's Dream*, originally composed in 1959 for the reopening of the Jubilee Hall at Aldeburgh. John Bury's sets were inspired, and the production, conducted by Haitink, ranks as one of Glyndebourne's greatest triumphs ever, as is evident from the video. The mixture of poetic imagination, of other-worldly magic (which included trees capable of moving about the stage) and of enchanting humour, all of them faithful to Shakespeare's genius, earned it the most wholehearted admiration and enjoyment, above all perhaps for the Tytania of Ileana Cotrubas and the Puck of Damien Nash. (Strange to relate, one of the animated trees, in this case a recumbent log, at one point ceased to move, and it is alleged, improbable though it seems, that he had actually fallen asleep on stage.) Also praised to the skies was Hall's economy, accuracy and alertness to the music. After seeing the production, Peter Pears said how much he wished the composer could have seen it too.

Following the total lack of sympathy between John Christie and Britten in the productions of the latter's works in 1946 and 1947, it was extremely satisfactory that the real qualities of Britten's work should now be so triumphantly manifested at Glyndebourne. An important part in the early stages of this rehabilitation was played by Brian Dickie, in con-

Moran Caplat in his box at Glyndebourne at the time of his retirement (1981)

Brian Dickie, who took over from Caplat, with George Christie (1981)

versations over the garden fence with his neighbour in Sussex Donald Mitchell, who just happened to be one of the Britten trustees. Back in 1960, Britten had written a piece in the *Observer*, most unusually for him, about the original production of the *Dream*, in which he commented: 'One hoped, after the war, that audiences would revolt at seeing opera performed with bad acting,' and admitted that it would have been better if he had given Glyndebourne due credit for bringing this change about. (Almost unbelievably he added, after 'bad acting', the words 'and in a foreign language'. How such a gifted composer could simply rule out the concept of operas being performed in the language in which they had been written seems very strange today; but in the 1960s the tide flowed strongly in favour of performances in the vernacular, for the benefit of wider audiences. Fortunately, in this case, his words went unheeded.)

In 1982 another major change came about with the departure of John Cox, Director of Productions, to become General Administrator of Scottish Opera. Like Ebert before him, Cox did not entirely sever his link with Glyndebourne. He returned a number of times: in 1983 to put on a new production of *La Cenerentola* which had not been given at Glyndebourne for twenty-three years; to revive *Intermezzo* in the same year; and in 1984 to direct the first Glyndebourne staging of Strauss's *Arabella*; and more recently, to revive *The Rake's Progress*. The production of *Arabella* was sponsored by Imperial Tobacco, bringing their sponsorships to the remarkable total of seven over the previous eight years. Also in 1982 came the appointment of Jane Glover as Music Director of GTO. She had only joined the music staff three years before, but had risen to be chorus director the following year, and was also a considerable musicologist. She conducted *Die Entführung* on the 1980 tour, and by 1984 shared the revival of *A Midsummer Night's Dream* with Haitink in the Festival. She went on to a wide-ranging and successful career with a number of orchestras, opera companies and choral societies, having gained invaluable early professional experience at Glyndebourne. In a newspaper interview she modestly claimed to have been taken on 'without one of their awful auditions, otherwise I'd never have got in'.

The other new production of 1982 was John Cox's exuberant *Il barbiere di Siviglia*, with John Rawnsley as an energetic Figaro, and Maria Ewing's wilful Rosina covering an almost unbelievable range of emotions and reactions, with numerous touches of sheer comic genius complementing her fine singing. She had an equal success as the Composer in *Ariadne*, also produced by John Cox, both at Glyndebourne and subsequently at the Proms (where Caplat's ingenuity in adapting it for the Albert Hall reached its final zenith). A triumphant year was rounded off by the revival of Peter Hall's *Fidelio*, where Haitink was described in *The Musical Times* as 'approaching Furtwängler in the nobility of his conception' of the work.

In addition to its full tour, GTO put on three works in the Kent Schools' Festival at Glyndebourne at the end of September. This scheme, which had been inaugurated two years earlier with a week of *Fidelio* and *Così fan tutte*, was now revived with *Figaro*, *Falstaff* and the *Dream*, and with Kent County Council taking responsibility for raising the necessary sponsorship. Afterwards the audiences were invited to go in for a competition: entries could take the form of an essay, a poem, or an expression of visual art such as a poster; the prizes were Festival tickets for the following season and a boxed set of records of one of the operas performed. The preparation by the children beforehand, their enthusiastic interest in the course itself, and the keenness of the follow-up, undoubtedly fostered an interest in and a love of opera which they would not have had the chance to develop otherwise: yet another example of the way in which the wider community was enriched by Glyndebourne's constructive ventures. The only cloud on the horizon was the fact that the Arts Council grant to GTO remained the same as in the year before, while other touring companies received an average increase of 12 per cent. The result was that the tour was cut by a week, though a serious threat that the grant would be abolished altogether was strongly and persuasively resisted by Glyndebourne, with sturdy support from the press. Had it come about, it would have meant the end of GTO.

The 1982 season was remarkable both for the first (and, to date, the last) appearance of a Prokofiev opera at Glyndebourne, and for the first example of sponsorship by a French company – and what could have been more appropriate than Cointreau paying for *The Love for Three Oranges*? It appeared under its French title, true to Glyndebourne practice, since it was first performed in French in Chicago in 1921. Peter Hall also created a new production of Gluck's *Orfeo ed Euridice*, with a wonderful performance by Janet Baker, her swansong on the operatic stage. It was conducted by Raymond Leppard, who used the version made by Berlioz for Pauline Viardot in 1859, and the production was recorded on the French label Erato. The part caused severe stress for Janet Baker, and she records in her book *Full Circle* that:

> Only I can ever know what this desperate journey of Orfeo's has done to me. In the test of will and discipline involved in bringing Euridice back from the dead and obeying the demand not to look at her, Orfeo fails. The gods know the fatal weakness in all of us and choose the very thing they know we cannot do. Of course Orfeo fails the test. Of course everybody does.

At the end of the performance, Orfeo clasps the hands of the chorus by turn, and describing the curtain call on the last night Baker added:

> We have exchanged more than hand clasps; we have touched each other with infinite tenderness and respect; we have looked into each other's hearts and souls; we have shared and communicated something indescribably precious. If any moment could sum up the beauty of my whole theatre experience it would be this one. . . . We all came through this moment with a glorious joy, regardless of the tears in many eyes. . . . The sense of exhilaration and joy I had felt all day rose to bursting point as the love of everyone surrounded me.

On a lighter note, she added the story of a man who was determined

The final curtain of Orfeo ed Euridice, *Janet Baker's farewell to the operatic stage (1982)*

to be first in the queue for returns for one of the performances. He staked his claim by placing a stuffed dog with a note in its mouth by the box office window at midnight. The note stated that the dog represented its owner who was asleep in the car park, and if this method of queuing was objected to, he was to be woken and would stand through the night in person. At dawn, the owner took his place and was later rewarded with the first ticket returned.

Handel once commented that his cook was a better musician than Gluck, and though no one would have agreed after hearing this *Orfeo*, it is quite possible that Janet Baker, with her rare depth of feeling for the part, put something into the music that had not been there before, at least since the days of Kathleen Ferrier.

With great imagination, Brian Dickie had acquired a letter written by Berlioz to Viardot when they had worked together on *Orfeo*, had had it bound, and presented it to Dame Janet on stage after the performance. There are moments of great drama and emotion every year at Glyndebourne, but the intensity of this occasion has seldom been exceeded there. As Harold Rosenthal commented: 'Genius, empathy, "star" quality; whatever it is called, Janet Baker possesses it . . . she can hold an audience enthralled just as Maria Callas did.' Significantly, she summed up by saying that she was, above all, grateful to Peter Hall for 'freedom within discipline'.

The revival of the Peter Hall production of *Don Giovanni* was a triumph for the American Carol Vaness as Donna Anna in her first appearance at Glyndebourne; and Richard Van Allan's Leporello, Thomas Allen's Don and Elizabeth Gale's Zerlina were highly praised. Max Loppert in the *Financial Times* described it as possibly the most exciting, most disturbing, most musically sentient *Don Giovanni* he had ever encountered. It was not only the top-class cast but the fusion of the various talents of Hall, Bury and Haitink that raised this production to the heights.

Excellent though 1981 had been, 1982 was in Rosenthal's opinion also a great vintage. He described the *Don Giovanni* revival as being 'as near perfection as one could possibly hope for', and Felicity Lott's Oktavian as 'near-ideal' in a *Rosenkavalier* 'conducted in the most exciting manner' by Simon Rattle. Rattle, incidentally, showed that it was not only singers who developed and blossomed as a result of working with GTO. He was to conduct – with 'magicianly ease', as one critic put it – a series of inspiring performances at Glyndebourne before deciding to return to his work with the City of Birmingham Symphony Orchestra. It is not really possible to put into words what distinguishes an exceptional conductor, who makes the hair on the back of the listener's neck stand on end, from a merely good one. Obviously he or she must be able to inspire the individual members of the orchestra and cast to give of their very best, and to combine together to produce an exceptional ensemble. For players to reciprocate fully, the conductor has to earn and retain their respect. Singers, in particular, would add a further requirement: that the conductor should not let the orchestra play so loud that an excessive strain is put on their voices if they are to make themselves heard. And finally, an exceptional conductor must have an overview of the work as a whole which will bring out the full significance of all its component parts, and produce harmonious balance between them. Simon Rattle, from an unusually early age, was widely acclaimed as having triumphed in all these departments. For those concerned with opera, it was just sad that his overriding interest lay in purely orchestral works rather than in the opera house.

This was also the year in which Peter Hall put his foot down with characteristic force on the question of who should direct the video recordings of his productions. The BBC took the line that this was a different professional skill from producing an opera on the stage, and one for which Hall was not qualified. Hall, however, had an absolute right to direct all his work at the National Theatre for video, and pointed out that while a live performance was an ephemeral affair which disappeared for ever when it was over, a video is a permanent record by which a producer will be judged till eternity. He announced that he had 'no intention of allowing other people to represent, or mis-represent, my work … so if Glyndebourne don't insist on me directing the videos, I cannot do the original production'. Hall won, but it was a foretaste of the clashes between an irresistible force and an immovable object that were to come.

The next year, 1983, saw the first production by Trevor Nunn, who had been Artistic Director and Chief Executive of the Royal Shakespeare Company for ten years, and, like Hall, was now spreading his wings in other directions. Much care had been taken to create a balanced programme of works, none of which was an obvious popular choice. Nunn directed *Idomeneo*, which, along with *Intermezzo* and *La Cenerentola*, was recorded for television, the two revivals, *Die Entführung* and *The Love for Three Oranges*, having already been recorded previously. The BBC, largely absent since its long run of broadcasts from 1951 to 1967, now returned. *La Cenerentola* was heavily (though not universally) slated, inspiring the critic Rodney Milnes to coin the useful term 'kimp', by kitsch out of camp. John Cox's *Idomeneo* in 1974 had not been a great success but Trevor Nunn's operatic debut was highly praised, even by those who tended to be critical of Glyndebourne. Nunn may not have played an instrument or even been able to read music, but nevertheless he is deeply musical. What he also brought to the stage was a fascination for Shakespeare's final plays, in which the triumph of love is paramount. The same is true of *Idomeneo*, and it was this that spurred him to accept Peter Hall's suggestion of taking it on. *Opera* magazine rated it 'the best production to have been seen or heard anywhere in recent years', with perfect co-ordination between Nunn and Haitink. There was special praise also for the chorus and their training by Jane Glover, and for the LPO, 'in top form', while Carol Vaness was reckoned to have been even more successful as Electra – one of Mozart's most demanding roles – than she had been as Donna Anna the year before.

Behind the scenes, a major improvement was made by Brian Dickie when he followed excellent advice in appointing Letheby & Christopher as caterers, thereby doing much for the morale of staff and performers alike, not to mention the audiences. Nine firms had applied to tender, and Letheby & Christopher were successful from a short-list of four. Although there had been few actual complaints about the food served in the dining-rooms (originally named Upper, Middle and Nether Wallop, after three villages on the estate of the Portsmouth family, of which John Christie's mother was a member), the difference was soon appreciated, and noted by Janet Baker in her diary ('The canteen was packed; it shows just how good the food is this year'). The firm may justifiably take pride in the satisfaction which, under the management at Glyndebourne of Sean Hall-Smith, they have given, almost without exception, to the present day. It must also be stressed that those who work at Glynde- bourne in whatever capacity (right down to the visiting author) should remember how lucky they are in the quality of the canteen now housed in the old Nether Wallop dining hall. It has for the last few years been presided over with authority and independence by Mrs Margaret Williams: in maintaining a wonderful standard, her eagle eye misses nothing. Long may she remain in charge. And, of course, none of this would be possible without the skill and imagination of Andy Barlow, the Head Chef. A further development followed in 1998 when Letheby & Christopher agreed to pay for the construction of a new catering block, opposite their old offices and close to Glyndebourne's own pub, the Pug and Whistle. This cost half a million pounds, in return for which the company's catering contract was extended for a further ten years. Both sides benefited: Glyndebourne got a fine new building with all the latest equipment. The caterers got a profitable new contract, and their staff will be enjoying conditions which could hardly be bettered.

Justice was also done to the Glyndebourne gardens in an attractive book by Christopher Lloyd and Anne Scott-James, a journalist of high reputation and the widow of Osbert Lancaster, whose designs had given such pleasure a number of years earlier. As Mary Christie pointed out in her foreword, no other opera house has a garden as its foyer, but keeping it at its best after late frosts, sometimes at the mercy either of drought or prolonged, battering rainfall, is anxious work. On the very rare occasions when things go wrong they are very soon put right, and the setting they provide adds enormously to the pleasure of audiences. Anne Scott-James's book was illustrated with attractive watercolours by Elizabeth Bury. She and John Bury, the designer who played such a crucial part in so many of Peter Hall's productions and, later, in the planning of the new theatre, formed one of the admirable husband and wife teams on which Glyndebourne, from the top down, has been so unusually lucky in being able to rely. It is also right to recognize the contribution made by Helen O'Neill, Head of Press and much more for many years, and managing editor of the annual programme book after Caplat's retirement. Her husband Guy Gravett was the official photographer at Glyndebourne from 1951 until his death in 1996.

Peter Hall was now officially appointed Artistic Director at Glyndebourne, as from the end of the year. For over a decade he had almost annually been fitting a new Glyndebourne production into the pattern of his extensive work elsewhere, but in 1983 had actually been absent from Glyndebourne, producing the *Ring* cycle at Bayreuth for Wolfgang Wagner. This new decision formally ratified his position, and he was provided with a house at South Chailey, not far from Glyndebourne. Nevertheless, his wider commitments sometimes prevented him from giving to Festival productions other than his own the attention which

Audiences in 1955, 1958 and 1981, enjoying the glorious gardens

might have been expected, and from time to time relations became strained.

Hall was to overlap with Cox for the jubilee year of 1984 before taking over fully in 1985. George Christie had informed Cox of the impending change back in 1980, and noted at the time that his reaction was 'extraordinarily philosophical and rational'. Cox had had a run of twelve years at Glyndebourne, roughly on a par with others who had held the post, and, after a spell at Scottish Opera, he went on to achieve some notable successes at Covent Garden – while returning, like Ebert before him, for an occasional production at Glyndebourne. There was also an important double development at GTO that year. First was the commissioning of a new version of *The Love for Three Oranges*, in English, from Tom Stoppard, who had by then reached the heights of the London theatre world; secondly, the whole tour, like several others, was sponsored by Barclays Bank.

If the 1983 Festival had its weaker moments, especially after the two preceding vintage years, 1984 was Glyndebourne's golden jubilee and opened on 28 May, the exact anniversary, with *Figaro*, just as it had originally. Among the invited guests were a few who had been there fifty years before, and a champagne reception was given for audience and company afterwards, following a firework display in the garden. Members balloted for tickets, and were rationed to two apiece. The Queen had expressed a wish to go to Glyndebourne to mark its jubilee, and the suggestion was made that she might like to attend *Figaro*. It is well known that opera is not one of her favourite forms of entertainment; but her astonishing memory for detail, in whatever field, extended to the moment in Act IV, when Barbarina finds the pin which the Count has given her to pass on to Susanna. The Queen enquired whether *Figaro* was 'the opera with the pin', and, on being told it was, replied that she had seen it before and would rather choose another. This turned out to be *Arabella* – though the legend that she was under the impression that it was the work of Johann rather than Richard Strauss has not been confirmed. It was the first time the opera had been put on at Glyndebourne. John Cox was at his very best, but the designer, Julia

HM The Queen with House Manager Geoffrey Gilbertson on her visit to mark Glyndebourne's fiftieth anniversary (1984)

Trevelyan Oman, though also in her element, was criticized for excessive clutter on the stage, and for hampering the singers with heavy and cumbersome costumes. Industrious though her research had been, she was accused of a lack of flair and imagination, not least in her choice of colours. There were two major last-minute cast changes, but the American Ashley Putnam thoroughly distinguished herself in the title role, as did John Bröscheler as Mandryka. And the revival of Britten's *Dream*, on the other hand, was praised even more ecstatically than in its first showing.

In Peter Hall's new production of Raymond Leppard's *Poppea*, Maria Ewing in the name part was described as 'unnervingly sure and subtle', and Robert Lloyd excelled himself as Seneca. Some of the passion and conviction of Leppard's original re-creation were thought to have been lost, and opinion was sharply divided about the extent to which subsequent scholarly findings had been taken into account.

175

GTO was not put in the shade by the jubilee celebrations in the Festival. Anthony Whitworth-Jones was determined to make new operas an integral part of Glyndebourne's activities. The first major work to be introduced was a one-act opera originally commissioned by the Brussels Opera in 1978, the so-called Year of the Child, with a libretto by the far-famed author and illustrator of children's books, Maurice Sendak, and music by the brilliant young composer Oliver Knussen – who had, as well as other experience, worked as a conductor with the London Sinfonietta, in close touch with Whitworth-Jones. *Where the Wild Things Are* was not finished in time for its première in Brussels, and the first complete performances were presented by Glyndebourne at the National Theatre, London, in January 1984. It is a charming story about an unruly, over-excited child who is sent to bed early for misbehaviour, and embarks on a magical journey by land and water to an island inhabited by weird creatures, half-terrifying and half-affectionate. It received, and fully deserved, a tremendous reception. Though the central character is a child, the opera was certainly not written only for children. It was neither frivolous, nor altogether serious. Quite simply, it made people happy. Like *Porgy and Bess* two years later, it was yet another example of Glyndebourne's versatility, and of the range of the imagination of those in charge, and wonderfully faithful to the plan that Audrey Christie had wanted. It also had a wider significance, which was well expressed in a letter from Brian Dickie to the Arts Council, intended to stiffen their often shaky resolve to support GTO:

> The project is the beginning of what we hope will be a series of serious attempts at something of lasting value in providing opportunities for composers, directors and librettists to come together to create new work under as near ideal conditions as possible, and providing them also with . . . an extended number of performances over a longer period of time than just a single series of repertory.

The intention was for a double bill by the same team, the second part

Two of the Wild Things under construction for Where the Wild Things Are *(1984)*

of which was to be the adaptation of another story by Sendak called *Higglety Pigglety Pop!* Knussen however, despite repeated promises to finish the score in good time for the GTO tour in September 1984, failed to do so. There are precedents in the history of opera. Rossini, on more than one occasion, delivered his music page by page at the very last minute and, in those free and easy days, more than once simply took over an existing overture from another opera. That however was long before the days of sponsors, and other financially interested parties. To resolve the crisis, George Christie asked his old friend and Cambridge contemporary, Bamber Gascoigne, for help. Gascoigne, as much at home on the stage as on the television screen (where years before, he had devised 'University Challenge'), stepped nimbly into the breach to read passages from the book of *Higglety Pigglety Pop!* from the stage, with such charm and aplomb that the audiences, who would have been justified in demanding their money back, were regularly disarmed. The double bill had been sponsored by Pearsons, the group where Lord Gibson was Chairman (as well as having been a Glyndebourne trustee and then Chairman of the Arts Council). All George Christie's reserves of tact and diplomacy were drawn on for the letter of apology which he had to write to Pearsons. Glyndebourne had been let down badly from time to time by singers breaking their undertakings, from Ina Souez in 1935 onwards. But singers can be replaced, whereas operatic music cannot be improvised. Though Knussen was only thirty-two, he had had orchestral works performed to great acclaim, his Third Symphony having been much admired by Simon Rattle, who took it on tour with the City of Birmingham Symphony Orchestra. He had also worked as an artistic director at Aldeburgh, so it was not as if Glyndebourne were putting its faith in an unknown quantity. By the time the double bill came to take its place in the 1985 Festival itself, teething troubles were resolved, even though the composer had still not completed the score. Audiences loved it, though most of them, as usual, were blissfully unaware of all the intense aggravation that had arisen. It was never revived at Glyndebourne, but the life of the production was, fortunately, prolonged through performances in America, and on video.

The jubilee year was also, most appropriately, marked by George's receiving a knighthood for his services to opera. When the excitements of the season had died down, it had been decided as far as possible to put on six operas per season. The plan for 1987 onwards was to be two new productions a year and four revivals: first, in order to reduce the excess of demand for tickets over supply; secondly to increase the value for money received by sponsors, who would be able to bathe in glory all over again when the productions they had paid for were revived in subsequent years; and thirdly, as George put it in the programme book, why bury a production long before it has outlived its useful existence?

In contrast to the complete novelty of *Higglety Pigglety Pop!*, there was in 1985 a great new Peter Hall production of *Carmen*, one of the oldest favourites of all, with Maria Ewing in a tempestuous and riveting performance. After the initial failure of *Carmen* in Paris, in 1876, Tchaikovsky had accurately predicted that: 'in ten years' time it will be the most popular opera in the whole world'. Both Brahms and Stravinsky admired it. Even Wagner liked it. But many changes had been made to the score since the composer had died, three months after its first performance and long before its worldwide success. This 1985 production used the version sold by Bizet to his publisher Choudens, and composed for a theatre about the same size as Glyndebourne. However, the production was on the whole considered much better on its revival two years later.

Hall's other new production in 1985 was *Albert Herring*, Britten's third opera, set in a Suffolk town of the kind he had known all his life. The world première had been staged at Glyndebourne in 1947, Eric Crozier, the librettist, was still alive, and Hall sent him a much-treasured postcard saying: 'Albert is a masterpiece – not least because of the wonderful libretto, witty but wise, tender but irreverent. If only you and Ben had done more *comic*

Albert Herring rehearsal, 1985: Peter Hall and John Graham-Hall

operas. There has been a shortage of laughter this century.' The 1985 programme book contains some letters written by Crozier during the composition of the work, in the bitter winter of 1946, to the soprano Nancy Evans, whom he later married, and for whom the party of Nancy in the opera was created. Though too long to print in full here, they are of great interest to anyone wishing to study this opera more fully. When the libretto was finished he wrote to her: 'Nancy is especially and particularly yours, for without you she either would not exist at all or would be someone quite different and nothing like so sincere.' *Albert Herring* is a work that is very easy to appreciate – it was once irreverently compared to 'The Archers' – and the popularity of this production was on a parallel scale.

It is of some interest to notice the share of tickets available for the general public at this stage after corporate and individual members had claimed their due. In descending order of popularity, the percentage available for the general public was as follows:

Carmen	6.25%
Arabella	8.6%
La Cenerentola	11.13%
Idomeneo	11.73%
Albert Herring	47.57%
Double Bill (Knussen)	71.08%

As far as GTO was concerned, Anthony Whitworth-Jones was careful to point out that, however closely intertwined it was with the Festival, its aims are different: to cast 'as many principal roles as possible with young singers either from the chorus or from the understudies'. In other words, artistically its policy is quite specific. Socially, of course, GTO attracts much more broadly based audiences by taking opera to different parts of the country at ticket prices similar to those of other touring companies.

The following year began with yet another departure from previous form. In January 1986, Peter Hall's famous productions of *Don Giovanni* and *A Midsummer Night's Dream* were taken to Hong Kong, sponsored by the Royal Hong Kong Jockey Club. The whole team of cast and technicians numbered 107, and predictably they were very warmly received.

George now emphasized a note of warning that had been heard at regular intervals before. Basically, public sector funding for the arts was not keeping pace with inflation. This did not affect the Festival directly, but GTO, now mutually interdependent on the Festival, was deeply vulnerable to the withdrawal of Arts Council support – a move that was threatened from time to time – or even to a failure to increase the level of such support. George also reproached the press for virtually never giving due credit to commercial sponsorship of the arts, and stressed its crucial role at a time when government support usually remained at best static (for which he was always careful, at this stage, to lay the blame on government policy rather than on the Arts Council itself).

The new departure in the year's repertory was new indeed: Gershwin's stirring *Porgy and Bess*, which had been written in the year in which Glyndebourne opera was born. The composer's aim, on which he laboured for three years, was for a combination of the drama and romance of *Carmen* and the beauty of *Meistersinger*. Indeed, the work has a locale as exotic and an atmosphere as dramatic as in the former, and choral ensembles almost on the scale of the latter. The composer's close friend Irving Berlin once observed: 'You must never forget that the rest of us were songwriters. George was a composer.' Other opera companies were competing to acquire the performing rights, but Brian Dickie, with characteristic energy and enthusiasm, went to Los Angeles and adroitly acquired them on the spot. He also auditioned for the principal members of the cast and some of the chorus at the Metropolitan Opera, in order to start creating the best available ensemble for the Glyndebourne pro-duction, which had to consist entirely of black artists. *Porgy* had created a sensation in a six-month run at the Stoll Theatre in London in 1952–3, and had then been put on in truncated form at La Scala, before disap-pearing from the major opera houses of the world. For Glyndebourne it was an inspired, and very successful, departure from anything in the past, and it was achieved in competition with English National Opera, who also wanted to put it on. In true Glyndebourne tradition, it was the way in which the tensions of a living, breathing community had so skilfully, and naturally, been brought into being (by Nunn) that had the greatest impact; and although there was not a single weakness in the whole cast, Willard White, who had had long experience of the part, identified himself more profoundly with Porgy than would have been thought possible, imparting to the whole glorious ensemble a unique and astonishing quality. The conductor, Simon Rattle, in his response to Gershwin's peculiar genius, inspired the fullest choral and orchestral delivery. Apart from White, Cynthia Haymon, as Bess, not only sang beautifully but acted the part without ever losing credibility or sympathy. Of the newcomers to Glyndebourne, Harolyn Blackwell, as Serena, sang 'Summertime' exquisitely, and was described by the *Financial Times* as having 'a face of heartbreaking sweetness', and as lighting up the stage every time she appeared. Gregg Baker's Crown was also a magnificent performance.

Hitherto, the programme book had seldom included a major article by a member of an opera cast. But the 1987 book contained one of the most moving pieces in all the issues that had appeared over the past thirty-five years. It was by Damon Evans, who played Sportin' Life, cool, and gleaming with mocking intelligence, in both the seasons of 1986 and 1987. In his article, he describes the doubts, fears and suspicions of a black cast assembled in Sussex not only from the USA, but from the vastly different communities in Britain, Italy, South Africa and Jamaica; and how these worries were gradually dissolved by the genius of Trevor Nunn in fusing the separate parts into a whole. When the cast assembled for rehearsals for the first time, his opening words to them were: 'Glyndebourne will never be the same again, and it shouldn't be'; while to their amazement Simon Rattle enabled them to rediscover music which they thought they already knew backwards. Mercifully, Damon Evans was unaware of Dennis Thatcher's question at one of the performances: 'Where do all these blacks come from?' Nevertheless, in view of the great differences between the various communities just mentioned, it was an interesting question.

At the beginning, the unvoiced question in the minds of the cast was: 'How do you white Englishmen dare to direct us in this piece?' By the time the first night arrived, they had answered it for themselves. *Porgy and Bess* had ceased to be a black story and had become a universally human one. 'Never before', wrote Evans, 'had I experienced such a sense of dignity and integrity from every member of the ensemble.' The intensity of the audience's standing ovation – almost unknown at Glyndebourne – which occurred not only on the first night but at all the subsequent performances, confirmed that these qualities had come across to them with triumphant force. Evans concluded that 'this British production of an American classic brought the opera to its full glory. Only a few Americans have realized it as yet, but at Glyndebourne last summer, *Porgy and Bess* finally came of age.' Who could ask for more? Such indeed was its success that the soundtrack, recorded by EMI, was used in a subsequent feature film released on video.

Peter Hall's production of *Poppea*, first heard two years before, was widely thought to have improved, largely thanks to an utterly convincing (and alluring) return by Maria Ewing. She was later replaced by her understudy, Anna Steiger, who stepped across successfully from the rather different role of the goddess Virtù. Hall's *Don Giovanni* was revived, as was *Albert Herring*, and he also produced *Simon Boccanegra*, the first of a Verdi series. In an interview, Hall stressed his preferred method of working, for which there is time at Glyndebourne but not elsewhere:

> The important thing to me is to get a group of people on the stage and ask a question – what does this scene mean, and how do we express it? . . . if you try various ways, then you could actually find an answer . . . the great international singers, one has to say, on the whole don't want to spend time asking questions, [and are keener on] collecting their fees and moving on to the next.

He added that a special fascination of *Simon Boccanegra* is that it is the work of:

an old and mature artist at the peak of his form, revising [in 1881] his early work [of 1857], keeping the strength and vitality of his youth but adding the complexity and wisdom of his age. . . . It is politics expressed in terms of human passion – the father finding his lost daughter, and the betrayal of the great leader by his colleagues.

This reduction to an intensely human scale was of course particularly appropriate for the still smallish Glyndebourne auditorium, and the possibility remains that Hall's particular talents work better with a small cast than with large choruses. Of the principals, Robert Lloyd and John Rawnsley were singled out for praise, and Carol Vaness in the only leading female part showed a thrilling dynamic range. Yet there were those who thought that there was not quite room on stage for the crowd scenes, which became 'not so much crowded as crammed'. In 1998 he directed a new production of the opera in the new theatre, and in an interview in *The Times* referred to the earlier production as follows: 'There were moments which were very effective when the right principals were together. Half of the cast was superb, and the other half was catastrophic, and I am certainly not going to say who fell into which category.'

A brand new dimension for Glyndebourne was also established about this time. Although it was an offshoot of the Festival, it was to acquire a distinctive essence of its own, and is best treated separately from other developments. Mention has already been made of the biennial Schools' Festival pioneered at Glyndebourne by Kent County Council in 1981. In 1983 there followed what was to be the beginning of a steady expansion of the scheme. Two performances of each of the three operas being toured by GTO were sponsored at Glyndebourne itself, and a supply of teaching materials was made available to the schools beforehand so that proper preparation could be made, enabling the children to derive the maximum interest and enjoyment from the works that they were to see and hear.

In 1986 Whitworth-Jones invited Katie Tearle to join Glyndebourne

The theatre interior as it was in 1934 and in 1957, showing
Oliver Messel's proscenium arch

and establish a full-time Education Department. Its purpose was to enrich and broaden public appreciation of opera, by adults as well as children; and not only to develop new audiences, but to generate an exciting, creative experience in each of the projects that it undertook. Initially, it held opera workshops at schools and sixth-form colleges in the cities which GTO was to visit (Oxford, Plymouth, Norwich and Manchester), featuring *Albert Herring*, a particularly accessible work. Five primary schools in Sussex also took part in one-day workshops, on the theme of a gigantic local landmark, a chalk figure on the downs known as the Long Man of Wilmington. With help from a composer, a singer, an artist and a producer, the children first made up stories about the Long Man, then composed songs and made simple props, costumes and scenery, finally putting on an 'opera' composed from these elements to an audience of children and their families. By increasing Glyndebourne's 'outreach' (to use a piece of jargon which is for once appropriate), it was yet another step forward, dispelling the old, out-of-date charges of 'élitism' which were still parroted from time to time among those who were unaware how far Glyndebourne had developed. This was followed in 1987 by the usual Schools' Festival at Glyndebourne itself, and by a major project, overlapping with the GTO tour, that involved taking workshops led by the composer, Nigel Osborne, on his new opera *The Electrification of the Soviet Union*, to schools in the cities visited by GTO.

A further extension of the programme followed in 1988, with adult workshops on all those operas toured by GTO. There was also a longer-term composition project for sixth-form music and drama students, involving a total of five hundred students working within reach of the cities visited. This was followed in the autumn by a composition project for GCSE and A-level candidates, centred on *Káťa Kabanová*. Sponsorship had originally been pioneered by a lively publisher of children's books, Sebastian Walker, but as the education project snowballed it attracted other benefactors including Trustee Savings Bank (for a period of five years), W. H. Smith and Exxon. In 1989 Glyndebourne began to work with schools for children with 'special needs', generally with emotional and behavioural problems, in deprived areas with little or no access to the performing arts. The response was highly enthusiastic, and this new outlet had an incalculable value for children whose needs were often difficult to satisfy by conventional means. To get restless, previously unmotivated children to concentrate on a chosen theme, *Animals in Danger* was an intensely satisfying achievement for all concerned, and also led in some cases to a general improvement in other areas of schoolwork. Elizabeth Gorla and Robin Tebbutt were the producers, and Peter Harvey and Angela Tennick of the LPO were among those who worked at the schools by day, before returning to the Glyndebourne pit in the evening for the rather different task of performing *Arabella*.

In the following year Glyndebourne Education ventured a step further by putting on a community opera in the ballroom at the end of Hastings Pier. The composer was Jonathan Dove, who had worked previously as assistant chorus master at Glyndebourne. The opera, entitled *Hastings Spring*, traced the development of Hastings from a haven for smugglers into a flourishing coastal resort, against the background of great hardship and social unrest following the Napoleonic Wars. Nigel Ridout was the librettist and Tim Hopkins the director. Four local secondary schools were involved, and six of the forty musical numbers were group compositions in which the performers themselves, whose ages ranged from ten to eighty-seven, communicated their ideas to the composer. There were no auditions: contributions came from sources ranging from Hastings Youth Orchestra to folk groups, and the composer easily accommodated a considerable rarity in the person of a yodelling accordionist. In spite of strong competition from stormy winds and waves, two of the three performances were sold out, with queues for returns stretching down the pier. It is pleasant to reflect how strongly Audrey Mildmay would have approved of all this. Her Children's Theatre project, soon after the war, was a first step in this direction, but she can never have dreamed of involving children as completely as this.

In the autumn of 1990, a further project for musical students and student teachers in East Sussex and Birmingham was based on the new Tippett opera, *New Year*. Another had been organized in June in Eastbourne for 16- to 18-year-olds, all from special schools, who expressed their ideas, many of them for the first time, about the four elements, earth, air, fire and water, through the medium of dance, drama and music, as opposed to words. Yet another, more structured, project was organized in HM Prison, Lewes, with the composer Nigel Osborne joined now by the writer-in-residence at the prison, Stephen Plaice. It took the form of a musical world tour, encompassing Irish jigs, Brazilian sambas, gamelan and ketchak in Java and Bali, shoshaloza in Soweto, and finally flamenco in Spain. This, too, was probably the first creative cultural experience for most of those taking part, and a sharp contrast with the champagne picnics on the lawns at Glyndebourne, only three miles away. Lewes prison was subsequently revisited every year, and other projects were devised at Dartmoor and Ford prisons. Work was also developed with the Probation Service in West Sussex: a team from Glyndebourne spent a week in 1993 at the Hawth Arts Centre in Crawley with sixteen men on probation, creating a piece of music theatre which was enlarged and repeated the following year.

In 1993, when the builders were hard at work at Glyndebourne, Eurotunnel was among the sponsors for a community opera for Ashford. Alistair Campbell was commissioned to inspire local imagination and harness ideas and memories into words, against a background of celebrations of the opening of the Channel Tunnel, to music by Jonathan Dove – following up his success at Hastings. Ashford's history had included decimation by the plague three hundred years earlier, and a railway boom at the time of the building of the London–Dover line; and now the young heroine appeared, 'emerging from the deep, inward tunnel each of us has to negotiate if we are to grow up'. (By contrast, another member of the cast, Roy Neale, was a local man aged eighty-five, who never missed a rehearsal.)

In 1994 a third and very different community opera, *In Search of Angels*, was generated at Peterborough. The composer and librettist were, once again, Jonathan Dove and Alistair Campbell, and they spent the spring and summer there running a series of workshops, looking and listening for the stories which the eventual cast wanted to tell, in image and song. The material was shaped into dramatic form in the autumn and winter of 1994; and, in true Glyndebourne style, there were nine weeks of rehearsal, from the following January to March. The treatment was an extension and amplification of what had been done in Hastings and Ashford. Beginning with prehistory in the transept of the cathedral, it moved on into the nave for the Cromwellian period, and eventually into the late twentieth century, in the Queensgate Shopping Centre. Over six hundred people took part in this vast undertaking. The sense of participation on this scale made it for many the most exciting involvement of their lives, thanks to the strong but friendly professionalism of the Glyndebourne team. It is difficult to think of anything that could do more to kindle young people's enthusiasm for opera, to extend by direct experience their knowledge of how it should work, and to make some of them better participators in, and others better judges of, performances. As for the composer Jonathan Dove, these early works led to a commission for *Flight*, a full-scale opera performed by GTO in 1998, which will take its place in the Festival in 1999: yet another example of a considerable musician beginning with a minor project at Glyndebourne and then spreading his wings. In his case this also included an imaginative commission from the BT Celebration Series for an orchestral piece, *Ringing Isle* (its title a neat reference to Handel's comments about the bell-ringing to be heard, in his day, all over Britain), to mark the fiftieth anniversary of the Association of British Orchestras.

Glyndebourne Education had by now acquired, over a decade, a strong momentum of its own, emanating originally from the Festival and GTO, but distinct from them. Its next venture was the ambitious children's opera *Misper*, created and staged with great success by a cast from various schools in Sussex at Glyndebourne itself in February 1997, and revived a year later. As one walked across from Mildmay Hall to the foyer before the performance, the atmosphere was similar to that of the summer, yet at the same time quite different: more excitement in the air, and a stronger feeling of participation, as the families and friends of the large cast rushed about, noisier and quicker on their feet than Festival audiences, and generating a greater sense of anticipation. During the performances, attention was riveted on the stage, and the applause at the

Above and right: two scenes from Misper *(1998)*

end must have been audible in Ringmer. Stephen Langridge directed, John Lunn was the composer and Alison Chitty the designer. Seeboard, the privatized South-East Electricity Board, were enthusiastic sponsors (as also the Opera Opportunity Scheme, which extends beyond the scope of this book). All this activity hammered further nails into the coffin which contains the stale accusations of 'élitism'.

To return to 1986, the GTO pre-tour season at Glyndebourne itself was that year extended from one week to two, thanks to the Trustee Savings Bank's sponsorship of an annual fortnight for four years. Demand for tickets had always exceeded supply, and several thousand more people were now able to enjoy the operas at a cheaper price than in the Festival, most of them living in the neighbourhood. This development, as it happens, fulfilled one of John Christie's earliest intentions, which he had expressed in his original manifesto in 1933. After mentioning the 'superb performances, assisted by a marvellous *Festspiel* atmosphere' which he had in mind, he had added that: 'expense would

prevent the admission of the poorer portion of the public, and so it may be desirable to give local performances after the *Festspiel* is over. . . . There are no vested interests, no traditions in the way.' Half a century later, this had come to pass.

In 1987 the sequence of Verdi continued with a new production of *La traviata* by Peter Hall, with an exceptional performance by Marie McLaughlin. Apart from her, the opera sometimes seemed rather far from home, since there were no Italians in the cast, and the stage business, especially in the case of the chorus, sometimes seemed overdone and inappropriate. Haitink handed over to Sian Edwards later in the season, and when McLaughlin moved on to Salzburg in July, the incomparable Ileana Cotrubas took her place in the Proms version. One particular management headache (of a kind that seldom reaches the ears of the audiences) was that John Gunter's designs for this production were four months late in completion, and, for various reasons, ran to £80,000 over budget. That aside, there was a Ravel double bill: *L'heure espagnole* and *L'enfant et les sortilèges*, the latter based on a story by Colette. Her intention had been that the audience should share in the child's fluctuating sense of wonder, but instead there was often a feeling that they were being asked to admire the cleverness of the various stage devices. Nevertheless, Simon Rattle was much praised for his handling of the music, and Maurice Sendak's designs for both operas were also inspired. Finally, Felicity Lott's performance as the Countess in the revival of *Capriccio* was exceptional. The richness and purity of her singing and the excellence of her characterization made it a performance that has become a legend in the annals of Glyndebourne.

The brave new departure for GTO in 1987 was *The Electrification of the Soviet Union*, with libretto by the poet Craig Raine and music by Nigel Osborne. It was the first production for Glyndebourne, in fact the first in the UK, by the American Peter Sellars, then director of the National Theater of America in Washington. It was – thanks to the persuasive energy of Anthony Whitworth-Jones – commissioned initially for GTO, and the following year for the Festival, with funds provided by the BBC; the production was sponsored with buccaneering spirit by a generous French supporter, Vincent Mayer.

There have often been producers, and composers, who have been unable to put into words what their work is about, for the benefit of ordinary mortals who may be no wiser after the performance than before. Sellars, in a last-minute programme note, stated that 'the events, impressions and responses which are found in the work are not reducible in a synopsis', but there is only 'the moment to moment life of the mind, the heart and the eye', which is not a bad description of the novella by Pasternak, *The Last Summer*, on which most of the opera is based. He added: 'The feet are already, almost of their own accord, moving in step to an increasingly insistent rhythm that will have been the march of history.' In fact, of course, the forced march of history in the Soviet Union tended to lead in the direction of the Gulag Archipelago of freezing slavery and starvation, especially for those in whom any spark of genuine artistic creativity (as opposed to obedient toeing of the line), any shred of independent thought or beliefs or even basic

Nigel Osborne, George Tsypin, Craig Raine and Peter Sellars discuss the forthcoming world première of Osborne's The Electrification of the Soviet Union *(1987)*

human standards had managed to survive. Admittedly, a tiny handful such as Bulgakov did so, on the personal whim of Stalin; and of these Pasternak was one.

The title of the opera is taken from an obscure and ultimately almost meaningless statement by Lenin: 'Communism is Soviet Power plus the electrification of the whole country.' If the opera's contention is taken to be that this process actually vitalized or electrically galvanized the country, with positive fruitful results, nothing could have been further from the truth. Rather, it turned out to be the kind of electrification to be found in the electric chair. In fact, however, the opera focuses on the heart-and-soul-searchings of a poet and dreamer based on Pasternak himself and on the running-together of two of his early works: *Spektorsky*, a long poem which he published in an incomplete form in 1931; and *The Last Summer* (1934), which was the original title of the opera and looked back to 1914. The story concerns Serezha, and his sense of guilt at only being a 'useless intellectual' by comparison with a decorated sailor and man of action, Fardybassov, and Lemokh, a political activist. It also examines Serezha's relations with a young widow who is an oppressed companion-governess in pre-war Moscow, and with a prostitute of mature years. There is also an epilogue set in 1920, by which time the governess has become a party functionary engaged in the confiscation of bourgeois property.

It might well have been better to have retained the original title (thought to be insufficiently arresting), and it certainly would have been helpful to the audience to have been given some insight in the programme book into the poetic quality of Pasternak's prose – more or less untraceable in the opera – which, as far as many were concerned, was more a case of mystification than electrification. However, so compelling was the influence of Peter Sellars in the genesis of the opera from its original sources, that both librettist and composer, in spite of the formidable intellectual individuality of each of them, had willingly fallen under his spell. *The Last Summer* is full of startling symbolist images which, barely intelligible at first, can at least be taken slowly and appreciated on the printed page, but which, to the average audience hearing it for the first time, are hopelessly fugitive in an opera. It would be surprising if *The Electrification* were ever revived, but that does not mean that the experiment was a mistake. When a company commissions an opera and appoints two talented creative artists and an exceptionally gifted director, it is an act of faith – brave or foolhardy as it may prove – but based on solid credentials: the management cannot have any precise idea of what the eventual outcome will be. But some people thought that it was just a pity that the opera failed to convey much of the admirable and truly progressive ideas and intentions behind the historical creation of the Soviet Union, ideas which Pasternak, of course, deeply shared. Nevertheless, the Berlin Festival invited the company to put on two performances of the work, which in the end, perhaps ironically, netted Glyndebourne additional revenue of about £15,000; while shortly afterwards both Rome and Reggio Emilia were treated to three performances of *Albert Herring* which yielded a satisfactory surplus of £25,000, as well as flying Glyndebourne's flag in Italy.

In the autumn of 1987, Glyndebourne, like the rest of the south of England, had been devastated by the severest gales in living memory. Innumerable mature trees in the garden and in the protective woods behind it were lost; but here, as elsewhere, within a couple of years what had seemed a catastrophe had somehow faded, so that, unless they were told of it, those not intimately familiar with the place would hardly realize there had been a hurricane at all. But at the time, the impact on the trees and those who lived and worked among them was shattering.

That winter an archive department was established above the Christies' garage. Under the expert management of Rosy Runciman, a huge collection of material relating to Glyndebourne's past which had been assembled over the years by Helen O'Neill was brought together from obscure cupboards and oubliettes all over the premises. Rosy Runciman wrote an article in the programme book for 1991, in response to which various friends of Glyndebourne helped to expand the records of the early days by donating rare programmes, photographs and other memorabilia. The archive was excellently organized under the management of her successor Jayne Fenwick-White, who also took charge of a collection of a staggering 18,000 photographs connected with Glyndebourne; and she in turn has been succeeded by Julia Aries. The department makes much information about the history of Glyndebourne infinitely more accessible than it was in the days when Wilfrid Blunt and Spike Hughes wrote their books.

The programme book for 1987 had contained the first hint from George ('merely a glint in my eye') of the biggest change that lay in store for Glyndebourne since its foundation. For a number of reasons (rehearsed in the next chapter) he had had the idea of actually demolishing the old and dearly loved opera house, now structurally shaky, and replacing it with something that would hold half as many seats again, 1,250 instead of 830. He added that this could not possibly happen 'in less than half a dozen years', a forecast which turned out to be uncannily accurate. This first intimation had caused great anxiety to those who dreaded the abolition of what they loved so dearly. George tried to calm their fears by reminding them in the following year that, if there were desecration, he and his family, who lived 'over the shop', would suffer far more keenly than occasional visitors, and would therefore be all the more on their guard against any such thing. He put his finger on the nub of the situation by adding that Glyndebourne is an establishment 'which retains the heart-beat of a family central in some degree to it'. It was to be five years before plans were finalized, the money raised, and the grand reconstruction begun.

A more immediate milestone arose with the end of Haitink's musical directorship at the close of that season. He had worked at Glyndebourne for eleven seasons, and he now left to take up a similar position at Covent Garden. However excellent and successful a musical director may be, he seldom wishes to remain in the same place for much longer than this; and sad though the parting must have been in some ways, there was for him, among other things, the very attractive prospect of conducting Wagner in a potentially ideal house. When he first went to Glyndebourne in 1972, he had previously only conducted two operas, in the Netherlands, and initially he was less interested in what happens on the stage than most conductors: this however soon changed. Despite having become one of the most sought-after opera conductors in the world, who not only attracted singers, aspiring conductors and music staff to work at Glyndebourne, he had retained his outstanding natural integrity and remained resolutely uninterested in star billing either for himself or anyone else. George also paid tribute to Haitink's having maintained a standard which had 'enormously enhanced Glyndebourne's position generally in the world of opera'. Two important ingredients of his triumph at Glyndebourne were his sensitivity in relation to the team around him, and the fact that he invariably put himself at the service of an artistic occasion, rather than imposing his control in the manner of the heroic conductors of the past, such as Toscanini, Beecham or Karajan. Nobody appeared to be less interested in being a star, however brightly he in fact shone. In an interview in *Country Life* he later recalled that 'a German colleague once said to me: "It's a miracle, and also heart-warming, that you made a career, because you had such odds against you. You never had an entourage or a publicity machine." ' His success was a case of sheer quality triumphing unaided.

Another departure was that of Janet Moores, the last survivor of John Christie's original 1934 team. After the war she was briefly Moran Caplat's secretary, but was soon promoted to assistant manager of the company, with a multifarious work load which she shouldered enthusiastically. She went far beyond the call of duty in her affection and concern for many colleagues, and was in fact a true embodiment of the cheerful team spirit that has been such a distinguishing feature of Glyndebourne life. Ian Wallace's tribute to her was particularly apt: 'a kind, familiar face that makes my last performance seem so much more recent than it actually was'.

An important change came when Brian Dickie left the following year, after a total of twenty-seven years at Glyndebourne, to become General Director of the Canadian Opera Company. George paid tribute to his flair for maintaining and raising standards of casting, and for selecting conductors, directors and repertory. His other major contribution had been on the financial side: on his arrival, he had introduced a system of costings beside which previous practices looked slack and distinctly old-fashioned. He had insisted that heads of the various departments should be involved in the calculation of the budget for each opera. This greatly reduced the danger of costs escalating (indeed separate budgets for each work had previously been unknown at Glyndebourne). He was a true professional, with a wide and passionate interest in the art form, and a formidable ability to achieve results both artistically and commercially. He richly deserved the farewell party laid on for him at Claridge's by a grateful Glyndebourne.

His successor, Anthony Whitworth-Jones, who had been in charge of GTO for the previous seven years, had obviously been working very closely with him and shared many of his intentions and targets, and indeed, his general vision of the future. During the next ten years he was to play the leading part in the ambitious task of preparing Glyndebourne for life in the twenty-first century. There were a number of different aspects to this process, the most monumental project being, of course,

*Anthony Whitworth-Jones, Glyndebourne's newly appointed
General Administrator, with Sir George Christie (1989)*

the rebuilding of the opera house itself. But closest to his heart was the commissioning of new works by living composers; and although some were more successful than others, and there were to be hot arguments about the balance between new and old repertory, no one can doubt that his general policy was the right one. The composers he commissioned to write for Glyndebourne included Oliver Knussen, Nigel Osborne, Michael Tippett, Harrison Birtwistle and Jonathan Dove. Conductors whom he introduced to Glyndebourne included Dietfried Bernet, William Christie, Mark Elder, John Eliot Gardiner, Knussen again, Yakov Kreizberg, Gennadi Rozhdestvensky and Franz Welser-Möst. He worked closely with the directors Nikolaus Lehnhoff and Peter Sellars and also engaged Tom Cairns, Richard Jones, Graham Vick (who was appointed Director of Productions in the new theatre), Jean-Marie Villégier and Deborah Warner. This is a roll call of which any opera house could be proud, and each of them was to inject something new and valuable into Glyndebourne's bloodstream. And apart from the commissioned works, he was to introduce the following operas which were new to Glyndebourne: *Cornet Christoph Rilke's Song of Love and Death*, *La clemenza di Tito*, *Ermione*, *Lulu*, *Manon Lescaut*, *The Makropulos Case*, *Owen Wingrave*, *Death in Venice*, *Peter Grimes*, *Theodora* and *Rodelinda*. In the GTO programme book he had already referred to the necessary and joyful responsibility of encouraging composers to renew the operatic repertory. Commissioning or discovering new works was the aspect of his role which he had concentrated on with almost missionary zeal – a phrase which he himself echoed in the 1997 programme book – since first taking over the running of GTO, and which had its origins in his work with the London Sinfonietta. He was to continue wholeheartedly in the same vein after his promotion, and among other results this championing of new works certainly helped to mitigate whatever anti-Glyndebourne feelings that there may have been at the Arts Council. As far back as 1939 Glyndebourne had revelled in innovation. What will always, and inevitably, be in dispute is the question of balance between new and old. Too much of the old leads to ossification, and to degeneration into the condition of the dinosaur. Too little, and insolvency will loom, combined with distaste, sometimes amounting to revulsion, on the part of the audiences.

Haitink was succeeded as Music Director by Andrew Davis, who came after eleven years as Managing Director of the Toronto Symphony Orchestra. Though his symphonic career had been largely in North America, Davis had already conducted no fewer than eight operas at Glyndebourne, going back to *Capriccio* in 1973. He generously acknowledges his debt to John Pritchard, and has commented that: 'Many things can go wrong in opera, and often do, but when it all goes right there's nothing like it.' His great rule of not forcing his own style on to the music goes back to John Christie's motto: 'Respect the work.'

Another important innovation at Glyndebourne was the introduction of the Orchestra of the Age of Enlightenment, the period instrument orchestra which featured in all the Mozart/da Ponte operas under Simon

Rattle over the next few years, and later in *Theodora* and other appropriate works. Remarkable and interesting though they are, these instruments are not an end in themselves: they do, however, provide a wonderful way of hearing music afresh, sounding more or less as it would have done in the composer's day. Nevertheless, it was essential for Glyndebourne to retain a strong connection with a permanent orchestra of twentieth-century proportions, namely the LPO; and it was agreed that the Orchestra of the Age of Enlightenment would only perform in one opera a year at Glyndebourne. More important still was the decision to assess during the year the financial feasibility of the design concepts produced by two short-listed architects for a new opera house.

In 1988 *The Electrification* took its place in the actual Festival, and attendances at these performances only fell from the usual average 98 per cent to 90 per cent. Whitworth-Jones is surely right in thinking that the introduction of a challenging new work preserves and enhances the vitality of an opera company. If such a work sometimes fails to come up to expectations, it is, however, the 'step in the dark' that provides a unique thrill – and probably also broadens the experience of some members of the cast. And even if such a bold experiment involves giving a large proportion of the audience an evening of what they may not fully appreciate, this, in moderation, is probably a price worth paying. It was in fact noticeable that corporate members responded particularly adventurously to the new repertory.

In sharp contrast to *The Electrification* was Janáček's *Káťa Kabanová*, a simple but poignant tragedy, set against a background of rural Russia at its most primitive and repressive. It was Brian Dickie who had sought out the director Nikolaus Lehnhoff at Bayreuth and had invited him to put on *Káťa Kabanová* and *Jenůfa* at Glyndebourne, with Andrew Davis conducting. These were to be followed by *The Makropulos Case* in 1995; and although the operas were all quite separate and do not form a trilogy, one of Lehnhoff's most successful achievements lay in his exploration of the network of relationships, mostly dominated by women, which are developed in each of the works. In *Káťa Kabanová* it is not simply a question of an unfortunate woman being destroyed by the social forces which surround her. The emotions and visions were much more complex, so that the personal pathos was all the more real. Janáček himself expressed his method and his longing very clearly in letters he wrote in 1928: 'One gate will always remain open in art: *emotion*. On the whirlwind of emotion, the music runs boldly forward . . .'; and again:

> One day I would like to take in my hand a pen filled only with my own passion; its nib sharp enough to stab, to create pain out of pain, pile bliss upon bliss, top wretchedness with wretchedness, darken fury with fury, caress love with love, so as to be able to say: this is my work, mine alone – and no one else's.

Although his work had been performed a good deal in England before, the emotional intensity of Janáček's drama was a powerful new experience for most of the Glyndebourne audiences. *Káťa* was broadcast live on Radio 3, and in the interval Andrew Davis made some illuminating comments in an interview, which were printed in the programme book when the production was revived in 1990. The opera was, of course, sung in the original Czech, a language familiar to few singers, and equally few audiences. Supertitles in English had been introduced for GTO in 1984, and they were now used for the first time in the Festival, with Lehnhoff strongly in favour. They were privately paid for by two of the trustees, Ingrid Channon and Leopold de Rothschild, who later also contributed to the more advanced system in the new house. Andrew Davis underlined their value in the 1990 programme book, as Isaiah Berlin had done in the case of GTO in 1984.

Janáček was deeply attracted to Russia and his visits there influenced him strongly, even to the extent of searching Russian literature for operatic themes. But it is above all his preoccupation with the heroic, freedom-loving rebellion by the younger generation against the narrow, strict obscurantism that permeated Russian life from the time of Nicholas I, that informs his most profound dramatic work. *Káťa* is a bourgeois version of *Anna Karenina*; yet it inspires more heartfelt sympathy, largely on account of the sharply outlined musical portrayal of Janáček's characters within what has been called 'the observed lilt and cadence of human speech'. The Russian background was even harsher and more oppressive than that of the composer's own Moravian villages, which were to be the setting for *Jenůfa* the following year. In that brooding slice of Moravian life, the composer's power to sympathize even with those guilty of the most repellant behaviour brings the characters to life with great strength and purity of feeling. For many, this was exactly the kind of innovation for Glyndebourne to tackle: unfamiliar, sometimes wild and exuberant, but never obscure or difficult to take in, and again wonderfully directed by Nikolaus Lehnhoff.

Apart from *Jenůfa*, the 1989 Festival included a revival of John Cox's *Arabella*, in which Felicity Lott gave an outstanding performance in the name part. She had widened her range by singing in Brussels, Florence and Munich, and was now on her way to New York as the Feldmarschallin, and to Vienna and Dresden, again for *Arabella*. The conducting of Graeme Jenkins, who had been Music Director of GTO since 1986, was also highly praised. Peter Hall's *A Midsummer Night's Dream* and John Cox's *The Rake's Progress* were also revived, the former with a notably strong cast. Particularly singled out were Michael Chance's Oberon and Elizabeth Gale's Tytania. The year's other revival was *Orfeo*, although this had some design adaptations by John Bury. Ivor Bolton made a very successful conducting debut, having previously worked as chorus master, and was soon to take over from Graeme Jenkins at GTO.

Simon Rattle conducted the Orchestra of the Age of Enlightenment in Hall's new production of *Figaro*. He explains that the strings used in the old instruments were gut, rather than the modern steel variety; that oboes and bassoons are 'hardly the same instruments at all now'; and the other wind instruments are also very different. The players could however let themselves go, without drowning the singers, to a remarkable and invigorating extent. And in Mozart, as well as all the elegance and wit, there is a full-hearted and full-blooded strength in the music, which can be given freer rein. Peter Hall summed it up by saying that hearing these instruments was like seeing a cleaned painting and discovering what was actually there. Despite Rattle's obvious commitment to authenticity in operatic accompaniment, he revealed in an interesting interview that his first priority was the City of Birmingham Symphony Orchestra, and that he had actually turned down Glyndebourne's invitation to succeed Bernard Haitink, partly because, apart from those of Mozart and Janáček, there were not many operas he wanted to conduct.

In the stunning new production of *Jenůfa*, Anja Silja made her Glyndebourne debut as the Kostelnička. The favourite soprano of Wagner's grandson Wieland, she had been chosen by Klemperer to sing in *Der fliegende Holländer* and *Fidelio*, and had been described as 'lighting Wagner's roles with a glorious new flame'. Her triumph here was sensational; and Philip Langridge as Laca ('twice as effective as at Covent Garden', according to *Opera* magazine) and Roberta Alexander in her Glyndebourne debut as Jenůfa both threw themselves fully into the production, so that the audience were relentlessly caught up in the action. Altogether, the Janáček works in those two years were rated among Glyndebourne's most remarkable successes, in which a major part was played by the outstanding designs of Tobias Hoheisel and his imaginative collaboration with Lehnhoff. Both were revived in the years following, and were taken on tour by GTO in 1991 and 1992.

The big excitement for GTO in 1989 was their production of Britten's *Death in Venice*, the libretto by Myfanwy Piper, whose husband had designed the premières of both *The Rape of Lucretia* at Glyndebourne back in 1946 as well as a memorable and characteristic *Don Giovanni* in 1951 and *A Midsummer Night's Dream* at Aldeburgh in 1960. The story was familiar to the many who had seen Visconti's film treatment, with Dirk Bogarde in the leading role of Aschenbach. The GTO programme book contained some rather dubious justification for this work. Faithfully following Thomas Mann (even though the central character is portrayed as a composer, rather than Mann's writer), both film and opera seem positively to revel in the seedy atmosphere of corruption and collapse, physical as well as moral, which closes in on Aschenbach; and its claims that he achieves 'redemption and liberation' by 'wisely' submit-

Librettist Myfanwy Piper at rehearsal for Death in Venice *with conductor Graeme Jenkins (centre) and Robert Tear, who sang the role of Aschenbach (1989)*

ting to his passion for the Polish boy Tadzio, and by yielding to 'chaos and sickness', are curiously hollow and unconvincing. The first performance had been planned for the Aldeburgh Festival in 1972, but was postponed till the following year owing to Britten's serious heart condition, which had originated, ironically, from an infection he had picked up in Venice in 1968. This intimation of mortality had already made it an intensely personal affair for Britten, and he had also been desperately keen to complete (before, as he put it, 'anything happened') what was to be the last major operatic part he was to compose for Peter Pears. The beautifully contrived Glyndebourne production, by Stephen Lawless, again with designs by Hoheisel, was found to concentrate rather heavily on death, to the virtual exclusion of Venice. The opera was vigorously and also sensitively conducted by Graeme Jenkins. After its tour, on which every ticket was sold, it was shown at the Festival in 1992, but has

After the 20 July performance of Capriccio, *a presentation was made to Hugues Cuenod by Anthony Whitworth-Jones and George Christie (1990)*

not been revived, though the range of compositional technique and the beauty of some of the music perhaps deserved better. GTO also took an adaptation of Peter Hall's *Figaro* on tour conducted by Sir Peter Maxwell Davies, with Graeme Jenkins taking over later.

For the revival of *Káťa Kabanová*, Andrew Davis insisted on performing it once again in the original Czech. However difficult this may be for both singers and audience, Janáček's distinctive 'speech rhythms' ensure that the music is wedded to the text, and that this close synthesis would be lost if the words were translated. Of course, singing in Czech raises considerable problems for the cast, but the coach, Ilya Bohac, was an immense help to them. Davis was also full of praise for the LPO, as were the critics, and Nancy Gustafson was considered to have developed and deepened her interpretation of the name part still further. The revival was as warmly applauded as that of *Capriccio*, which also inspired endless superlatives, above all, once more, for Felicity Lott, who made audiences feel that they were looking into the very heart of the role: her voice and the emotional focus seemed to be exactly what the composer had intended. The third revival was *Albert Herring*, also described as 'an evening of pure joy', and now back at Glyndebourne, having been transplanted to Covent Garden the year before.

The new productions were – rightly so, in theory – more controversial. To sample for once the full range of press reactions: the *Financial Times* considered Peter Sellars's *Die Zauberflöte*, which was sung in German, 'the flattest, laziest, emptiest piece of work in festival history', and to one degree or another the British press mostly concurred. But the *New Yorker* loyally described it as 'one of the keenest, most energetic, most engaging performances of the work' in the critic's experience; and the highly respected Michael Kennedy in the *Sunday Telegraph* felt that uprooting and updating the setting did no damage to the essence of the work, which is after all a mixture of pantomime, fairy-tale and religious symbolism. The production was set in an imaginary Los Angeles landscape, where gas stations become Hindu temples; but notwithstanding these departures, Andrew Davis has attested to the fact that Sellars always knows the score of any work that he directs 'inside out', and that his interpretations invariably start from the music. Davis himself is, it should be remembered, a faithful follower of John Christie in his insistence on respect for the composer's intentions.

As for Sellars, his ideas certainly had their roots in the music rather than the words – to the extent that he actually cut all the spoken dialogue. It was replaced by an electronic text display, which supplied spasmodic translation during key arias and choruses. There were many who were prepared to swallow the loss of the dialogue but who jibbed at the endless dumb show that accompanied every word expressed by every character, described by one critic as 'first fussy, then silly, then exasperating'. Sellars's aim was to link Mozart's operas into the lives of the audiences, a large number of whom were very different animals from those of the 1950s and 1960s. It is unlikely that those at Glyndebourne, even in the 1990s, have much in common with those at Pepsico

18. *The extensive and immaculate gardens provide a charming counterpoint to the buildings, and a tranquil setting for alfresco relaxation and picnicking*

19. *From 'A Mozart Sketchbook' by Peter Brookes, for the Mozart bicentenary year programme book, 1991*

20. *Carl Ebert's 1950s production of* Falstaff *with felicitous designs by Osbert Lancaster*

21. *David Hockney's stunning cross-hatched designs, based on Hogarth, complemented John Cox's 1975 production of Stravinsky's* The Rake's Progress. *It strongly impressed audiences, was most recently revived in the opening season in the new theatre, and remains in the repertory*

22. Britten returns to Glyndebourne.
Peter Hall's magical staging of A Midsummer Night's Dream, *with inspired sets*
by John Bury and sympathetic conducting by Bernard Haitink.
Peter Pears remarked that he wished the composer could have seen this production

23. Trevor Nunn's Porgy and Bess *(1986) was sensational.*
The magnificent cast, led by Willard White, was conducted by Simon Rattle;
as Nunn said: 'Glyndebourne will never be the same again, and it shouldn't be'

24. *Graham Vick's first Glyndebourne production (1992) was of* The Queen of Spades, *with designs by Richard Hudson*

25. *In Vick's* Yevgeny Onyegin *(1994), his first staging in the new theatre, the chilly atmosphere of aristocratic St Petersburg contrasted with the tragic humanity of the ill-matched lovers*

26. *Janáček's* Káťa Kabanová *(1988) was Nikolaus Lehnhoff's first production for Glyndebourne. His skill in exploring its complex network of relationships brought the pathos of the work to the fore, especially in the final scene: the death of Káťa*

27. *Lehnhoff's staging of* Jenůfa *(1989) again focused on the composer's ability to sympathize even with those guilty of the most terrible crimes*

28. *Lehnhoff's third Janáček production (all of which were designed by Tobias Hoheisel and conducted by Andrew Davis),* The Makropulos Case *(1995) was rapturously received. The hypnotic performance of Anja Silja was especially memorable*

29. *John Cox's 1980* Der Rosenkavalier, *with designs by the veteran French designer Erté, was described as resembling 'a sort of milliner's bandbox'; the singing of the principals, however, transcended such distractions*

30. *Cox's 1987 revival of* Capriccio *featured Felicity Lott in a legendary performance combining beauty of tone and exceptional insight*

31. *Maurice Sendak's charming children's book became the basis of Oliver Knussen's opera* Where the Wild Things Are, *which was premièred by Glyndebourne at the National Theatre in 1984*

32. Ermione, *a striking* opera seria *by Rossini, had flopped at its première in 1819, but the 1995 Glyndebourne revival, staged by Graham Vick, was an unqualified success*

33. The Second Mrs Kong, *by Harrison Birtwistle, was commissioned by Glyndebourne (1994). It was too far-fetched for some audiences (and critics), although it explored the traditional operatic preoccupation with the nature of love through Russell Hoban's libretto, Tom Cairn's imaginative setting and the composer's austerely beautiful music*

34. *As one enters the new auditorium, its mellow, golden pine interior provides an atmosphere of well-being and welcome for both audiences and performers*

Summerfare in New York State, where Sellars had put on a number of his earlier productions, but is it not better for the former to be asked to make the imaginative leap necessary to accept that there are many different directorial approaches, rather than allowing them to sit back and enjoy what has been tailor-made for them and presents no challenge – and gives no idea of the sheer breadth of Mozart's appeal in different contexts? Few accepted this principle on the first night, and there was some booing, though less at later performances. In any case, it often seems likely that some clap simply because others boo, and others in order to show how clever they are at seeing some quality the rest have missed. More significantly, Peter Hall resigned as Artistic Director on the opening night, after a number of previous disagreements of varying severity. This time, he felt that he should have been consulted about the removal, at a late stage in rehearsals, of the dialogue from a production for which he, as Artistic Director, was ultimately responsible. He added that the first he had heard of this was on the opening night. Perhaps the most sensible reaction was that of Rodney Milnes, simply that the Los Angeles setting of *Die Zauberflöte* was 'just fine in theory, but inadequate in execution, with the cutting of the dialogue an insuperable hurdle'.

To a greater degree than perhaps can be said of any previous director at Glyndebourne, you either loved Sellars or you hated him. The basis of his approach was to pose questions to which the audience must find answers – and thus, to give them new and rewarding perceptions. This was in keeping with his belief that the director's first duty is to *challenge* the audience; but not surprisingly many audiences found the form of that challenge too far-fetched, and the production consequently too far removed from the original work to be acceptable – in short, not reinterpretation but violation. They would have pointed to the validity of the modernist architect Mies van der Rohe's observation: 'I don't want to be interesting, I want to be good.' 'New' does not necessarily mean 'good', though operas undoubtedly cannot go on being 'good' in exactly the same way for ever. Experiments must be made, but if informed audiences (and critics) regard them as total failures they should feel free to say

so, and to point out that, for them, the Emperor's new clothes are
simply not there. It is, however, possible for a director to disturb
without actually repelling (as Lehnhoff, for example, has shown so successfully in his Janáček productions). If he or she is simply content to say:
'This will make them think', and after careful thought their verdict is still
one of revulsion, then it is at least a possibility that it is the innovator
who should have done the thinking in the first place. Certainly Sellars
had a near-hypnotic effect on those who worked with him, such was his
eloquence and enthusiasm; but looking back a few months further on,
there were those among his collaborators who could no longer see what
had originally been so compelling about his ideas. And sooner or later
his insistence that everything must be Californianized begins to pall on
all but his blindest admirers.

George himself, and Whitworth-Jones too, showed a rock-like loyalty
to Sellars and to his 'enormous creativity', and they were richly
rewarded when his production of Handel's *Theodora* was a triumphant
success, in the new theatre in 1996, when Dawn Upshaw's performance
in the title role, together with those of Lorraine Hunt, David Daniels
and Richard Croft, were as moving as anything seen at Glyndebourne
for many years. The production, which was revived with almost equal
success in the following year, was an *inspiring* experiment, as opposed to
a *repellent* one, and very few were unmoved by its great profundity. It
provides also a wonderfully apposite example of Glyndebourne's capacity
to influence the musical taste and appetite of the public. This brand new
approach to Handel struck a responsive chord not only at Glyndebourne
itself, but was applauded by full houses when it went on tour in the
autumn. George publicly stated that Glyndebourne had known Sellars
was a hot potato when they hired him, but 'we did it deliberately and
we're still happy about it'. In his turn, Sellars commented: 'You can't
imagine how supportive Glyndebourne is to its directors. . . . The level
of coaching [and] the attention to detail is so high. Nothing is faked, no
one is short-changed.'

The other new production in 1990 was a commissioned opera from
Michael Tippett, *New Year*, making four twentieth-century operas out of

six put on in that year. It was a co-production (the only such shared production in Glyndebourne's history) with Houston, Texas, where it had
first been performed in the previous October, and where the director,
Peter Hall, had been involved from the start. It is the story of Jo Ann, an
orphan with a dream of helping and comforting all the other orphans in
the world. She has a (black) foster-brother Donny, a rougher character.
They are visited by a space-ship containing the heroic Pelegrin, a trav-
eller in time as well as space, whose mission is to rescue Jo Ann from the
anxieties which have been threatening to prevent her from fulfilling her
own philanthropic dream. Dance also plays an important part in the
action.

Part of the message which Tippett, at the age of eighty-five, wanted
to deliver was that – in the words of Rodney Milnes – 'There's little
point in planning a glossy future if you can't sort out the present, and
you can't sort out the present without a vision of the future.' The theme
of 'one humanity, one justice' is vastly ambitious, and Glyndebourne
showed great skill in handling it. The production was an unusually
expensive one, and budgeting problems were exceptionally testing, even
though some costs were shared with Houston. Some found it incoherent
as an opera (*The Times* said it might have been devised by a committee
consisting of Steven Spielberg, R. D. Laing and the Delphic Oracle).
But one of its justifications was the feeling of constructive optimism that
inspired it, which attracted critical attention all over Europe and also in
Australia: Glyndebourne once again making an impact on the world
opera scene. Helen Field as Jo Ann, and Philip Langridge as Pelegrin
were highly successful, but Krister St Hill, dancing as well as singing in
the very challenging role of Donny, was triumphant. Tippett's own brief
imprisonment as a conscientious objector in 1943, his sense of isolation
intensified by the production of the atomic bomb, and his acute horror
at the revelation of the nature of the concentration camps: all these had
been major influences on his world-view, from which emanated the
unique contemporary element in this particular work, as well as in
others. Glyndebourne was well rewarded for its courage in presenting it;
new and unfamiliar works such as this may sometimes attract bigger

audiences, both in the Festival and afterwards on tour, than they would elsewhere, thanks to Glyndebourne's own unique reputation. The problem remains that massive resources have to be devoted to them, and the management is constantly worrying about whether they can be financially afforded.

The 1991 season, marking the bicentenary of Mozart's death, could hardly have been a greater contrast to the year before. All six works put on were by Mozart, as had been the case in the bicentenary of his birth back in 1956. In that year W. H. Auden (whose work at Glyndebourne had ranged from the ultra-successful co-operation in *The Rake's Progress* to the mutual hostility with Rennert in *Elegy for Young Lovers*) had written a poem which neatly expressed one side of the argument about the extravagant experiments which at that time lay in the distant future:

> Operas, God knows, must stand enough.
> What greatness made, small vanities abuse.
> What must they not endure? The Diva whose
> *Fioriture* and climactic note
> The silly old composer never wrote;
> Conductor X, that overrated bore,
> Who alters tempi and who cuts the score,
> Director Y who with ingenious wit
> Places his wretched singers in the pit
> While dancers mime their roles, Z the designer
> Who sets the whole thing on an ocean liner,
> The girls in shorts, the men in yachting caps
> Yet genius triumphs over all mishaps . . .

Auden need not have been so pessimistic. In 1991 Trevor Nunn did indeed set *Così* on board ship in the Bay of Naples. But even those who had misgivings in advance loved what they saw on the night, and the ingenious designs of Maria Bjørnson made perfect sense in what was described as 'the Arcadia of frothy musical comedy'. This was truly a

All aboard for Nunn's Così, *set by Maria Bjørnson in the Bay of Naples (1991)*

break with the past, and some of the pain and profundity brought out in other versions may have been missing; but if every production concentrated on the elusive psychological depths so deftly and convincingly explored by Peter Hall in the 1970s, the work might begin to suffer from the ultimate un-Mozartian fault of ultra-seriousness. Amanda Roocroft's Fiordiligi was most beautifully sung, and a reliable critic said that he had never heard a better Don Alfonso than Claudio Desderi. In spite of its Edwardian appearance, it was a 'modern' production in that it underlined the way Mozart and Da Ponte removed women from the pedestals on which they were often conventionally placed by men, delved deeply into character relationships, and treated them as all-too-human. One could not help but feel that Auden would have approved after all.

Enough has already been said to vindicate the claim that Glyndebourne was the first company in the twentieth century to put Mozart opera on the map in England, under the inspired direction of Busch and

Ebert. In the 1950s and 1960s the standard was maintained, with John Pritchard conducting and with such brilliant artists as Berganza, Jurinac, Lorengar, Söderström, Freni, Lewis, Simoneau, Bruscantini, Bacquier and Evans. And in the 1970s and 1980s, under Peter Hall, Trevor Nunn and John Cox, and with the inspired conducting of Bernard Haitink, great singers like Margaret Price, Elizabeth Harwood, Frederica von Stade, Kiri te Kanawa, Carol Vaness, Thomas Allen, Philip Langridge, Jeremy Hadley and Claudio Desderi kept the torch burning. Happily, there does not seem to have been any falling off in the 1990s, as the careers of Amanda Roocroft, Kurt Streit, Elena Prokina, Gerald Finley, Renée Fleming and Alison Hagley, among others, have taken off. In the bicentenary year, Hall's *Don Giovanni* was revived under Stephen Medcalf, with Alison Hagley's Zerlina a striking success. Trevor Nunn's *Idomeneo* and Sellars's *Zauberflöte* were also revived. The other new production was *La clemenza di Tito*, the only major Mozart opera never before to have been performed at Glyndebourne. For once, the tempi of Andrew Davis were criticized, but the director Nicholas Hytner was hailed on his first appearance at Glyndebourne. He made excellent use of space to underline the formality of the opera's context, while giving full rein to the romantic passions that rage below the surface. On the other hand, in the revival of *Die Zauberflöte*, this time in a new English translation by Alice Goodman, with the dialogue restored, a good cast worked hard in a version which was (almost) universally condemned as not being properly thought through, though many of the complaints were a great deal more severe than that. To be fair, it also had its strong supporters.

That year also marked the retirement of Geoffrey Gilbertson, who had been an integral member of the permanent team since 1957, originally in stage management and then for many years as front-of-house manager. His devotion to Glyndebourne, and the way in which, like others already mentioned, he treated his work there as far more than an ordinary job, made his contribution outstanding. His middle name, Theodore, was given to an important new meeting room in the new house, partly in recognition of a generous and almost unique legacy which he bequeathed to Glyndebourne on his death, in the year following his retirement. As well as programme books and brochures dating back to the Festival's earliest days, it included a complete set of *Grove's Dictionary*, and some fans and gloves which had belonged to Dame Adelina Patti. But of more direct relevance was his collection of paintings of Glyndebourne by Mary Fedden and opera designs by, among others, Elizabeth Bury and Martin Battersby. In 1974 he had played the silent role of the Guest in *Intermezzo*, and his legacy included the design for the curious hermaphrodite costume made for it, a man's when walking from right to left, and a woman's when walking from left to right (see p.141). He had begun his stage career at the Connaught Theatre, Worthing, where he met and worked with June Dandridge, following her to Glyndebourne and succeeding her as stage manager in 1957. His warmth and kindness and concern for his staff and colleagues, as well as his perception of their natures, were a by-word, but his sense of fun and mischief also made him a character who left a big gap behind him. He would make ordinary announcements from the stage, for example about singers' indispositions, with a wit and drama that were all his own. He sometimes echoed John Christie's 1939 Eton and Harrow match announcement by informing the audience of Test Match scores, and after an exciting Wimbledon final, he let them know that 'McEnroe won!' As an actor and an extrovert, he was the choice to give the address at the service of thanksgiving which was held in Ringmer Church (where he was a regular server at the early Communion Service) to mark the fiftieth anniversary of Glyndebourne Opera.

By the time the 1992 season approached, the demolition men were already breathing down the necks of management, casts and audiences alike. With a typically imaginative and thoughtful touch, special holes were cut in the hoarding surrounding the huge excavation where building works had started, so that in the supper interval, or before performances, members of the audience could peer through and see what was going on. The final opening night in the old theatre was three weeks earlier than usual, on 2 May. On top of all the other pressures connected with the rebuilding, one of the scenery stores burned to the ground on the night of 16 May. Sets of *Falstaff*, *The Rake's Progress* and

Figaro, as well as much else, were partly or wholly destroyed, along with some of the props for Trevor Nunn's new production of *Peter Grimes*, which was mercifully the only work in the current year's programme to be affected, and which proved to be an impressive success. But still greater success attended Graham Vick's production of *The Queen of Spades*, another setting by Tchaikovsky of a Pushkin story, which had failed to impress in its only previous staging at Glyndebourne in 1971. This time it was described by Max Loppert in the *Financial Times* as 'one of the outstanding events in festival history'. An interesting newcomer to Glyndebourne was Sergei Leiferkus in the role of Tomsky, whose training at the Leningrad Conservatoire had taken no less than seven years, the first two being entirely taken up with 'breathing exercises, technique, scales, theory and the history of the Communist Party'. This glacier-like process makes the famous Glyndebourne preparation period look like one mad rush, but in this case at least the results were wonderful. As for Yuri Marusin as Hermann, it was a manic performance of prodigious proportions.

Plans for the dark year had originally included possible expeditions to Japan and America, but for various reasons these had come to nothing. Instead, 'as if in answer to prayer', as George put it, a series of three concert performances of each of three operas was given in the Royal Festival Hall. Among other advantages was the preservation of uninterrupted collaboration with the LPO, which might otherwise have suffered; and Glyndebourne Festival Opera in general and the chorus in particular were able to preserve their momentum to some degree, however different the circumstances might be; and in the dark year Glyndebourne successfully kept faith with its audiences.

Two of the three works put on were new to Glyndebourne. One was *Béatrice et Bénédict*, a comedy by Berlioz. It was sung in French, but instead of the dialogue passages a narrative was written and delivered by John Wells, no mean comedian himself, and in general an immensely popular figure, with a wide range of literary as well as musical expertise. Though some of the audiences enjoyed it very much, most of the critics felt, perhaps rather stuffily, that his brand of humour was intrusive and jarring, and that the comedy needed to be played straight for the humour to make its maximum impact. The fairest of the critics felt that it was not that Wells's jokes were irrelevant or out of place; it was simply that they went on far too long, losing the thread of the ravishing music. There were also regrets at the lack of the semi-staging which had been such a successful feature of the Prom performances over the years. On the credit side, the singing of Dawn Upshaw and Jean Rigby in the first-act duet which is the musical highlight of the opera was beautiful, and Anne Sofie von Otter as Béatrice was consistently remarkable in every nuance of the part. One member of the audience wrote in to complain that the composer Somarone was awful, not having realized that this was the whole point of the role. Anthony Whitworth-Jones replied in masterly style that it was 'very difficult to sing so badly so well', and that Richard Van Allan had managed it with remarkable success, of which Glyndebourne was proud.

The other novelty for Glyndebourne was *The Merry Widow*. The richly inventive narrative by Tom Stoppard avoided what might have been regarded as the excesses of John Wells, and was well delivered by Dirk Bogarde, while the operetta itself was sung in the original German. The mixture of sex, class and money had remained as absorbing for most people as in the days of Franz Lehár, and both Thomas Hampson as Danilo and Felicity Lott as the widow acquitted themselves as wonderfully as ever. *Fidelio*, the other work performed, was beset, right up to the last week, by casting problems from which Glyndebourne had seldom if ever suffered more acutely. The intention had been to provide exceptional artists in *Fidelio*; however, two of the star attractions were obliged to cancel. The great conductor Klaus Tennstedt fell ill after the first rehearsal, in which he had expressed himself very happy with the Glyndebourne chorus. Unfortunately, he never conducted in the concert hall or theatre again, and died five years later. Also lost to the production was Julia Varady, the first choice as Leonore; and while Roger Norrington was at least the second choice as conductor, no fewer than four other Leonores fell by the wayside before Carole Yahr was successfully engaged. Those who are more interested in the music than

Bert Pullen (Chief Technician) and Ivor Green discuss alterations to the stage, winter 1983–4

The house from the front (1990). Note that the opera house is barely visible

The Press Office picnic, during the interval of the old theatre's
final performance (23 July 1992)

in the staging of opera were richly rewarded by the playing of the LPO, though the singers had to battle against the disadvantage of being placed above and behind them on the stage. Despite all the setbacks, *Fidelio* was warmly received.

GTO, in its silver jubilee year, made an enterprising choice with *Cornet Christoph Rilke's Song of Love and Death*, by the East German composer Siegfried Matthus, a first performance in Britain. Lasting only ninety minutes, and with an eleven-piece orchestra, its chief impact, not inappropriately, was choral rather than orchestral. It was put on initially at the company's temporary home at Sadler's Wells before going on tour. The story owed its origins to the experiences of an earlier member of the family of the poet Rilke, ending with the protagonist's death in action. Composed in the immediate wake of the Second World War, it made a strong impact on audiences, even though it had had to wait half a century to be performed in Britain.

On top of all the other upheavals and problems that arose in the year of the rebuilding, a massive furore erupted over the Arts Council's threat to withdraw its funding of GTO. A vigorous protest campaign was mounted, with Nicky Webb, who was in charge of press, marketing and publicity, playing a crucial role. When the tour began on 16 September, George made a protest from the stage, and on every night of the tour itself Sarah Playfair, the Administrator of GTO, devoted herself to the cause with passionate attachment, though this episode was only a very small, if crucial, part of her work: in 1995 George paid a tribute in the most public way possible (that is to say, in the programme book) to the artistic quality of the GTO productions under her administration. Her energy, professional verve and decisiveness continue to prevent the impetus of GTO from flagging. Both she, and subsequently the Music Director, Ivor Bolton, and Aidan Lang, the Director of Productions, went on stage to urge members of the audience to protest against the threat, which at the very least seemed intended to force GTO into smaller theatres where fewer tickets would be available. Press reaction was passionately loyal to Glyndebourne and uniformly hostile to the Arts Council. The *Financial Times* commented that 'GTO has already met every possible Arts Council criterion and measurement of quality', while local papers in the areas in danger of losing their visits from GTO (such as Plymouth, Oxford and Southampton) also complained bitterly, and there was strong support from the theatres themselves, who knew how secure the demand for tickets for GTO performances always was. Copies of a draft letter of protest were put on each seat at every performance on the tour, for members of the audience to send either to the Arts Council itself, or to influential people who might intervene effectively.

But it was in the professional magazines that reaction was on the most violent scale. *Opera Now* accused the Arts Council of betraying thousands of opera-goers by axing Kent Opera and by 'breaking every promise to provide theatres and audiences with undiluted opera of comparable distinction'. And in a powerful editorial in *Opera* magazine itself, the editor, Rodney Milnes, pointed out that on the very afternoon of 16 September the touring department of the Arts Council had issued 'a hurried, defensive, ultimately meaningless' press release in a hopeless attempt to contradict what was being said by its own client. The editorial went on to applaud the fact that the major regional opera companies had banded together in declining to tender for touring dates that could or should be GTO's, 'a smack in the face to the "divide and rule" policy emanating from the government itself and permeating the Heritage Department and, alas, the Arts Council'. More strongly still, the magazine declared elsewhere that:

> Since everything the Arts Council had done recently has been both muddled and destructive, major decisions ought really to be taken out of their hands. . . . Only the appointment of a shrewd, tough Chairman to replace . . . Lord Palumbo can save the institution itself, and the gloomiest of all summer thoughts is whether or not it is worth saving.

Since that unhappy time, the Arts Council has become in some ways a different animal, but this episode supports the view often expressed far beyond the world of Glyndebourne, that the Arts Council contained at that time a number of weak, politically motivated people who resented Glyndebourne's consistently high standards and who obstinately and wrongly persisted in seeing it as an 'exclusive' enterprise. They expressed their resentment by totally ignoring the manifest preferences of opera-goers who consistently voted for GTO at the box offices up and down the land. Finally, and most significantly of all, the threat to GTO was attacked in more measured tones by all four previous music directors of the Arts Council, who between them covered the years 1948–88. John Denison, John Cruft, Basil Deane and Richard Lawrence, in an authoritative letter to *The Times* on 4 December, commended in particular GTO's commitment to new works, and the training ground it provided for first-rate young singers, 'many of whom have attained the highest level of national and international recognition'. All this had often been said before by Glyndebourne itself, and also by the critics, but it was exceptionally rewarding that it should be spontaneously confirmed in this independent and highly relevant way. From the Continent, further support for GTO came from Gérard Mortier, by then Director of the Salzburg Festival, and Hugues Gall, then head of the Geneva Opera – two of the leading figures in opera in Europe. There was much other lobbying in high places, and by the middle of December, when the tour was over, the Arts Council had abandoned its threat. Had it gone ahead, GTO might have ceased to exist, and the effect on the Festival itself would have been extremely damaging.

7

THE REBUILDING

In the programme book for 1987 George had for the first time put forward the possibility of complete transformation for Glyndebourne. The old and dearly loved opera house was now structurally shaky – he would have been only too delighted had it collapsed in the great storm of 1987, and that insurance money could have been collected – and he saw the need to replace it with a larger house within the next 'half a dozen' years.

Many devotees reacted with disbelief and then with deep disapproval at such a shocking plan. Before any appeal was actually launched they were given two years to get used to it, and to take in the incontrovertible reasons for it: first, to ensure the future of Glyndebourne's all-round financial security; secondly, to modernize the facilities in the face of increasing competition from other opera houses; and thirdly (softening the blow to devotees), to do something to meet the ever-increasing and excessive demand for tickets, which so often created chagrin and disappointment among the opera-loving public. Finally, if the rebuilding had not been undertaken, a major refit of the old building, including the whole of the backstage area, would have been required within ten years, and the increase in ticket income provided by the new house would not have been there. From now on, George's opening statements in the programme books became rather less formal and detached, less like the Queen's Speech at the Opening of Parliament, and began to take the reader rather more into his confidence – though they had always been warm in paying tribute to those who were departing from Glyndebourne (or indeed, who had left this world altogether).

Prudence, according to Stendhal in his life of Rossini, kills music. Some of the Glyndebourne trustees, on the other hand, felt that a lack of prudence might kill Glyndebourne. That is what trustees are for, and they were right to point out the risks. But their urge for caution only strengthened George's determination to mastermind the awesome task of fund-raising, and then to choose, and brief, the architects, the consultants and the project manager, and to lay down their timetable. It should always be remembered that an important element in his extraordinary achievement as a leader is his ability to make his presence felt in the background, without interfering with the responsibilities of individuals, except as a last resort. For the rebuilding, he now abandoned his usual position as constitutional monarch, in order to take full charge. His general contacts in the more civilized areas of the business world, as well as among individual patrons of the arts, had snowballed over the years, and his invitations to the Glyndebourne box throughout each season were of course greatly coveted and enjoyed. Virtually no one who was invited because they might be of use to Glyndebourne would be likely to decline one of these invitations if they could help it.

Looking back after a decade, he claims never to have lost any sleep during the long process of the rebuilding. To put it much more bluntly than would have been appropriate at the time, the message that he delivered in 1990 to the members of the Festival Society was as follows:

> We are going to pull down the opera house, before it falls down, because we feel an acute need for more ticket income, and in order to accommodate as many more of you as possible. The old Festival Society will therefore cease to exist. But I hereby invite you to become members of the new Society, in any one of a variety of categories.

1992: George and Mary Christie on site

Anthony Whitworth-Jones, Andrew Davis and George Christie on site

Of course, this was put across with infinitely skilful diplomacy and tact. It was one of the most respectable, necessary, and ultimately successful forms of blackmail ever devised, and it owes everything to George himself. He is however always anxious to give boundless credit to others, and above all to John Botts, the former Chairman of Citicorp in Europe, later to become Chairman of the trustees. Just as Alex Alexander had built on and developed the original efforts of Miki Sekers, so the torch was now firmly grasped by Botts, with magnificent results.

The first requirement, that of financial stability, had to be satisfied in a subtle and sophisticated fashion. A considerable increase in total ticket income was needed, as well as access to a larger body of corporate members, but this had to be achieved without destroying the balance between the two sources of revenue and, above all, without damaging the whole atmosphere of Glyndebourne. First, the possibility of increasing the seating capacity of the old house was carefully looked at and rejected. It would have involved altering the size of the proscenium arch, but this in turn would have made it necessary to enlarge the stage areas and therefore the fly-tower, a step which was recognized as impracticable. The only alternative was to build a bigger and better theatre, but without sacrificing the sense of intimacy so fundamental to the appeal of the old house. When examined, the cost of building a brand new house, on the site of the old one, but with the stage at the opposite end, came to a staggering £34 million. In the end, this sum was raised entirely from companies (about 75 per cent) and individual members and well-wishers (25 per cent). There could be no more striking proof of the passionate attachment that had been built up over the years among Glyndebourne's audiences, which inspired them to dig deep into their pockets. Even so, the project could never have been achieved without George's sheer will-power (sometimes mistaken by those who disagreed with him for obstinacy, an echo, perhaps, of what Ebert had detected in John Christie back in 1934) and his extreme skill in presenting his case. Mention must also be made of Mark Beddy, who had arrived as finance director from Arthur Andersen on 1 January, 1988 and was to add essential refinement to the fund-raising strategy, and to provide the really strong financial management essential not only for the rebuilding but for the continued welfare of Glyndebourne in general.

The first stage in the fund-raising process was the appeal to the existing corporate members. Capital contributions were invited at three different levels, £90,000, £60,000 and £30,000, which would guarantee benefactors a supply, respectively, of 120, 80 and 40 tickets in each season. They would also be charged an annual subscription of £4,800, £3,200 or £1,600. The next stage was an appeal to 300 companies which had already shown interest in corporate membership, and their capital contributions were set proportionately higher, at £150,000, £100,000 and £50,000, with an additional category of £30,000, carrying a guarantee of 24 tickets per season, and with a pro rata annual subscription. In this way, the old corporate members were rewarded for their past support by being able to join the club at a rate 40 per cent lower than the newcomers.

The first appeal was launched in January 1990, and by the following year the total capital pledged from companies, came to £22,723,680, contributed by 230 of the original members, and 87 newcomers. The next stage was an appeal to raise the balance from existing and potential individual members, and George reassured them that the number of tickets allocated to the corporate members would be a distinctly lower proportion of the total than had been the case in the old theatre. Here again, the existing individual members who had supported Glynde-bourne, many of them for years, were offered preferential terms. A down-payment of £15,000 would secure four tickets for each opera in every season and £7,500 would secure two. Four other options for con-tribution were also on offer: life membership; the right to continue their annual subscription during the closed year; donations; and support for specific requirements. Life membership involved a single down-payment of £2,500, with no further subscriptions to come, in return for the same booking rights as they had enjoyed before. The great attraction of this was the protection it gave existing members against possible future increases in annual subscription as a result of inflation; but those who preferred could continue to subscribe annually as before, at a starting rate of £100, the subscription during the closed year being a contribution to the rebuilding. The third category, donations, was intended for those who might simply want to help the future of Glyndebourne in general. Apart from Gift Aid relief from tax, single donations of less than £600 could also attract tax relief if covenanted over four years. Thus loyal but less prosperous lovers of Glyndebourne could also make their contributions to the cause, in a tax-efficient way.

Provision was also made for newcomers to become founder members, with an annual guarantee of tickets. This category was limited to three hundred, so as not to set aside an intolerably high proportion of the total supply of tickets. In return for a minimum down-payment of either £15,000 or £20,000, new members were guaranteed two or four tickets for each opera per season, to be paid for in the ordinary way, on top of an annual subscription at the going rate. Later, when 85 per cent of the target had been reached, but with fewer than three hundred of the new founder memberships having been taken up, the entry price was raised from £20,000 to £30,000, and the lower category at £15,000 for two tickets was dropped. As previously, if members of any category wished to resell any of their allocation of tickets, they might only do so at face value, on pain of expulsion from the Society.

Later, those interested were sent a list of costed items relating to the new house which they might generously wish to donate. Thus it may be seen that the net of the appeal was spread as wide as possible, to cover major international companies looking for business entertainment on a large scale, and at the other end of the spectrum individuals who wanted a guarantee of getting a small number of tickets of their choice. At the outset, the whole scheme might have seemed wildly optimistic, entered into on the basis of evidence that could only be guessed at, rather than known to be there. However, some market research was carried out by a firm managed by Dennis (now Sir Dennis) Stevenson which confirmed that the appeal strategy was on the right lines; and it proved George's estimate of the strength of the general desire to go to Glyndebourne, on a variety of scales, to be absolutely correct. His personal commitment to the fund-raising process can be measured by the fact that he is calculated to have signed no fewer than *eight thousand* personalized letters, at first inviting support, later thanking for it. It was in the end a triumph, first of initial courage, then of inspired ingenuity in the planning and execution of the campaign, and finally of personal warmth in expressing gratitude, so that all contributors from the largest to the most modest had the satisfaction of knowing that they were genuinely appreciated.

All along, the trustees' nightmare was of finding themselves embarking on a project without the certainty of funds being available to complete it. But by the time of their meeting on 1 May 1991, pledges had been received for almost 60 per cent of the target, and reserves and other borrowing facilities were available to cover the remainder. The trustees' decision to go ahead was made public at a press conference held on 7 May.

Meanwhile, much work had already been done on the design of the new house and the construction programme. In this George was greatly helped by the property developer Stuart Lipton, of Stanhope Properties. George confined the choice of architects to British firms. He believed that they could be as good as any in the world, and he did not want to find himself working with 'an architect in (say) Nicaragua'. A list of twelve architects was drawn up, of which ten came for interview. In August 1988 George sent them what he modestly described as his 'idle thoughts' on what he wanted. The preamble ran as follows:

> Glyndebourne is a country house which has bred an opera house. There is emphatically no need in rebuilding the theatre to be slavish to the existing theatre which has grown piecemeal over the last fifty-odd years and which is architecturally a complete hybrid.

His second point was that he was looking for a design which would justify itself to the audience and which would 'convince all of us using it (both back-stage and front of house) of its practicability', and, significantly: 'It can be controversial to a point that does not alienate the majority.' Thirdly, 'Any good piece of architecture must "make a state-

ment", but the style has got to convince in the first year of the building's existence as well as for the next hundred years . . . something that would neither provoke violent reactions nor be depressingly reactionary.' On the subject of the old house he was characteristically blunt: it was 'in quite large measure of such architectural indifference' that any change would be for the better – hence the approval by English Heritage for its demolition.

The original nine names on the short-list for Glyndebourne were all leading architects. Robert Adam, who had stuck to the classical tradition; Peter Ahrends, a respected modernist; Edward Cullinan, highly responsive to local materials and traditions; Norman Foster, renowned for high technology; Sam Lloyd, for sensitive designs in historic settings; Richard MacCormac, a modernist producing designs with an individual character; James Stirling, the best-known post-modernist; Nicholas Thompson, of Renton Howard Wood Levine, the practice with the widest experience of theatres in Britain; and finally Michael and Patty Hopkins, who came forward with apparent reluctance but eventually won the appointment against James Stirling. They were told by George that what was wanted was 'a building which works like a dream and which makes your own architectural statement without flying in the face of the downland context'.

To turn to details of the design, the most obtrusive, and the most indispensable in practical opera terms, was the fly-tower. Everything possible was done to reduce its inevitable impact on the eye, starting with the decision to dig deep into the hill, which consists of chalk, not only easy to excavate but also a naturally stable foundation. George himself made a rare personal intervention to have the height of the tower slightly reduced. One of the advantages of turning the new house round through 180 degrees on the axis of the old one is that the fly-tower is situated 33 metres further away from the garden, and nearer the sheltering hill and wood behind it. It appears solid and uncompromising at first sight; but no substitute for it would have been possible. It looks at

The girders of the new, impressive fly-tower are lifted into place (December 1992)

its most overpowering to those who reach the new house by way of the arch to the left of the private house. (As it happens, decreasing numbers do so as a result of the addition of the new driveway to the north of the theatre.) From the gardens, too, it looks fairly large, though by comparison the original fly-tower was also quite dominant, and yet everyone had become accustomed to it soon after it had been built. What is particularly harmonious is the way in which the very shallow circular roof of the new auditorium appears, from the garden, to melt into the tower, and reduces its rectangular impact. The tower (which, like the roof, is clad in lead) is at present darker in tone, but is likely to lighten under the impact of wind and rain. The original plan was to build it in brick, but Bovis, the contract managers, explained that to do so would lengthen the contract disastrously.

It is true that in the case of the load-bearing steel trusses which crown it, something less stark and industrial-looking might have been devised; but subjective aesthetic judgement has to be measured against the puritanical honesty of the architects, and their determination that their practical solution of the requirements of the building should hit the beholder in the eye. Many of those who are, or were, shocked by their first impression of the tower feel differently when they reflect on the elements required for the building to be as effective as possible. A number of enterprising spirits have loved it at first sight, and others have grown accustomed to it. But reactions at Glyndebourne are seldom purely logical: emotional considerations have always played a large part. Others resented the new building, and there are a few who continue to do so.

The bulk of the fly-tower is also softened by two projecting bows which contain a variety of technical equipment. But the most important advance of all is that the auditorium is twice the size of that in the old theatre, while the number of seats has only been increased by half. The volume of space per seat is therefore much more generous, and the resulting improvement in the acoustics is enormous.

The first 'idle thoughts' that George had put to the architects had soon taken on a very definite form, while leaving scope for a wide range of designs. He had insisted on a timber-clad auditorium, in natural wood and without any of the gilt or plush echoes redolent of many of the opera houses built in the previous two centuries. He had also demanded the atmosphere of intimacy which had been so much valued in the old house, and a quality of friendliness, so that people feel at home there from the beginning; and this was in the end achieved by skilful design work, in spite of the great increase in size. A major contribution was made by the guidance of Derek Sugden of Arup Acoustics, who had achieved similar success at the Maltings at Snape, among other places, and who worked closely with Andrew Davis on the structure of the orchestra pit; together they contrived that there would be much more warmth and resonance to the orchestral sound than in the old house. Iain Mackintosh, of Theatre Projects, was the consultant who gave important guidance on technical equipment, sightlines for the audience and other aspects of theatre design, while Michael Coates, of Gardiner and Theobald, was the cost consultant whose advice on budgetary requirements was indispensable.

The overriding principle dictated by George was that the new house should be designed to meet the needs of the performers first, and those of the audience second. Only thus would the final object be achieved, from which everything else would follow; and there were in due course huge improvements as far as the audience was concerned. In addition to the elements mentioned above, there is a wonderful system of insulation from external sound; and the increased areas of space both backstage and in the wings is of the greatest value both to designers and directors; while the new rehearsal stage was another invaluable improvement which had a variety of beneficial repercussions. Finally, the orchestra benefited from an increase in the size of the pit which in the old house often became cramped. It would have been better if the pit had been larger still. This may turn out to have been the only significant design fault in the whole project, but the problem will depend to some extent on the future repertory.

Out of doors, more picnicking space would be required by the larger audiences, and an extended series of gardens was planned by the well-known garden designer and writer Mary Keen, who initially worked in difficult circumstances, in competition with the heavy plant and machinery required for constructing the foundations of the new building. Approaching the opera house from the enlarged car park at the back, visitors first cross the walled Mildmay Garden, flanked on the right by Mildmay Hall, the new restaurant which doubles as a pre-performance tea-room, and is a valuable venue for outside organizations between October and May. The Mildmay Garden leads into the Figaro Garden, with square beds and wide pathways of recycled paving-stones. Finally comes the Bourne Garden, leading down from the far end of the foyer, where the bar, box office and shop are situated, with a ramp for wheelchairs and generous landings between the flights of steps. A profusion of very large shrubs such as gunnera, bamboo and acanthus, and trees including eucalyptus, figs and acacias, provide a suitably impressive setting for the opera house, where smaller plants might have been overwhelmed by the bulk of the auditorium rising above a smallish sunken site. The Bourne Garden also contains a reclining figure by Henry Moore, which came to Glyndebourne through the Kahnweiler Bequest and is on loan from the Tate Gallery. These three new gardens form a delightful series leading from car park to foyer, at the other end of which lies the original garden, which still stretches outside the windows of the Organ Room and the main house, all the way to the main road; and although the larger audiences can enjoy the gardens without feeling overcrowded, there is still a feeling of intimacy, and plenty of shelter on windy summer evenings. Picnics nowadays vary from the most modest of spreads on the grass to what look like formal alfresco banquets, complete with the finest table linen and even silver candlesticks on special tables (not encouraged) in what the *Wall Street Journal* once described as 'the world's most elegant picnic ground'.

The 1992 season ended on 24 July, with the demolition men waiting in the wings. That evening consisted of a gala concert, for which Mary Christie had for some months borne the brunt of the arrangements. It was attended by the Prince of Wales and starred some of the greatest names to have appeared in the Festivals, going back over many years. All

Mary Christie in discussion with Chris Hughes (head gardener) and garden staff (1994)

of them generously waived their fees: artists featured included, among others, Montserrat Caballé, Frederica von Stade, Benjamin Luxon, Felicity Lott and Ruggiero Raimondi, with both Bernard Haitink and Andrew Davis conducting, the only disappointment being a late cancellation by Pavarotti. Although priced at £1,000 and £750, the tickets were quickly sold out, and the evening included a champagne reception (thanks to Veuve Clicquot), a sit-down dinner for one thousand given by Letheby & Christopher in a marquee, and a display of fireworks to console the mourners for the old house. Including the sale of television rights, and many donations from supporters who were not able to attend, the huge sum of £841,457 was raised towards the cost of the new building.

George compered the evening, and mentioned the affirmation made by Semper, the nineteenth-century architect at the Burgtheater in

Vienna and of that greatest of all theatres, the Semper Oper in Dresden, that all opera houses burn down after sixty years. Characteristically George added the words: 'no such luck here'. Of course there was infinite sadness at the impending disappearance of something so greatly loved by so many for so long. But Geraint Evans's prophecy from the stage at the gala that Glyndebourne's soul and spirit would remain the same in the very different context of the new house was in due course found to be triumphantly true. In sharp contrast was Sir Edward Heath's grumpy and mistaken prediction that the new building would have 'no atmosphere'. It was not, incidentally, his only brush with Glyndebourne. When he complained, like many others, about the Sellars production of *Die Zauberflöte*, the director remarked airily that 'it was like being savaged by a hot water bottle'.

As regards the actual design of the new house, the contribution of John Bury, who had designed no fewer than ten operas at Glyndebourne between 1970 and 1988, including many of Peter Hall's triumphs, was of great importance. The architects themselves, though eminently successful in other fields, had never worked on a theatre before. Bury had spent many years on theatre work, and was therefore well able to explain various requirements, technical and otherwise, that might have caused problems. His was very much a 'hands-on' approach; indeed, when he was designing *La Calisto,* a leading singer had enquired: 'John Bury, he is so nice, but why is he always so dirty?' Iain Mackintosh of Theatre Projects has already been mentioned. He had invaluable experience of the characteristics of various older theatres and opera houses from the point of view of performers and directors, and George had made it quite clear that it was their interests which were to have top priority. Theatre Projects had not only breathed new life into old theatres by introducing modern technology, but had also created some of the most advanced new theatres, especially in North America: witness the auditorium at Los Cerritos in Los Angeles, 'which can change overnight from a 900-seat theatre into a 2,000-seat concert hall'. As well as advising on technical equipment and sightlines, it was Mackintosh who convinced everyone else to choose a horseshoe shape for the new theatre: acoustically it could be as good as anything else, and to give a feeling of intimacy, with the audience 'forming part of the spectacle' (as Count Algarotti put it in Mozart's day), it could not be bettered. And the Hopkinses put his ideas into practice.

The foundations and substructure consisted of massive concrete slabs, cast *in situ* and supported on the chalk subsoil. The excavation for these went deep into the hill on the north side of the site, to lower the perceived height of the building and the fly-tower. The upper-level floor beams and ceiling panels were of high quality precast concrete, with a fine mica-speckled surface finish. In order to keep the construction time to a minimum, they were manufactured off-site by Dynaspan in Northern Ireland, and by Trent in Nottingham.

After studying many local buildings in stucco, flint and tiles, the architects decided on brick for the walls of the building. The bricks were made at a brickworks at Selborne in Hampshire, taking its entire output for about twelve months. Imperial-sized bricks, smaller than usual, were used, and lime mortar, which, being flexible, dispenses with the need for unsightly expansion joints in the load-bearing walls. Around forty bricklayers laid the one and three quarter million bricks. The almost-flat brick arches round the foyer were self-supporting, but required considerable skill in manufacture and laying, and a full-scale mock-up was built on site in order to test the method.

The fly-tower, which is at the heart of the building, could not have been built in brick in the time available. The superstructure above the concrete supporting beams is consequently made of steel. The concrete panels for sound insulation were also supported with steel, and with lead-covered cladding panels to match the lead-covered 'coolie hat' roofs of the backstage and auditorium spaces. Crucially, this steel structure contained all the theatre equipment. Like others involved in the project, the Dutch steelwork contractor, Hollandia, demonstrated a strong commitment to the project, and was particularly keen on the exposed steel mass at the top of the fly-tower, regarding it as symbolic both of the industry and the century, and also of their own skills. Not all those who live and work under its shadow share this enthusiasm, but, pre-

The roof of the new auditorium taking shape (May 1993)

dictably, it has become less oppressive as people have grown accustomed to it.

A single tower crane was used for lifting the concrete beams, the fly-tower and roof steelwork, and the panelling and cladding. During the critical stages of construction the main steelwork for the fly-tower was lifted into position by night, under floodlights, and concrete lifting was carried out by day; the work continued round the clock in order to keep to time. The crane was positioned in the centre of what was to be the auditorium, and served the whole building area. When the work was complete and the crane removed, its base remained as part of the foundations.

As for the interior, the intention had always been to build it of wood, in the spirit of the old Glyndebourne. But the effect, and not least the colour, was to be entirely different. The auditorium of a magnificent theatre in Parma, where the inside was of stripped pine, golden orange in

General view of the backstage area, looking towards the main auditorium (1994)

colour, was held up as a model by the Hopkinses and this example was embraced by the Christies. The timber at Glyndebourne was sourced from the north of England by Nelson's Sawmill in Romney Marsh, which delivered it to Cheeseman's, a firm of joiners at Aylesford in Kent. Most unusually, it was all reclaimed pitch pine, *pinus palustris* and *pinus picea*, most of it over a hundred years old, grown on the banks of the Mississippi, brought back in British trading vessels, and recently salvaged from disused warehousing and other industrial buildings. Planing revealed a smooth, mellow texture and this, together with its warm, orange glow, provides a remarkable feeling of welcome and well-being as one enters the auditorium, essential for creating the right mood in the audience, and not easily brought about. It is also worth noting that in the new house the back row of the audience is actually nearer the stage than it was in the old house. The increase in size has been achieved more in the vertical than in the horizontal plane, and although there is a feeling of much greater space all round, the new proscenium is only seven feet wider than in the old house. But a far greater improvement for the audience is that each seat is individually air-cooled: there can be many hot evenings in a Glyndebourne summer, but those who sweated or even slumbered in days gone by at least sweat no more. The seating layout was planned on the principles that had been established in the opera house at Edinburgh that was designed, and later cancelled. To add to the welcoming effect, George had the idea of installing what became known as 'twinkle lights' on the balcony fronts, which brighten the auditorium pleasantly before and after each performance.

As regards the timing of the whole enterprise, Glyndebourne once more had the luck which it so richly deserved. The money for the new house had been in large measure pledged in a period of boom, but the building process was carried out in a recession. As George put it: 'We were able to pick up the cream of the trades.' Alan Lansdell, the Bovis construction manager, had the awesome task of getting the building completed in the space of sixteen months, a period which had been ruthlessly reduced from an original twenty-two, and this was helped by stockpiling materials at Glyndebourne itself and prefabricating some of the main constituent elements elsewhere – and by vigorous management. The formidable job of completing it within budget fell to Eric Gabriel, the client's project manager, who had masterminded the National Gallery extension in London and came with a glowing recommendation from Lord Rothschild, then Chairman of its trustees. The mechanics of Gabriel's role are of some interest, in that he acted as the single link between construction management (Bovis, who had responsibility for the rebuilding project) and the management at Glyndebourne. All expenditure had to be authorized by him, particularly any design changes which inevitably result in additional costs. Such changes, when allowed by Gabriel, had to be balanced by corresponding savings elsewhere. Seldom have client and his two heads of operations got on so well as George with Lansdell and Gabriel, something which does not come about by chance but only by unflagging determination. Every day of the building period, George would be on site in his hard hat, checking everything that could be checked, and thinking about the implications of each stage of the construction as it was completed. When it was all over, he summed up, briefly and generously: 'Eric Gabriel was gold dust for us. Bovis I can't fault. Alan Lansdell is a gritty individual with a huge heartbeat, a man of incredible confidence, dedication and passion.' The way in which Gabriel reciprocated this tribute is reflected in a letter which he wrote to the Christies after a lunch given for those involved in May 1994:

> Most of all I must say what a privilege and pleasure it has been to know and be accepted by you both, in work & socially. To say that this has been the highlight of my life is an understatement. With hindsight the whole of my career appears to have been a preparation for Glyndebourne . . .
>
> The Glyndebourne Project will never be repeated or be equalled. For these reasons above all I could not contemplate working on another major project. It could only be a disappointment, and would interfere with our memories, which is unthinkable.

The unique success of The Grand Plan springs directly from yourselves, and you are unique, that is my logic. The crowning kindness was the gift of membership to enable us to enjoy this Great Place for the rest of our lives.

There could be no better evidence of the exceptional rapport, both professional and personal, that George had created with his chief of staff. It originated from the ever meticulous attention to detail which was at least as crucial to the rebuilding as it has been to individual opera productions, and to the warmth of personality above the underlying steel. And this distinctive strain of dedication spread, almost like an epidemic, from the Christies themselves to all those who were to work on the project. It should be stressed that George's gluttony for work was also generally tempered with his own brand of humour, of which there are many examples in the programme books. It could lighten the most laborious tasks, often in original and unexpected ways, and constantly strengthened the loyalty and devotion of all who worked at Glyndebourne. George observed at one point, after one of his penetrating daily visits to the site, that he had never before seen a work force all of whom were actually working all the time, rather than enjoying regular intervals for reflection. It appears that the Bovis team came to feel the same sort of commitment to their exacting task as members of cast, chorus and orchestra do to their roles in the operas. Without it, the huge undertaking could certainly not have been completed in the time specified, which was always a major preoccupation. To have lost all, or even part, of a second season would have been crippling, and this was only avoided by everyone's magically infectious enthusiasm. Subsequently, recognition poured in from a number of organizations, beginning with the British Construction Industry itself. The new theatre won too many awards to mention them all here, but Glyndebourne scooped the pool. Most appropriately, these successes are recorded on a series of admirably carved plaques in the covered arcade of the foyer circle.

The opening of the new theatre in 1994 was a thrilling experience, and the fact that all five productions put on were generously sponsored did much to dispel any lingering uncertainties. With a fine touch of symmetry, the season in the new theatre began with *Figaro* on 28 May, sixty years to the day after it had been presented on the Glyndebourne Festival's first night of all. It was described as a 'newly mounted' production under Stephen Medcalf, John Gunter's new sets replacing those that had been destroyed in the fire two years before. The garden in Act IV was distinctly sparse, and hardly suited to the action, which calls for a good deal more in the way of camouflage. Apart from that, the details of the production pleased everyone, as did the timing and impeccable clarity of Haitink's conducting, with Ivor Bolton taking over successfully in July. In describing the production as a whole as *'tout pour la musique'*, *La Belgique Libre* put it in a nutshell. Renée Fleming, the Countess, is widely regarded as one of the world's greatest living lyric sopranos; Alison Hagley was hailed as 'a world-class Susanna', and Gerald Finley's Figaro and Robert Tear's Don Basilio were also singled out.

The other Mozart production, *Don Giovanni*, was as new as the most ardent iconoclast could desire. It was Deborah Warner's debut at Glyndebourne and she was determined to portray the Don as mad, volatile and dangerous, 'with a constant threat that there is nothing he may not do next, just for the hell of it', as one reviewer put it. The scene that caused most offence was where the Don subjected a statue of the Madonna to various lascivious indignities, which not surprisingly appalled and nauseated many of the audiences (and to caricature them as 'toffee-nosed stick-in-the-muds', as one reviewer did, was the height of absurdity). Ironically, the scene caused no offence to a Catholic priest who was in the audience one night and was asked for his opinion. He felt that the scene involving the Madonna simply indicated that the Don despises women to such an extreme degree that he wishes to ill-treat even the purest and noblest of them all; and the fact that the statue remained on the stage after the action was over, in a position which it might well occupy in a church, serves to show that the dignity of the Blessed Virgin, and consequently of all women, was reinstated after the Don's perdition; and that in any case something done to a statue cannot, in view of the sanctity of life, be worse than something done to a human being.

Bernard Haitink in rehearsal for the opening production in the new theatre, and (below), Alison Hagley as Susanna and Gerald Finley as Figaro

This highly intellectual view can hardly be expected to be shared by those whose initial reaction was one of shock and horror, although perhaps, when recollecting in tranquillity, many might well come round to it. However, objections to the production, its grimness and drabness, its lack of any sense of place or of atmosphere, went far beyond this particular scene. In addition, it was difficult to be interested in any of the characters as human beings. (Leporello, in part at least, is one of the librettist's and the composer's great comic creations.) Was the director's treatment controversial and interesting, or merely drab and boring? Was it a real challenge for the audience, in keeping with the general philosophy of Whitworth-Jones, or a bogus, empty one? Would Mozart and da Ponte really have wanted the *giocoso* element in the drama to be so brutally cut out? Can this treatment honestly be described as respecting the composer's intentions? Would he really have approved of a large false stage looming up from floor to ceiling, and hopelessly distracting the audience from Don Ottavio's sublime aria '*Dalla sua pace*'? Even giving the director the maximum benefit of the doubt, the answer must surely be no, though *Opera* magazine disagreed entirely. Yet the question remains to some extent a subjective one, and no doubt justification could be found for cheers as well as boos, counter-cheers as well as counter-boos. Some experienced opera-lovers also feel that there is a more general danger of what might be called 'over-theatricalization' on the part of directors. The difficulty here is that when a director is appointed by the management, the latter (and perhaps even the former) only has a hazy idea of how the production will turn out. It is an act of faith on the part of management, made on the basis of the director's previous record. Andrew Davis has also pointed out that nowadays there is far less discussion between director and conductor than in the days of Busch and Ebert. And it would be a matter for regret if directors came to interpose their own ideas or whims in such a way that the audience are hindered from appreciating the composer's music, and the usually wonderful way in which the singers and orchestra perform it.

The row about *Don Giovanni* was exceptionally fierce, but the enthusiasm which greeted Graham Vick's *Yevgeny Onyegin* was universal. The elegance and economy of Pushkin, as well as his irony, with a classical absence of clutter, was most faithfully expressed by Vick, as was the grace and restraint of Tchaikovsky's music in the hands of Andrew Davis and the orchestra. The chilly, stylized atmosphere of aristocratic St Petersburg contrasted well with the profound humanity of the tragically ill-matched lovers. The duel was fought beyond the open doors of a large barn, so that the audience heard the shot but were unaware of who had been killed until Onyegin reappeared alone, destined always to remain so. The reviews were rapturous. To give but one example: 'Frankly, you haven't seen the opera until you've seen this production.' They were a tribute to all concerned, but the purity and subtlety of Elena Prokina's Tatyana and the beauty of her voice were in a class of their own, while the nuances of her phrasing, which might well have been lost in a larger house, were most perfectly provided for by Glyndebourne. Not for a second could the most perverse of critics have suggested that the intentions of composer and librettist were not being faithfully and convincingly respected. Richard Hudson's designs were truly evocative, and the effects of Thomas Webster's lighting were inspired. As a good example of Glyndebourne's production standards, the ballet in the ballroom scene was danced by Stephen Jefferies and Bryony Brind, two of Covent Garden's most dazzling stars. And to satisfy their needs, a considerable area of new flooring was inserted on the stage, at a cost of £13,000 – a good example of the lengths to which Glyndebourne will go in the pursuit of technical perfection.

John Cox returned to revive *The Rake's Progress*. Nineteen years after their first appearance, Hockney's stunning sets had been retouched by the artist after having been rebuilt following the fire two years earlier, and greatly impressed those who had never seen them, while bringing back happy memories to those who had. One reliable critic described them as being 'among the most unforgettable strokes of genius in modern theatre design'.

The production of *Peter Grimes*, which rounded off the season, had been created for the old theatre two years before. Franz Welser-Möst, then Music Director of the LPO, conducted with considerable musical

Simon Rattle and Deborah Warner in rehearsal for Don Giovanni *(1994)*

intelligence and sophistication, and Anthony Rolfe-Johnson gave Grimes the poetic, visionary quality intended by Britten, but which some others have not brought out in the role. Though various thuds and bumps were audible during the scene changes, it was observed that the most challenging of the season's five operas was cheered the most loudly.

Altogether it was a triumphant new season in a triumphant new house, borne out by the fact that in the Prudential Awards for the Arts Glyndebourne won the Opera Award for the 'commitment to quality shown in the creation of the new opera house and in its first season's productions'. And to underline his role, the *Evening Standard*'s award for opera was given to George himself, much though he would have preferred it to be shared with others who were responsible for the season's success. In the programme book for 1995 he admitted his relief that the new house had had such a good press.

Opera magazine had commented that, in the previous June, 'one or two people tried in a desultory fashion to find fault with Michael and

Patty Hopkins's new theatre – but they soon gave up', though if they had spoken to some of the backstage staff they might have heard something less than complete approval. Scene-shifting is still done by human teams, and the sort of mechanization to be found at the Théâtre de la Bastille in Paris could simply not be afforded. But given the level of finance available, what had been achieved for those who were to work in the new theatre was an extraordinary triumph. Above all, it was honest and practical. There are no frills. The reaction of older Glyndebourne lovers was, not surprisingly, more mixed. At one extreme, an elderly lady who had not heard much about the rebuilding, arrived for a performance and saw the new house, at which she burst into tears and went straight back to her car. But even at the time, most people were filled with admiration, and when 'the shock of the new' had passed, enthusiastic approval became more or less universal.

Of all the seasons in Anthony Whitworth-Jones's time as Administrator, 1995 is the one of which he is proudest, and it is not difficult to see why. Each of the works put on expressed, in one way or another, his conviction that opera is, and must be, more than mere entertainment. It must show audiences either something new or something familiar in a new light or a new context, and make them think more seriously about the implications, rather than allowing them to stroll out into the garden in the interval, vaguely murmuring: 'How lovely!' If this seems an excessively solemn or earnest approach, exceptions may be (and are) allowed. It is all a question of balance. The season began with a new production by Graham Vick of *Ermione*, an *opera seria* by Rossini which, since its première in 1819, had never been performed in Britain before, and nowhere else either until ten years previously. It was a classic example of Whitworth-Jones's successful desire to break new ground – though in this case from a source so familiar that the box office was not going to suffer. In fact, it was more of a challenge for the performers than for the audience, and Anna Caterina Antonacci, in the name part, led a hugely successful cast. The cold, classical surface of Racine, on whose *Andromaque* the work is based, was less in evidence than the passionate feelings that blaze beneath it. Rossini had observed mysteriously that it was a

Russell Hoban, Harrison Birtwistle and Anthony Whitworth-Jones before a performance of The Second Mrs Kong *(1995)*

work for posterity rather than for the Naples audiences of 1819. How right he was. Then, it was taken off after one night; but the Glynde-bourne audiences of 1995 and 1996 loved it. Graham Vick, who had wisely decided to concentrate on operas which, for reasons of scale, work better at Glyndebourne than elsewhere, was described by one leading critic as having, 'these days, the touch of someone who can do no wrong'. He remained concerned that the seriousness of the tragedy should survive, however reminiscent some of the music was of the com-poser's comic creations, such as *Le comte Ory* (which was restaged in 1997). It was no mean feat.

The second novelty could hardly have been more different. Harrison Birtwistle's *The Second Mrs Kong* had been commissioned for GTO the year before, and had been a considerable success on tour. The plot con-sists of a romance across the centuries between King Kong, a gorilla who is only a figurative representation of a lost and lonely child, yearning for normal relations with his surroundings which he can never attain (and who is therefore an object of sympathy rather than of terror) and Vermeer's *Girl with a Pearl Earring*, who is also, in her way, an imaginary creation. The idea of the librettist, Russell Hoban, is that it is not love that moves the world, but the longing for what cannot be.

As usual with such an innovative piece, reactions were divided. Critics such as Alexander Waugh, who consider that opera is a great art form simply and solely because it 'provides a unique means of enriching our understanding of human emotion and human character', disliked it because they found that here, 'inhuman protagonists are used only as mouthpieces for intellectual ideas'. And of the more forward-looking critics, Tom Sutcliffe also disliked it, though on musical grounds, accusing the composer of 'using the human voice as if it were a slightly recalcitrant, enfeebled brass instrument'. One regular Glyndebourne attender was heard to say on leaving that she found it discordant and difficult, and added: 'My daughter is in it and she hates it too.' But many people found it possible to detect the feeling of a real love story beneath the opaque surface, with much visual imagination going into Tom Cairns's production. It included wonderful watery images as well as luminous cityscapes, and the critics were enthralled by his setting for the austere beauty of Birtwistle's world of sound. The production was backed by magical lighting by Wolfgang Göbbel. George himself calmly observed that he was aware of pushing back the bounds further than they had been for some time, but that this was part of the ancient Glyndebourne tradition of broadening the recognition of operatic repertory. As so often with adventurous novelties, one man's meat was regarded as poisonous by others. The music, like many masterpieces (such as the late Beethoven string quartets), requires a great deal more than one hearing to be appreciated.

The other new production, Janáček's *The Makropulos Case*, was greeted with rapture all round. Here too there was an element of fantasy since the central character, Emilia Marty, is some 337 years old. Anja Silja, who looked a very great deal younger, and who had already taken Glyndebourne by storm in *Jenůfa* in 1989 and 1992, gave a towering, hypnotic performance, which those who saw it either in that year, or in

Così fan tutte *rehearsal, 1998: Director of Productions Graham Vick with Natale de Carolis, Daniela Mazzucato and Roberta Saccà*

its revival two years later, will never forget. Anyone who needed reconfirmation of their belief in opera as 'one of the sublimely satisfying manifestations of the human spirit in art', as Michael Kennedy put it, found it in abundance here. As with his earlier Janáček stagings, Nikolaus Lehnhoff's production, with Hoheisel's designs, was inspired and inspiring; and the supporting cast was strong enough not to be put entirely in the shade by Silja, while Andrew Davis was at his dramatic, forceful best, and the LPO rose to the occasion with the fiendishly difficult score. Even the more capricious critics (to name no names) were at a loss for superlatives, and one of them, who had sometimes been arbitrarily dissatisfied in the past, asked: 'Is there consistently better opera anywhere in the world?'

The revival of *Don Giovanni* seemed less shocking than the year before, perhaps simply because it *was* a revival. But although some individual performances were excellent, the old objections, already described, retained their force, and there were many who thought that, by depriving the opera of its character relationships, the production also robbed it of some of its strength and its interest.

8

THE FUTURE

What lies ahead for Glyndebourne? Its history, as has been seen, tends to be cyclical. The six pre-war seasons came at a time when professional competition in Britain was at a very low ebb, and the productions at Glyndebourne, thanks to Ebert and Busch, came up to John Christie's most exalted aims, exceeding the hopes of well-wishers, routing the many sceptics, and establishing Mozart's operas in England. After the war, because of financial restrictions, there was a muted start with the Britten premières, followed by an increasing momentum developed via Edinburgh. Then, thanks first to John Spedan Lewis, and then to the Treasury (of all people), and finally to the invaluable enlistment of commercial sponsorship by Miki Sekers, the Festival was successfully re-established at Glyndebourne itself in the 1950s. Later, there was a perceptible downturn during a period when those in charge either died (in the case of Andrey Mildmay, John Christie and Busch), retired (Ebert), grew old (Gui), became lazy (Pritchard) or had simply been in the same job long enough: Moran Caplat admitted in his memoirs that he had stepped down in 1981 with a sense of relief, and that he was becoming too set in his ways 'to adapt readily to the changing conditions, social, commercial and technological, that lay ahead'.

After this time of uncertainty, there had followed the crucial formation of GTO, and an injection of energy and power of innovation from Brian Dickie in the 1980s, built on and further amplified by Anthony Whitworth-Jones from 1988 up to the time of writing. The momentum that had been built up, and the state of morale that had been generated, had made the rebuilding possible, under George's inspired and irresistible leadership. Various adventurous novelties had been introduced into the repertory, not all of them popular, but most of them invigorating. Now, however, very important changes were in the air. Brian Dickie has observed that the job of General Administrator should only be held for as long as the holder has the requisite energy and enthusiasm, and that ten or twelve years may usually be about the right limit. Whitworth-Jones had done the job for two years longer than Dickie, and now decided, on the most amicable basis, to move on to new pastures, so far unidentified. Nicholas Snowman, who has been appointed to succeed him, has been Chief Executive at the South Bank Centre for the last six years, where he had been host to Glyndebourne in the year of the rebuilding. He had previously been the co-founder and, like Whitworth-Jones, General Manager, of the London Sinfonietta. In his youth he had been a founder of the Cambridge University Opera Society, before working at Glyndebourne for three seasons as assistant to Jani Strasser, actually succeeding Brian Dickie in that post. Later, he had also been Artistic Director of IRCAM at the Centre Georges Pompidou in Paris from 1972 to 1986, while acting as co-founder, with Pierre Boulez, of the Ensemble InterContemporain. His enthusiasms and commitments are therefore not hard to guess. Quite what form they will take at Glyndebourne remains to be seen, but it is hard to imagine any great change from the recent policy of striving for the right balance between the traditional repertory, with Mozart at its centre, but also including the revival of neglected works: operas by Weber and Schumann have been tentatively mentioned, and, after all these years, Wagner. And of course, there will be the introduction, and commissioning, of new operas, with or without the collaboration of the BBC or other partners.

Thanks partly to the Glyndebourne Chorus Scheme, and the emergence of fine singers on the tours, there is no shortage of talent available

Theodora *rehearsal, 1996: Peter Sellars and Lorraine Hunt;*
and in performance, 1997: Jean Rigby and chorus

there. Human nature being what it is, conflict between loyalty and self-interest, real or imagined, is a recurring problem for singers, directors and conductors, especially now that more opera is being performed elsewhere, and even young and comparatively inexperienced singers are less willing to commit themselves to GTO than in the days when there was a more regular progress from chorus or understudy to principal parts on tour, and ultimately, in some cases, back to the Festival itself.

It should also be remembered that the scale of operations has increased enormously. By 1997 Glyndebourne was in action for nine months in the year. Festival rehearsals begin early in April, and in that year the Festival itself ran from 18 May to 24 August. The GTO rehearsals started only a week later, and the tour, beginning with the performances at Glyndebourne itself, lasted from 6 October to 11 December. In that year, too, over a thousand young people attended Glyndebourne Education workshops and GTO productions, thanks to Seeboard's Opera Opportunity scheme, already mentioned. GTO has to compete with such companies as Welsh National Opera and Opera North, and it is bringing in more established singers instead of relying heavily on the Festival chorus, as originally. Indeed, as Michael White pointed out in an interesting contribution to the 1997 programme book, the average age of the cast for *Theodora* on tour in 1996 was slightly higher than that of the Festival cast. Festival and tour now run to 120 performances, which is more than many a European company, powered by generous subsidies, gives in a full year.

The bad news, however, was that in 1997 GTO received the same grant from the Arts Council as in every previous year since 1993, a period when costs had risen by 12 per cent. Without the help of the Foundation for Sport and the Arts in 1996 it is difficult to see how GTO could have maintained the full range of its tour. While on the subject of what Glyndebourne does away from home, it is worth noting that even if Festival productions are now no longer taken abroad, sets, costumes and staging arrangements are regularly hired out to foreign companies. However, Glyndebourne is understandably careful about whose hands their productions fall into, so that they can be confident that as near as possible the same amount of care will be taken when they are put on abroad as was the case at home. Exports of this kind ultimately arise from the tradition of producing both sets and costumes at Glyndebourne and to John Christie's fascination with the building and engineering side of opera production. They either came with the original director, or with one who followed him or her closely. Glyndebourne's *The Rake's Progress* was given in Spain, as *La Cenerentola* and Hall's *Don Giovanni* had been earlier. And in 1996 both *Lulu* and *Theodora* were shown on television not only in Britain but in Japan, Canada, Mexico, Germany, Italy, North Africa and Israel, continuing an operation which had begun some years earlier; while in the following year both *Manon Lescaut* and *Le comte Ory* had similar exposure. Indeed, in one way or another, Glyndebourne now reaches out, with influential results, to a range of audiences and opera companies all over the world undreamed of in the early days.

Success on the scale to which Glyndebourne has become accustomed sometimes leads to self-centred complacency. Glyndebourne has usually avoided this simply because each year brings new productions, new challenges (above all in the years since 1988), new problems and new solutions. Everyone is kept on their toes, and the danger of resting on laurels is limited. Nevertheless there have been, from time to time, those who have sensed an element of corporate self-esteem, even of self-veneration. The feeling that 'we are not as others are' stems partly from a general increase in corporate strength, a situation arising from a string of successes only occasionally interrupted by disappointments or failures (and there are always some who find good qualities in productions which are widely disliked). It also stems partly from the sheer physical seclusion of Glyndebourne, and the segregation of those who work there – though nowadays there are far more commuters than in the past. And it is largely a matter of personal response. Most of those who work there (nine out of ten was the estimate of Martin Isepp) throw themselves joyfully into the spirit of the place, even if an exceptional few will recoil from it. The diversity of human nature is endless, and great artists are often also great individualists. But generally speaking, and making allowances for egocentricity, Glyndebourne remains to this day a happy and contented place of work, where imagination is controlled but not stifled by discipline. The innovations introduced by Whitworth-Jones, and the creation of the new theatre, have probably made Glyndebourne a better place of work for most of the few creative artists who might previously have felt uncomfortable there. If there are sometimes those who feel that Glyndebourne swallows them up and takes over their lives to an excessive degree, the same applies in many super-successful enterprises in other fields, such as the law, the armed forces, finance or the media. Some sort of sacrifice is always the price to be paid for excellence. Every ounce of commitment is extracted all round, even though those who work there now live in a far less authoritarian world than in the days when all Glyndebourne trembled before Ebert or Rennert, like Rome before Scarpia in *Tosca*.

Not long ago, the Board of Covent Garden surprisingly (but perhaps in despair at its own difficulties) invited George to join it, without reflecting that conflict of interest would inevitably prevent him from accepting. They failed to improve matters by then issuing a similar invitation to Mary, in whose case the same obstacle also obviously applied. She pointed out gently that if they had wanted her services, they would have done better to invite her in the first place. However, on the basis that it is nice to be wanted, she also felt grateful that Covent Garden should look to either of them as potential directors.

The Christies emphatically lead from the front. The load they bear is enormous, week in, week out, and their schedules are often almost as punishing out of season as in. Dame Janet Baker has described them as 'the people who perhaps sacrifice more than anyone else in the amount of time, energy, privacy, and heart's blood they pour out on Glyndebourne'. Consequently, no change at Glyndebourne will ever be more fundamental than when George steps down as Chairman of Glyndebourne Productions at the end of 1999, his sixty-fifth birthday falling neatly on 31 December. His second son Augustus, universally known as Gus, will succeed him at the age of thirty-six, eleven years older than his father was when taking over as Chairman. His professional experience includes working on some very successful wildlife films for television, and, more relevantly, as Acting Finance Director after Mark Beddy left in 1997, and before the arrival of his successor Sarah Hopwood.

In the thirty-six years since his father's death, George has guided Glyndebourne through a transformation scene which has passed off remarkably smoothly. The autocracy which he has exerted has always been masked by much real consultation and co-operation with the Board, the trustees and the General Administrator and, as he himself has put it, 'by keeping his head below the parapet'. Be that as it may, thanks to ever-watchful planning, and attention to the minutest detail, the beginning of the new millennium will find Glyndebourne stronger and better able to face the future than at any other time in the sixty-six years of its existence, a period which coincides almost exactly with George's own lifetime. But the conditions necessary for this will include support, at a level that keeps pace with any future inflation, from the individual and corporate members of Glyndebourne, and crucially, from the Arts Council for GTO.

There are however other favourable omens. Among its many talents, Glyndebourne has shown a capacity to learn from its mistakes, to spot warning signals in good time, and to use forceful ingenuity in dealing with threats and dangers. There are, of course, three elements which it would allow to deteriorate at its peril, and which have been emphasized earlier: first, the concentration on the sheer quality of production details which is made possible partly by the long rehearsal periods and partly by the calibre of the music staff; secondly, the ability to attract new sponsorship on a sufficient scale; and thirdly, the energy and skill it has in the past shown in identifying, at the formative stage in their development as artists, those who may become great singers, and in attracting them to Glyndebourne, partly on the strength of what they will learn there, and

George and Mary Christie, with Gus and Imogen Christie and twins
Romulus and Jackson

partly thanks to the working conditions and the warmth of the welcome they receive when they join the Glyndebourne 'family', for however long or short a time. This sense of well-being is created by the physical beauty of the place, the freedom from urban stress while working there, and the personal qualities of those in charge. Nothing as good as what happens at Glyndebourne is easy, and it will not be a simple matter for the various people who follow George and Mary Christie to maintain the standards and the atmosphere which they have maintained in the last forty years. But it will not be impossible.

Glyndebourne can be likened to a goldmine, with the important difference that sooner or later a goldmine is worked out, and all that is left is an empty shell. Glyndebourne on the other hand is constantly being replenished and rejuvenated by the introduction of new ideas and new talent on all fronts, which ferment and blend together to produce the results that have been described. Given its history, the conditions just mentioned, and the steady introduction of the right new blood, there appears to be no reason why the development traced in these pages should in the foreseeable future ever come to an end.

COMPLETE LIST
OF WORKS GIVEN BY
GLYNDEBOURNE FESTIVAL OPERA
1934–1996

(Dates given in bold for new or redesigned productions.)

BEETHOVEN	*Fidelio:* **1959**, 1961, 1963, **1979**, 1981, 1993 (South Bank)
BELLINI	*I puritani:* **1960**
BERG	*Lulu:* **1996**
BERLIOZ	*Béatrice et Bénédict:* 1993 (South Bank)
BIZET	*Carmen:* **1985**, 1987
BIRTWISTLE	*The Second Mrs Kong:* 1995
BRITTEN	*The Rape of Lucretia:* **1946** (world première), 1947 *A Midsummer Night's Dream:* **1981**; 1984, 1989 *Albert Herring:* **1947** (world première), **1985**, 1986, 1990 *Peter Grimes:* **1992**, 1994 *Death in Venice:* 1992 *Owen Wingrave:* 1997
BUSONI	*Arlecchino:* **1954**, 1960
CAVALLI	*L'Ormindo:* **1967**, 1968, 1969 *La Calisto:* **1970**, 1971, 1972, 1973, 1974
CIMAROSA	*Il matrimonio segreto:* **1965**, 1967
DEBUSSY	*Pelléas et Mélisande:* **1962**, 1963, 1969, 1970, **1976**
DONIZETTI	*Don Pasquale:* **1938**, 1939 *L'elisir d'amore:* **1961**, 1962, 1967 *Anna Bolena:* **1965**, 1968

GAY	*The Beggar's Opera*: **1940**
GERSHWIN	*Porgy and Bess*: **1986**, 1987
GLUCK	*Orfeo ed Euridice*: **1947**, **1982**, 1989
	Alceste: **1953**, 1954, 1958
HANDEL	*Jephtha*: **1966**
	Theodora: **1996**, 1997
	Rodelinda: **1998**
HAYDN	*La fedeltà premiata*: **1979**, 1980
HENZE	*Elegy for Young Lovers*: **1961**
JANÁČEK	*The Cunning Little Vixen*: **1975**, 1977
	Káťa Kabanová: **1988**, 1990, 1998
	Jenůfa: **1989**, 1992
	The Makropulos Case: **1995**, 1997
KNUSSEN	*Where the Wild Things Are*: 1985
	Higglety Pigglety Pop!: 1985
LEHÁR	*Die lustige Witwe*: 1993 (South Bank)
MASSENET	*Werther*: **1966**, 1969
MAW	*The Rising of the Moon*: **1970** (world première), 1971
MONTEVERDI	*L'incoronazione di Poppea*: **1962**, 1963, 1964, **1984**, 1986
	Il ritorno d'Ulisse in patria: **1972**, 1973, 1979
MOZART	*Le nozze di Figaro*: **1934**, 1935, 1936, 1937, 1938, 1939, 1947, **1950**, **1951**, **1955**, 1956, 1958, 1959, 1962, 1963, 1965, **1973**, 1974, 1976, 1981, 1984, **1989**, 1991, **1994**, 1997
	Così fan tutte: **1934**, 1935, 1936, 1937, 1938, 1939, **1948**, 1949, 1950, 1951, 1952, 1953, 1954, 1956, 1959, 1962, **1969**, 1971, 1975, 1976, **1978**, 1979, 1984, 1987, **1991**, 1992, 1996, **1998**
	Die Entführung aus dem Serail: **1935**, 1936, 1937, **1950**, 1953, **1956**, 1957, 1961, **1968**, **1972**, 1973, **1980**, 1983, 1988
	Die Zauberflöte: **1935**, 1936, 1937, **1956**, 1957, 1960, **1963**, 1964, 1966, 1970, 1973, **1978**, 1980, **1990**, 1991
	Don Giovanni: **1936**, 1937, 1938, 1939, 1948, **1951**, 1954, 1955, 1956, **1960**, 1961, **1967**, 1969, **1977**, 1978, 1982, 1986, 1991, **1994**, 1995
	Idomeneo: **1951**, 1952, 1953, 1956, 1959, 1964, **1974**, **1983**, 1985, 1991
	Der Schauspieldirektor: **1957**
	La clemenza di Tito: **1991**, 1995
OSBORNE	*The Electrification of the Soviet Union*: **1988**

POULENC	*La voix humaine*: **1960**, **1977**
PROKOFIEV	*The Love for Three Oranges*: **1982**, 1983
PUCCINI	*La bohème*: **1967**, 1978 *Manon Lescaut*: **1997**
PURCELL	*Dido and Aeneas*: **1966**
RAVEL	*L'heure espagnole*: **1966**, **1987**, 1988 *L'enfant et les sortilèges*: **1987**, 1988
ROSSINI	*La Cenerentola*: **1952**, 1953, 1954, 1956, 1959, 1960, **1983**, 1985 *Il barbiere di Siviglia*: **1954**, 1955, 1961, **1981**, 1982 *Le comte Ory*: **1954**, 1955, 1957, 1958, **1997**, 1998 *L'italiana in Algeri*: **1957** *La pietra del paragone*: **1964**, 1965 *Il turco in Italia*: **1970** *Ermione*: **1995**, 1996
STRAUSS	*Ariadne auf Naxos*: **1950**, **1953**, 1954, 1957, 1958, 1962, **1971**, 1972, 1981 *Der Rosenkavalier*: **1959**, 1960, 1965, **1980**, 1982 *Capriccio*: **1963**, 1964, **1973**, 1976, 1987, 1990, 1998 *Intermezzo*: **1974**, 1975, 1983 *Die schweigsame Frau*: **1977**, 1979 *Arabella*: **1984**, 1985, 1989, 1996
STRAVINSKY	*The Rake's Progress*: **1953**, 1954, 1955, 1958, 1963, **1975**, 1977, 1978, 1989, 1994
TCHAIKOVSKY	*Yevgeny Onyegin*: **1968**, 1970, 1975, **1994**, 1996 *The Queen of Spades*: **1971**, **1992**, 1995
TIPPETT	*New Year*: **1990**
VERDI	*Macbeth*: **1938**, 1939, 1947, 1952, **1964**, 1965, **1972** *Un ballo in maschera*: **1949** *La forza del destino*: **1951**, 1955 *Falstaff*: **1955**, 1957, 1958, 1960, **1976**, 1977, 1980, **1988**, 1990 *Simon Boccanegra*: **1986**, **1998** *La traviata*: **1987**, 1988
VON EINEM	*The Visit of the Old Lady*: **1973**, 1974
WOLF-FERRARI	*Il segreto di Susanna*: **1958**, 1960

HISTORIC AND FIRST PERFORMANCES OF OPERAS AT AND BY GLYNDEBOURNE AND GLYNDEBOURNE TOURING OPERA

1938   *Macbeth* (Verdi) – first professional production in England.

1946   *The Rape of Lucretia* (Britten) – world première; production by Britten's group (later known as the English Opera Group) but rehearsed and performed at Glyndebourne.

1947   *Albert Herring* (Britten) – world première; production by English Opera Group at Glyndebourne.

1950   *Ariadne auf Naxos* (R. Strauss) – first version; with preceding play *Le bourgeois gentilhomme* translated (for this Glyndebourne production at the Edinburgh Festival) by Miles Malleson.

1951   *Idomeneo* (Mozart) – first professional production in Britain.

1953   *The Rake's Progress* (Stravinsky) – first professional stage performance in Britain. Staged by Glyndebourne at the Edinburgh Festival.

1954   *Arlecchino* (Busoni) – first stage production in Britain.

1957   *Der Schauspieldirektor* (Mozart) – story and spoken dialogue newly devised for this production, after G. Stephanie by Hans Hammelmann and Michael Rose; at Glyndebourne's instigation.

1960   *La voix humaine* (Poulenc) – first performance in Britain; by Glyndebourne at the Edinburgh Festival.

1961   *Elegy for Young Lovers* (Henze) – world première in original language.

1962   *L'incoronazione di Poppea* (Monteverdi) – realization by Raymond Leppard; first professional production in England.

1967   *L'Ormindo* (Cavalli) – score arranged by Raymond Leppard; so far as is known this was the first time *L'Ormindo* had been performed anywhere since 1644.

1970   *La Calisto* (Cavalli) – score arranged by Raymond Leppard; so far as is known this was the first time *La Calisto* had been performed since 1651.

1970   *The Rising of the Moon* (Maw) – world première; first opera to be specially commissioned by Glyndebourne.

1972   *Il ritorno d'Ulisse in patria* (Monteverdi) – first performance of Raymond Leppard's version.

1973   *The Visit of the Old Lady* (von Einem) – first performance in England.

1974   *Intermezzo* (R. Strauss) – first professional stage performance in England.

1983   *The Love for Three Oranges* (Prokofiev) – first performance in an English translation made for Glyndebourne by Tom Stoppard for Glyndebourne Touring Opera.

1984   *Where the Wild Things Are* (Knussen) – performed by Glyndebourne at the National Theatre. Originally commissioned from Knussen by Brussels Opera in 1978, it was produced for them in an incomplete form in 1980. In 1982 London Sinfonietta gave a concert performance of the revised but still incomplete work. Glyndebourne then commissioned the completion of the work as premièred in 1984.

1984   *Higglety Pigglety Pop!* (Knussen) – world première; commissioned by the BBC for Glyndebourne and performed in an incomplete edition in 1984 by Glyndebourne Touring Opera. A more complete version performed in the Glyndebourne Festival, 1985.

1986   *Porgy and Bess* (Gershwin) – first British production in Britain (previously toured to Britain by an American company at the Stoll Theatre, London, 1952–3).

1987   *The Electrification of the Soviet Union* (Osborne) – world première; commissioned for Glyndebourne by the BBC; performed by Glyndebourne Touring Opera.

1990   *New Year* (Tippett) – European première; commissioned by Glyndebourne, Houston Grand Opera and the BBC, receiving its world première at Houston Grand Opera, 1989.

1991   *La clemenza di Tito* (Mozart) – with newly composed *secco* recitatives by Stephen Oliver.

1993   *Béatrice et Bénédict* (Berlioz) – Glyndebourne at the South Bank in concert; sung in the original French but with dialogue passages in English by John Wells specially commissioned for these performances.

1993   *Die lustige Witwe* (Lehár) – Glyndebourne at the South Bank in concert; sung in the original German but with new English narration by Tom Stoppard specially commissioned for these performances.

1993   *Cornet Christoph Rilke's Song of Love and Death* (Matthus) – British première, given by Glyndebourne Touring Opera.

1994   *The Second Mrs Kong* (Birtwistle) – world première; commissioned by Glyndebourne, given by Glyndebourne Touring Opera.

1995   *Ermione* (Rossini) – first staging in Britain.

1996   *Theodora* (Handel) – first staging in Britain.

Many tapes, cassettes and other desirable items relating to Glyndebourne are available from the Glyndebourne shop there. For details of opening hours etc., ring 01273 – 812321.

GLYNDEBOURNE FESTIVAL OPERA: TICKET PRICES 1934–1997

1934 | **Stalls** | **Box (Seats 9)**
First nights — £2 — 20 guineas (1 guinea = £1 1s.)
Subsequent perfs — £2, £1 10s. — 20 guineas

1935
First nights — £2
Subsequent perfs — £2, £1 10s.

1936
29 May, 1 June
& Saturday perfs — £2
Sunday perfs — £2 10s., £2
Weekday perfs — £2, £1 10s.
(4 subscription rates ranging from £6 15s. to £13 10s.)

1937	**Stalls**	**Balcony**
19 May &		
Saturday perfs	£2	£2
Sunday perfs	£2 10s., £2	£2 10s.
Weekday perfs	£2, £1 10s.	£2

(6 subscription rates ranging from £7 to £13 10s.)

1938	**Stalls**	**Balcony**	**Box seats**
Saturday &			
Sunday perfs	£2	£2, £1 10s.	£2
Weekday perfs	£2, £1 10s.	£2, £1 10s.	£2
June 5 & 6	All seats £1 10s.		

(6 subscription rates ranging from £7 to £11)

1939	Stalls	Balcony	Box seats
Saturday &			
Sunday perfs	£2	£2, £1 10s.	£2
Weekday perfs	£2, £1 10s.	£2, £1 10s.	£2

(7 subscription rates ranging from £7 to £11)

1940–5	No opera performances at Glyndebourne

1946	Stalls	Balcony	Box seats
All perfs	£1 5s.	£1 5s., 15s.	£1 5s.
Restricted view seats	12s. 6d., 7s. 6d.		

1947			
All perfs	£2 2s.	£2 2s. & £1 5s.	£2 2s.
Restricted view seats	£1 1s. & 10s. 6d.		

1948–9	No opera performances at Glyndebourne

	Stalls	Balcony	Boxes
1950	2gn, £1 5s., 1gn	3gn, 2gn, £1 15s., £1 5s., 17s. 6d.	2gn, £1 5s. per seat
1951	£2 12s. 6d., 2gn, £1 11s. 6d., 1gn	3gn, £2 12s. 6d., 2gn, £1 11s. 6d., 1gn	£2 12s. 6d., £1 11s. 6d. per seat
1952	3gn, £2 12s. 6d., 2gn, £1 11s. 6d., 1gn	3gn, £2 12s. 6d., 2gn, £1 11s. 6d.	3gn, £2 12s. 6d. per seat
1953	3gn, £2 12s. 6d., 2gn	3gn, £2 12s. 6d.	£39 7s. 6d., £23 12s. 6d., £15 15s.
1954	3gn, 2gn	3gn, 2gn	£39 7s. 6d., £23 12s. 6d., £15 15s.
1955	3gn, 2gn	3gn, 2gn	£39 7s. 6d., £23 12s. 6d., £15 15s.
12 perfs	3gn, 2gn	3gn, 2gn	£31 10s., £18 8s., £12 12s.
1956	3gn, 2gn	3gn, 2gn	£39 7s. 6d., £23 12s. 6d., £15 15s.
14 perfs	3gn, 2gn	3gn, 2gn	£31 10s., £18 18s., £12 12s.

	Stalls	Balcony	Balcony /Box Seats	Boxes
1957	3gn, 2gn	3gn, 2gn	2gn	20gn, 15gn
12 perfs	3gn, 2gn	3gn, 2gn	£1 11s. 6d.	16gn, 12gn
1958	4gn, 3gn, 2gn	4gn, 3gn, 2gn	2gn	27gn, 24gn, 15gn
12 perfs	4gn, 3gn, 2gn	4gn, 3gn, 2gn	£1 11s. 6d.	16gn, 12gn
1959	Gala Performance (25th Anniversary) of *Der Rosenkavalier* on 28 May. All seats 6gn			
	4gn, 3gn, 2gn	4gn, 3gn, 2gn	2gn	27gn, 24gn, 15gn
12 perfs	4gn, 3gn, 2gn	4gn, 3gn, 2gn	£1 11s. 6d.	18gn, 16gn, 12gn
1960	4gn, 3gn, 2gn	4gn, 3gn, 2gn	2gn	27gn, 24gn, 15gn
12 perfs	4gn, 3gn, 2gn	4gn, 3gn, 2gn	£1 11s. 6d.	18gn, 16gn, 12gn

	Stalls	Balcony	Upper Balcony	Boxes
1961	4gn, 3gn, 2gn	4gn, 3gn, 2gn	2gn	24gn, 15gn 3gn per seat
12 perfs	4gn, 3gn, 2gn	4gn, 3gn, 2gn	£1 11s. 6d.	16gn, 12gn
1962	4gn, 3gn	4gn, 3gn, 2gn	£1 11s. 6d.	24gn, 15gn 3gn per seat
1963				
1964	£4 17s. 6d., £3 15s.	£4 17s. 6d., £3 15s., £2 12s. 6d.	£2	£30, £19 10s. £3 15s. per seat
1965	5gn, £4	5gn, £4, £2 15s.	2gn	£32, £24 £4 per seat
1966	5gn, £4	5gn, £4, £2 15s.	2gn	£32, £24 £4 per seat
1967	£5 10s., £4 10s.	£5 10s., £4 10s., £3 10s.	£2 10s.	£36, £27 £4 10s. per seat
1968	£5 10s., £4 10s.	£5 10s., £4 10s., £3 10s.	£2 10s.	£36, £27 £4 10s. per seat

	Stalls	Balcony	Upper Balcony	Boxes
1969	£6 10s., £5 10s.	£6 10s., £5 10s., £4	£3	£44, £33 £5 10s. per seat
1970	£6 10s., £5 10s.	£6 10s., £5 10s., £4	£3	£44, £33 £5 10s. per seat
1971	£7, £6	£7, £6, £4.50	£3.50	£48, £36 £6 per seat
1972	£7, £6	£7, £6, £4.50	£3.50	£48, £36 £6 per seat
1973	£8, £7	£8, £7, £5	£3.50	£56, £42 £7 per seat
1974	£9, £8	£9, £8, £6	£4	£64, £48 £8 per seat
1975	£11.90, £10.80, £9.70	£11.90, £10.80, £9.70, £7.55	£4.30	£10.80 per seat
1976	£12, £11, £10	£12, £11, £10, £8	£5	£100, £75 £11 per seat
1977	£13.50, £11	£13.50, £11	£5	£100, £75 £11 per seat
1978	£15.50, £12.50	£15.50, £12.50	£6.50	£115, £85 £12.50 per seat
1979	£17.50, £15	£17.50, £15	£8	£140, £105 £15 per seat
1980	£21.50, £18	£21.50, £18	£10	£170, £130 £18 per seat
1981	£26.50, £22	£26.50, £22	£13	£210, £160 £22 per seat
1982	£31, £25	£31, £25	£15	£250, £185 £25 per seat
1983	£35, £27.50	£35, £27.50	£16.50	£280, £210 £27.50 per seat

	Stalls	Balcony	Upper Balcony	Boxes
1984	£38, £30	£38, £30	£18	£304, £228, £30 per seat
1985	£38, £30	£38, £30	£18	£304, £228 £30 per seat
Sendak double bill – morning performances	£20, £15	£20, £15	£10	£160, £120 £15 per seat
Sendak double bill – evening performances	£30, £20	£30, £20	£15	£240, £180 £20 per seat
1986	£46, £36	£46, £36	£22	£368, £276 £36 per seat
1987	£50, £40	£50, £40	£25	£400, £300 £40 per seat
1988	£60, £45	£60, £45	£25	£480, £360 £45 per seat
Half-price tickets for all performances of *The Electrification of the Soviet Union*				
1989	£65, £48	£65, £48	£28	£520, £390 £48 per seat
1990	£75, £54	£75, £54	£30	£600, £450 £54 per seat
1991	£85, £60	£85, £60	£33	£680, £510 £60 per seat
1992	£90, £65	£90, £65	£35	£720, £540 £65 per seat

(Limited number of wheelchair spaces in the Stalls at £35)

NEW THEATRE TICKET PRICES

	1994	1995	1996
Stalls & Foyer Circle	£100, £75	£105, £78	£110, £80, £55 £35
Foyer Boxes	£100, £50, £30	£105, £52, £32, £20	£110, £55, £35 £20
Circle	£100, £75, £50	£105, £78, £52	£110, £80, £55,
Circle Boxes	£75, £50, £30	£78, £52, £32, £20, £15	£80, £35, £20, £20, £15
Upper Boxes	£50, £30	£52, £32, £20	£55, £35, £20
Slips	£15	£20, £15	£20, £15
Standing	£10	£10	£10

	1997	1998
Stalls	£114, £83	£118, £86
Foyer Circle	£114, £83, £57, £36	£118, £86, £59, £37
Circle	£114, £83, £57	£118, £86, £59
Foyer Circle Boxes	£114, £57, £36, £21	£118, £59, £37, £21
Circle Boxes	£83, £36, £21, £16	£86, £37, £21, £16
Upper Circle	£57, £36	£59, £37
Slips	£21, £16	£21, £16
Standing	£10	£10

Further Reading

The following are the chief printed sources: although they are all out of print, they are obtainable from good libraries and second-hand booksellers.

Rudolf Bing: *5,000 Nights at the Opera* (Hamish Hamilton, 1972). Autobiography, with much interesting detail of the early Glyndebourne years.

Wilfrid Blunt: *John Christie* (Geoffrey Bles, 1980). Authorized biography.

Paul Campion and Rosy Runciman: *Glyndebourne Recorded* (Julia MacRae Books, 1994). Comprehensive record of all Glyndebourne audio and video recordings 1934–1994.

Moran Caplat: *Dinghies to Divas* (Collins, 1985). An autobiography containing much first-hand information.

John Higgins: *The Making of an Opera* (Secker and Warburg, 1978). Follows the creation of Peter Hall's production of *Don Giovanni*.

John Higgins (ed.): *Glyndebourne: A Celebration* (Cape, 1984). Thirteen contributions, including one of special significance by Peter Hall, for fiftieth anniversary.

Spike Hughes: *Glyndebourne* (Methuen, 1965; updated new edition, containing 42pp. David & Charles, 1981). A thorough and lively general history, especially down to 1964.

John Julius Norwich: *Glyndebourne* (Cape, 1985). Lively text, many illustrations, to celebrate Glyndebourne's fiftieth anniversary.

Rosy Runciman and Marcus Binney: *Glyndebourne: Building a Vision* (Thames & Hudson, 1994). The story of the original building and the rebuilding.

Ann Scott-James and Christopher Lloyd: *Glyndebourne: The Gardens* (Peterhouse Press, 1983). Charming guide (illustrated by Elizabeth Bury) to the gardens, with a Foreword by Mary Christie.

There are informative references to Glyndebourne in the memoirs and published diaries of many singers and others who have worked there. Those of Dame Janet Baker, Sir Geraint Evans, David Franklin, Sir Peter Hall, David Hockney, Raymond Leppard, Elisabeth Söderström, Robert Tear and Ian Wallace will be found especially rewarding; while a more general book, *The Joys of Opera* by Nigel Douglas, is a glorious goldmine not only of excellent anecdotes but of thoughts on opera, from the horse's (or more accurately the tenor's) mouth.

A biography of Carl Ebert by his son Peter will appear in 1999.

In addition, those seriously interested may apply for access to the complete run of annual programme books in the Glyndebourne archives. These books contain a mass of fascinating information about the operas performed in each season, as well as being profusely illustrated, and effectively edited at first by Moran Caplat and, since his retirement, by Helen O'Neill. The Glyndebourne shop stocks many of them, as well as other merchandise relating to Glyndebourne.

INDEX

Note: *Italic* page numbers indicate illustrations